DECISIVE BATTLES

Also by John Colvin

Nomonhan
Lions of Judah
Volcano Under Snow
Not Ordinary Men
Twice Around the World

JOHN COLVIN

DECISIVE BATTLES

OVER 20 KEY NAVAL AND MILITARY
ENCOUNTERS FROM 480 BC TO 1943

headline

First published in 2003
by HEADLINE BOOK PUBLISHING

10 9 8 7 6 5 4 3 2 1

The extract from 'Little Gidding' from *Four Quartets* by T. S. Eliot (1944)
is reproduced by kind permission of Faber and Faber Ltd

Cataloguing in Publication Data is available from the British Library

ISBN 0 7553 1070 5

Typeset in Caslon Regular by Avon DataSet Ltd,
Bidford-on-Avon, Warwickshire

Printed and bound in Great Britain by
Clays Ltd, St Ives plc

HEADLINE BOOK PUBLISHING
A division of Hodder Headline
338 Euston Road
London NW1 3BH

Every effort has been made to fulfil requirements with regard to
reproducing copyright material. The author and publisher will be
glad to rectify any omissions at the earliest opportunity.

www.headline.co.uk
www.hodderheadline.com

the Soviets at Nomonhan. Then, after sweeping the board from 1941 in a brilliant twentieth-century series of campaigns, she succumbed unconditionally to superior Allied industrial and military power, giving up all her Pacific conquests. India, however, at Plassey losing both liberty and the subcontinent, regained them by negotiation in 1947. Other subject states – Burma, Philippines, Malaysia, French Indo-China, Netherlands East India – also reacquired 'independence', sometimes peacefully, sometimes after protracted battle, as in Vietnam and the Protocol States.

The Battle of Britain, Kursk, Singapore, Midway, the Battle of the Atlantic, fateful encounters of the Second World War, provide little guidance for the future, while the wars of decolonisation must now be mostly over except in certain former Soviet Islamic states.

It seems likely, however, that one category of future wars will be small in compass, sometimes literally underground, as in the Cu Chi tunnels, or conducted by venomous individuals transporting and employing a range of weaponry from nuclear to conventional, suicide or other; poisoning public amenities; hideously destroying such buildings as the World Trade Center, the target countries' defence arrangements designed and appropriately deployed with a leading role for intelligence and counter-intelligence.

Conventional war across frontiers, as in the Middle East and the Balkans, cannot be excluded. Neither can the massive aerial and artillery confrontations of the Gulf War. Yet armour, although increasingly vulnerable to hand-held and simple weapons, is still essential. So is infantry – with a large contribution from Special Forces – in order to hold and dominate battlefield and objective. Most conflicts will, nevertheless, be fought asymmetrically, at different levels, with varying degrees of intensity, according to whatever plan is currently in force. This strategy, practised with infinite sophistication by the Politburo in Hanoi, has been noted by al-Qaeda, observing the vulnerability of democracies with complex infrastructures.

Later, by April 1241, Chinggis Khan's Mongol descendants controlled all eastern Europe from the Dnieper to the Oder and from the Baltic to the Danube, overwhelming Christian armies five times their strength. Next winter, Subatei planned to invade Italy, Austria, Germany, then doubtless France and England, against panic-stricken and uncoordinated western forces. Only chance, or divine providence, saved Christian Europe. The call came from Karakoram for the return of all troops to Mongolia, to elect a new great khan on the death of Ögedei, Chinggis's latest successor. The armies went bloodily home, crushing Serbia and Bulgaria en route, suffering obscure defeat by Egyptians, never to return.

Others believe that the recall was strategic, a sudden realisation that the conqueror could never muster enough horses to control so vast a populated area. The horror was over for western Europe, but the White and Golden Hordes oppressed western Asia and Europe – including Russia – east of the Carpathian mountains, for 150 years thereafter.

Four centuries later, faced with a subsequent invader of ethnic similarity, it was the aim of Jan Sobieski, Polish nobleman and elected king, 'to drive the Turk from Europe, to hurl him back into the deserts, to exterminate him, to raise upon his ruins, the Empire of Byzantium'. That empire, it will be recalled, after Saladin's military victory against the Franks in 1187 at the Horns of Hattin, had been deliberately destroyed with papal connivance by the Fourth Crusade itself.

On 11 September 1683, after marching 220 miles from Warsaw in fifteen days, Sobieski's 30,000 Poles defeated and almost eliminated the Sultan's army besieging Vienna, 150,000 men under Kara Mustapha. The Turks did not come again. Europe was safe and the long Ottoman decline proceeded. But, as with Subatei, it had been close.

Asian countries in the eighteenth century and after included victors as well as victims. Japan sank the Russian fleet at Tsushima, but her attempt in 1939 to take Siberia was massively rebuffed by

At sea, 'The Royal Navy hath ever been [England's] greatest defence and ornament: it is its ancient and natural strength, the floating bulwark of the island.' The role has somewhat shifted from open ocean warfare to power projection ashore in national and international operations, these also often asymmetric, high-intensity war-fighting in one area of the battle space, and 'constabulary or peace support' in another. New landing ships and associated installations are being acquired, and plans made for a new generation of much larger aircraft carriers.

Decisive Battles is a broad sweep through history. It does not claim to be definitive; rather, it is illustrative of how our civilisation has been shaped by the ebb and flow of conquest and retreat, victory and defeat. It is a book for the layman, not the professional soldier or military tactician; for the general reader with an interest in historical perspective and in contemplating the fascinating possibilities of 'what if . . .?'

CHAPTER ONE

SALAMIS, 480 BC

M arathon was not a decisive battle, 'rather a brilliant prologue to [the] grand drama' performed ten years later at Salamis.

In Greece, 2,500 years ago, on the eastern shore of Attica, the forces of Darius, king of Persia, lay encamped by the plain of Marathon, surveilled with uncertainty by 10,000 Athenians hidden in the surrounding mountains. Only a thousand loyal Plataeans had come to Athens' aid, since Sparta's troops, although promised, could not be released until the full-moon ceremonies.

Under the prior guidance of Hippias, son of Pisistratus, exiled enemy of the Greeks and Persia's friend, the seaborne forces of the Great King numbered some 45,000, of whom 15,000 under Datis had been landed at Phaleron in the Bay of Marathon, there to entice the Athenian army out of its city twenty-five miles southwest. Thus would be liberated the Persian fifth column, and battle with a superior Persian army enforced. Victory achieved, Athens taken, Darius would move on Thrace and Macedonia with Hippias as his vassal, then conquer Sparta and the rest of Greece for Persia.

In the Greek camp, Miltiades, once prince of the Chersonese under Persia, now tactical commander of the Greek army, learned of treachery at Eretria. Miltiades knew that although the enemy at Phaleron did not intend to attack Athens directly, the loss of Eretria would free the Persian general Artaphernes to do so under cover of Datis' holding action in the bay. On the afternoon of 21 September 490 BC, therefore, he gave the order to attack the Persians and their galleys on the shelving beach, their depots the occupied islands astern on the turquoise, wind-ruffled Aegean Sea.

In order to avoid outflanking or charging from the rear by Persian cavalry, Miltiades decided with Callimachus, the war archon or supreme commander, to extend the Greek line by weakening the centre from eight to four ranks, distributing the excess to the wings. Callimachus commanded on the right, Miltiades his regiment of ten tribes in the centre; the gallant Plataeans fought on the left. (Among them, in the ranks, was the poet Aeschylus.) The Greeks moved in two parallel columns in line ahead, wheeling to line abreast on entering the plain, less than a mile from the Persian hordes parallel to the shore.

In this region, sacred to Hercules and to Theseus, the Greeks were armed chiefly with long spears as well as shields, breastplates, greaves and shorter spears. Their usual formation, amended on this occasion to four ranks in the centre, was a phalanx accustomed to move slowly and deliberately at eight long spears' depth to the music of flutes. The eighth rank, at least at Plataea, was of helots who clubbed to death the enemy wounded and succoured their own. But the requirement to hide from the enemy until the very last moment – albeit aided by the irregularity of the terrain – was paramount. Miltiades therefore decided to pre-empt both the arrow fire of massed Persian archers and the menace of heavy Asian cavalry. The Greeks took the mile between the mountains and the sea – the 'beaten zone' – at the double, chanting to the trumpets: 'Oh, sons of the Greeks! Strike for freedom . . .'

'When the Persians', said Herodotus, 'saw the Athenians running down on them, without horses or bowmen, and scanty in numbers, they thought them a set of madmen, rushing upon certain destruction,' the first Greeks ever to charge at a run. Against enemy resilience, the Greek centre gave at first but, after retreat, rallied and re-formed under Themistocles and Aristides, the heroes later of Salamis and Plataea. The Greek wings, meanwhile, routed their Asian opponents, rejoining in a single unit to cut down the enemy, whether Persian, Sacae, mountain men from Afghanistan, horsemen from the steppes of Khorassan, black archers of Ethiopia or dusky swordsmen from the Nile, Euphrates, Oxus and Indus.

But '. . . no national cause inspired the Great King's men', little trained in drill, with only scimitars, wicker shields, short weapons, lacking armour. At the water's edge by Marathon, because of superior Greek arms, equipment, morale and command, as well as the inability of Datis' cavalry to prepare themselves in time – saddle and bridle their horses and form line – 6,400 Persians died, but only 192 Athenians. Seven Persian ships were taken. The myth and experience of Persian invincibility were broken, the road to Salamis and Plataea opened, the careers of Xenophon and Alexander assured.

The battle over, at last came the Lacedaemonians from Sparta, having marched 150 miles in three days to witness the dead bodies of the Medes, praise the Athenians, and return to their home.

Darius died in the following year. His son, Xerxes, was soon persuaded to invade Greece by marching out of Asia into Europe from a bridge of boats, 'a ribbon of lashed timbers and nailed planks', across the Hellespont, as his father had bridged the Bosphorus on the advance to Scythia. (In a dream, the Magi told Xerxes that his plan foretold the conquest of the world and its total subjection to Persia.) For four years thereafter, Xerxes assembled his armies and his fleets from the provinces of the empire, cutting too a canal from Mount Athos to the mainland, bridging the Hellespont between Abydos and Sestos. When the work was damaged in a storm, Xerxes threw a pair of fetters into the water and gave it 300 lashes, the men with whips abusing it as they struck. Later, as offering or apology, Xerxes threw in a golden goblet and bowl . . .

At Sardis, the Lydian capital, the king established his first headquarters. Here he had a young man cut in half to punish the father for seeking the son's release from duty: the army marched out between the two halves. After the baggage train and a host of mixed nationalities came spearmen with weapons reversed and golden pomegranates on the spears' butt ends, then ten of the huge, sacred, Nisaean horses: the holy chariot of Zeus, drawn by eight white horses, followed the king in his own royal chariot.

After Xerxes marched the Persian infantry, of whom 1,000 had golden pomegranates instead of spikes on their weapons, some with golden apples, and 9,000 with silver pomegranates. These 10,000 infantry preceded 10,000 Persian cavalry, then the great ethnic, miscellaneous mass of the rest of the army. First of these came the Persians, of supposed descent from Perseus, in 'tiaras' or soft felt caps, embroidered tunics with sleeves, scaled mail coats and trousers, armed with wicker shields, cane bows and arrows, daggers swinging at the belt by the right thigh. The Medians, or Arians, were accoutred like the Persians, as were the Cissians, although those wore turbans, not caps. Assyrians had intricate bronze helmets. They carried spears and wooden clubs studded with iron: with them were the Chaldeans.

The Bactrians had caps like the Medes, while the Sacae (Scythians) wore trousers and tall pointed hats: the son of Darius, by Cyrus' daughter, commanded. Present in the ranks were Parthians, Chorasmians, Sogdians, Sarangians in leather jackets, Caspians in highly coloured clothes, Arabians, Ethiops in leopard and lion skins, their bodies smeared with chalk and vermilion. The headdresses of some Ethiops were horses' scalps, ears and mane attached, their shields of crane skin. Accompanying them were the Phrygians, dressed like the Paphlagonians; Cappadocians, Libyans, Matteni; 'soft-skinned' Lydians uniformed like Greeks and carrying small shields and javelins; Thracians with fox-fur headdresses, long bright cloaks, fawn-skin boots. Pisidians in bronze helmets with the ears and horns of oxen, crimson leggings. Moschians, Tibareni, Macrones, Colchians, and Mossineeci with wooden helmets. The helmets of the Marians were plaited. The Indians were dressed in cotton. Arabs wore the belted *zeira*.

These troops – the Persians glittering with unlimited quantities of gold – numbered, according to Herodotus, 1,700,000 infantrymen and 80,000 horsed cavalrymen, camels additional and separated from the horses. The *true* infantry strength is, however, unlikely to have been more than 180,000 and the cavalry considerably fewer.

Apart from transport, about 1,000 galleys and others, Herodotus estimated the Persian battle fleet at 1,207 triremes or three-deckers, a figure agreed by Aeschylus, these vessels contributed also by Phoenicians, Syrians, Egyptians, Cypriots, Cilicians, Pamphylians, Lycians, Carians, Ionians (Pelasgians), Aeolians, the first three greatly preponderant. Crews were largely Persian, Mede and Sacae: for speed, the Phoenicians' ships gained the palm. A woman, Artemisia, furnished five ships and commanded the Halicarnassians. Xerxes, having reviewed in his chariot the various national contingents, from one end of the army – both horse and foot – to the other, then embarked. Under a golden canopy, the king inspected the fleet drawn up 400 yards from the beach, bows turned shoreward: 'the diadems and yellow buskins of Persia, the scarlet cloaks and brilliant ostrich feathers'.

The first omens on the march to Greece were unfortunate. A mare gave birth to a hare, meaning that Xerxes would soon come running back to his starting point, and a foal was born with male and female sexual organs. Xerxes ignored both, nor did he send demands for submission – traditional demands for 'earth and water', representing surrender on land and sea – to Athens and Sparta. His father's messengers, on a similar mission, had been stuffed into a pit in Athens and down a well in Sparta; Spartans seeking atonement had, however, refused submission in exchange for life and land, telling the Persians: 'You have never experienced freedom . . . if you ever did, you would advise us to fight for it, not with spears only, but with axes too.' Xerxes spared them. Some Greeks, of course, submitted – Thessalonians, Achaeans, Thebans,

Boeotians – although warned by Athens that, the war once won, all men of Greek blood would be punished who had yielded to the Persians without duress.

The great Persian host moved on, victualled and accommodated at vast compulsory expense by the oppressed Greek inhabitants, with poultry, wheat and barley flour, cattle, cups and bowls of gold and silver. In the mornings, after spending the night at their hosts' open hand, the soldiers would 'pull up the tents, seize the cups and table-ware and everything else that they contained, and march off without leaving a single thing behind'. One victim said that his friends should be grateful that the king did not order *two* dinners each day. At one point, Xerxes' camels were attacked by lions, although not by the wild oxen with enormous horns which were imported into Greece at that time.

After Athens had attempted the recruitment of Argos, Corcyra, Crete, and Gelo at Syracuse, Xerxes sought the conquest of all Greece by invading Thessaly through the passes of Olympia and Ossa at Tempe, which the Athenians had also calculated as the most likely point for Persian assault. The Macedonians under Alexander II covertly advised withdrawal because of the gigantic strength of the Persian army and fleet, to which the Athenians agreed, choosing a narrow pass, no more than fifty feet wide, in which the enemy's numbers, in particular its famous cavalry, might flounder. This was Thermopylae, Gate of the Hot Springs. And Alexander's warning was confirmed by three Greek spies captured and tortured by the Persians, but released by Xerxes precisely so that they *could* confirm to Themistocles, the Greek commander, the terrifying magnitude of Persian power. The Greeks refused this tacit invitation to surrender without a fight since, if they did not stand, although Sparta might resist unto death, Greece would be lost to the Asians. But the choice of Thermopylae lost Athens the support of Thessaly, who lent their cavalry to Xerxes henceforward.

The Oracle at Delphi had pronounced twice, the first advice gloomy, if not forbidding:

Wretches, why sit you here?
Fly, fly to the ends of creation.
Quitting your homes and the crags which your city
Crowns with her circlet.

But the second saying, referring favourably to 'the wooden wall,'
interpreted as the fleet, ended:

Holy Salamis, thou shalt destroy the offspring of women
Where men scatter the seed, or where they gather the harvest.

If the Greek army must stand at Thermopylae, the fleet had to
navigate in the Euboean channel, Euripus, or at Salamis, so as to
hold Greece as far north of the Isthmus of Corinth as possible,
thus discounting clumsy Persian numbers in the narrow sea while
simultaneously protecting the isthmus. (In the meanwhile, Xerxes
had tried to strengthen his strategic position further by persuading
the Carthaginians to bolster his own attacks on the Greeks
of Greece, by subduing the Greeks of Sicily and Italy.) The
Persians moved their army to Thermopylae and their main fleet
to the northern entrance of the Euboean channel. Two hundred
Phoenician ships would, at the same time, sail round the east and
south coasts of Euboea and bottle up the Greeks at Salamis.

The allied fleet of over 300 triremes, of which 180 were
Athenian, sailed for Artemisium. A Spartan army under Leonidas,
king of Sparta, sailed for Thermopylae with 8,000 hoplites and
300 men of the royal bodyguard, not enough to hold the line. In
the pass were rocks, boulders, juniper, thyme: the crags held birds
of prey in the cliffs off the little track. The hot springs, known as
'basins', rose among broken walls and gateways. Eurybiades,
Spartan commander of the Greek fleet, took fifty-three ships to
the mid-point of the channel at Chalcis, to hold the Phoenician
squadron. To the north, in a ferocious southeaster – 'the
Hellespontian' – 400 Persian ships were wrecked in a sea 'like a
pot on the boil', caught in lines eight deep. In the moonlight,

drowned men and splintered spars floated in bloodied water. (The Athenians, in celebration and thanksgiving, built a shrine to Boreas, the wind, perhaps also for the Persian treasure in gold and silver recovered after the fierce three-day storm.) 'The water was green, but shoreward it was a dirty red and *things* bobbed about in it.'

On land, Leonidas, in direct descent from Hercules, decided to ignore a proposal to retreat, instead choosing to stand and seek reinforcement, observed, however, by Xerxes' spies who watched the Spartans combing their hair, their practice when about to risk their lives. (As well as Spartans, Leonidas commanded Arcadians, Corinthians, Boeotians and Thebans.) Xerxes, astonished at the temerity of the little band, sent the Medes and the King's Immortals forward with the short spear at great loss. Leonidas and his men were soldiers. They knew and understood war. One among their feints was to turn in apparent confused flight, to round then with the long spear on the yelling pursuers, felling them to the rocky hill, a sort of infantry Parthian shot.

Xerxes, after two days of struggle, was at a loss, all assaults useless: three times, in terror for his army, he had leapt to his feet in preparation for withdrawal. Wave after Persian wave broke, but the Greeks did not slacken. Just then, however, Ephialtes of Trachis betrayed his Hellene countrymen by telling the Great King of a mountain track beginning at the Asopus river, along the mountain through a gorge to Black-Buttons Stone and Alpenos, the narrowest part of the pass at Thermopylae.

The Persians took this pass at night 'about the time of the lighting of lamps', the mountains dark at Oeta, those of Trachis to the left, through the sheltering oak woods whispering in the cool night breezes until, at dawn, the Phocian Greek guards heard the loud swishing and rustling of their marching feet in the fallen leaves. Under Persian arrows, the Phocians fled high into the mountains. The enemy bypassed them, hurrying at speed down the falling track.

Lookouts, deserters, and a seer reading Greek doom in sacrifices, all warned Leonidas. The army split and, whether Leonidas himself dismissed them or they panicked, some companies bolted for home, leaving only Thebans and Thespians with the Spartans. Herodotus believed that Leonidas, finding no heart for the fight among his allies, dismissed them to prevent unnecessary slaughter: although he admitted that at least the Thebans were held by the general against their will. The Thespians, certainly, refused to desert him and his men, and stayed and died with them.

In the morning, after Xerxes had poured a libation to the rising sun, the Persian army advanced. The Greeks, knowing that they were about to die, renounced sorties from the wall into the narrow neck of the pass, to fight instead in the wider reaches. Under the lash of the Persian whip from the rear, the barbarians fell dead, or into the sea to drown, or trampled one another to death. The Greeks fought with fury and desperation, discarding broken spears, killing Persians by the sword. Leonidas fell, pierced by six lances, his arm shattered, blinded, his helmet destroyed by axe blows, his shield still on his useless shoulder.

After four attempts, his dead body was rescued by his men before the survivors withdrew into the narrow pass behind the wall. In a single compact Spartan and Thespian body on the little hill at the entrance to the pass, 'where the stone lion in memory of Leonidas stands today', they made their last stand with swords, teeth and hands. Here the Persians, thrusting from front and back, by archery and, at the end, brute force, finally overran them.

A Spartan, told that there were so many Persian arrows that they blotted out the sun, had said only: 'If the Persians hide the sun, we shall have our battle in the shade.' The dead were buried where they fell. Over them the old inscription read:

> Go tell the Spartans, thou who passest by,
> That here obedient to their laws we lie.

Demiratus, overthrown king of Sparta, and advisor to the Great King, who had nevertheless betrayed to the Greeks the news of Xerxes' invasion of Greece, advised Xerxes to isolate Lacedaemon and Sparta by making the island Cythera his base, thence spreading terror over Lacedaemon. The Spartans then would have no opportunity to help the other Greeks. Xerxes declined, but, in an outrage to chivalry, broke the rules of decency by placing Leonidas' head on a stake.

The Persians had thus taken and cleared the pass of Thermopylae, opening the road to Athens. Xerxes marched on the Athenian capital, where citizens had heard the tragedy of Leonidas' defeat and death, yet expected help from their Peloponnesian allies. These, in fact, continued instead uselessly to fortify the Isthmus of Corinth. The Great King seized and burned the Acropolis, massacring the defenders, marching on from Doris to Phocis, burning and destroying the Phocian cities.

Themistocles, thirsty for fame, had been elected to the Greek command. He, a rival of Aristides because of a childish struggle for the affections of Stesilaus, a native of Ceos, had already seen the necessity for mastery of the sea and, with the revenue from the silver mines at Latrium, had built 200 triremes, the ships which won back Athens after its fall to the Persians. Themistocles had also aroused admiration by outlawing internal strife between the Grecian cities, and by executing an envoy from Xerxes for daring to use the Greek tongue to transmit the barbarians' demands for 'earth and water', at last levied on Athens.

He turned the Athenians, for better or worse, from 'steadfast hoplites into sea tossed mariners'. His intuition and good judgement led him to make his countrymen evacuate Athens and Attica, and to subsidise civilian refugees, the old, women and children, while urging the young, at eight drachmae a head, to man the 200 triremes in being. After the fiasco at Tempe, the Athenians sent this rich, amoral and sometimes loved leader to guard the straits at Artemisium, where he surrendered command, in the interests of unity, to the Spartan Eurybiades, although the latter had considerably fewer vessels.

At Artemisium was a small temple of Artemis in a grove within a ring of white marble stones, scented like saffron, on one of which was written:

Here by this arm of the sea, the valiant children of Athens
Sailed their ships into battle and shattered the fleets of the Mede,
Conquering a many-tongued host from the furthest confines of Asia
These are the tokens of thanks to victorious Artemis paid.

Here the Greek squadron in a close circle, bows outward, captured thirty Persian ships. After dark came violent rain and thunder, from Mount Pelion; dead bodies and wreckage drifted to Aphetae, whither the Persian survivors of the sea-fight had returned. Down on the beach at Artemisium, mingled with the sand, was a dark ashy powder produced by fire. It was believed that wrecks and dead bodies were buried here, to add to those fouling the bows and oar-blades at Aphetae. Yet graver disaster overtook the 200 Persian vessels sailing round Euboea, nearly every ship over-powered by storm and driven on to the rocks of the eastern shore.

Xerxes, nevertheless, attacked again at Artemisium, still in numbers greatly superior to the Greek fleet, attempting in crescent formation to surround them. Losses were heavier on the Persian side. Themistocles took the fastest vessels south, appealing en route to Ionians and Corians to desert the Great King and join their compatriots. But naval reinforcements joined the Persians.

After sailing from Artemisium, the Greeks under Eurybiades joined those at Salamis, Aegina and Troezen, who had been evacuated from Athens even before Xerxes from the hill called Areopagus had shot his burning arrows into the Acropolis and destroyed the temple. At Salamis, Themistocles persuaded Eurybiades not to withdraw to the isthmus, that open sea where the Greek ships would be at a disadvantage, and where conflict would also draw the Persian army upon them. Instead, the Greeks should fight in the narrow waters of Salamis. 'As for you,' he had cried to Eurybiades, 'if you stay here and play the man, well and good; go, and you'll be the ruin of Greece . . . if you refuse, we will sail for Italy. Where will you be without the Athenian fleet?' Eurybiades rapidly changed his mind, but argument broke out again over the Salamis proposal and the construction of a wall across the isthmus.

Themistocles had to use several tricks to convince those Greeks fearful of a naval battle with the Persians: disappearance of the sacred snake at the Acropolis, removal of the Gorgon's head from the breastplate of Athena, Apollo's reference to Salamis as divine . . . After Xerxes had decided on a battle at sea with the Greeks, challenged only by the woman Artemisia on the grounds of Athenian superiority in sea warfare, the Spartans once more took fright and concentrated on fortification at the isthmus, knowing the Athenian squadron to be only 180 strong, without its Corinthian and other allies.

The enemy's fleet, now 1,000 vessels, arrived off Attica, and occupied the Bay of Phalerum. 'The great host of their ships quite blotted out the surrounding coastline.' As a final throw, therefore, Themistocles sent Sicinnus, one of his slaves, in a boat to Xerxes. Sicinnus told the king that 'Themistocles, a well-wisher who hoped for a Persian victory, wanted Xerxes to know that the Greeks were afraid and were preparing to slip away, although divided in their counsels. Only prevent them from fleeing, destroy them before they could join forces with the army, and success would lie with Persia.'

The Persians believed this disinformation, landing troops in silence and at night at Psyttaleia, an islet between Salamis and the coast. The Egyptian contingent of 200 ships was despatched to block the western passage. The remainder of the Persian fleet lay in three lines between Cynosura and the Piraeus, the whole, it was hoped, sealing in the Greek navy around Salamis Island. The faster Persians (Ionian Greeks and Phoenicians) now broke into columns to pass Psyttaleia on either hand, in order to meet the Athenian, Spartan and other allies between Salamis and Heracleion. The Greeks at last found out that they were truly surrounded.

The Persian naval columns, however, because of rough seas, excessive numbers and poor steersmanship, were in disorder and confusion. The Greeks, including the Corinthians, in action against the large Egyptian contingent deceived by Themistocles' ruses into facing the naval battle which he had advocated, and they had feared, finally prepared for action. The whole fleet now got under way and in a moment the Persians were on them. The Greeks checked their way and began to go astern until an Athenian ship drove ahead and rammed an enemy or, as some say, until a phantom woman's voice cried, 'Strange men, how much further do you propose to go astern?'

The Persian vessels, difficult to manoeuvre with their high decks and towering sterns, tended to swing broadside on to their opponents, the Phoenicians facing the Athenians at Eleusis, the Ionians against the Spartans, the Greeks working together as a fleet. The Persians began to lose formation, without a battle plan although fighting bravely, fearing Xerxes' disapproval. The king watched from a golden throne at an eminence either near the temple of Heracles or on hills known as The Horns, where his secretaries wrote down his orders and observations.

Themistocles was careful not to engage his triremes head on with the Persians, until the wind blew from the sea, producing a heavy swell through the narrows. This motion, unfavourable to the huge Persian vessels, favoured the small, powerful, low-freeboard Greeks racing close alongside the enemy, shearing off their oars before ramming amidships with the great bronze beaks in the prow. The sheer bulk of the Persian fleet, furthermore, caused its vessels to foul one another in the crowded stream of the straits.

The Persians suffered severely in the battle, the decisive action being on the Greek left. Here the Athenians and islanders from Aegina turned the Phoenician right until the centre itself of the

Persian fleet was encircled, threatening the total destruction of the Ionians on the Persian left. Aristides meanwhile cleared the enemy out of Psyttaleia. The Ionians fell back and were not pursued, the Greeks sailed to Salamis, and the Persians, or such of them as still floated, were left to seek the army's protection at Phaleron.

At this point in the action, a great light shone from Eleusis and a loud cry rang out across the plain to the sea. A cloud rose slowly, drifted out from the land and descended on the triremes. 'Phantoms and shapes of armed men came from Aegina with hands outstretched to protect the Greek ships. The Greeks believed these apparitions to be the sons of Aeacus to whom they had prayed before battle. Earlier, a divine voice from Eleusis, in a cloud of dust, died away toward Salamis where the Greek fleet lay. The naval power of Xerxes was doomed to destruction.'

The Greeks lost 40 ships, and the Persians 200, sunk or otherwise destroyed: there is no figure for those captured. Simonides described the battle as 'that able and famous victory, the most glorious exploit ever achieved by Greek or barbarian, and they owed it to the courage and determination of all those who fought their ships, but not least to the surpassing skill of Themistocles'. Greek casualties were light. Most crews could swim, including the eighteen marines, archers and infantry attached to each trireme who fought the battles hand-to-hand. Many Persians drowned. In the end, the Greeks had put them to utter rout.

Diodorus the topographer quoted the poet Plato as claiming that a monument near Piraeus, shaped like an altar, housed Themistocles' cadaver:

> There on a noble height they heaped your tomb
> Above the shore and there the merchantmen
> Shall hail it as they pass: there you look down
> Upon the inward and the outward bound
> And the galleys crowding sail as they race for home.

More prosaically, it does seem that the strength of the two fleets, on the evidence of Herodotus and Aeschylus, was between 1,000 Persian and 300–380 Greek triremes (trieres). Themistocles had accomplished his first task – to ensure that Eurybiades did not weakly retreat to the Isthmus of Corinth – by the various ruses described. His second, the deception operation mounted against Xerxes through the slave Sicinnus, caused the desired division of the huge Persian force, when the Great King ordered the fleet to sail.

Two hundred and seven fast Persian triremes thus rowed to the sea coast of Salamis, while two squadrons patrolled the straits on either coast of Psyttaleia island at dawn. Two hundred Egyptian triremes sealed the Megarian strait to bar any potential Greek escape or withdrawal to the isthmus.

The captains of the great three-deckers of the Persian squadrons around Psyttaleia, twin masted, sails furled, high prowed, with bronze rams, had expected the Greeks to flee. It was, therefore, with surprise if not trepidation that they then met at dawn the whole strength of the Greek fleet, rested after a night's sleep, while the Persians had been rowing since midnight to reach the channels. The relative slowness of the Greeks was thus balanced by the exhaustion of the Asiatics. Moreover, because of the narrow channel, the Persian superiority in numbers could not be exploited.

Aeschylus said that 'the Greek right wing led in orderly formation, then the whole fleet followed, and after a clash', probably a change from line abreast to line ahead, 'moved through behind the Persian ships and surrounded them'. Presumably, slower though they may have been, they broke through on the left and, after the sea wind and swell, rammed the enemy in the narrow seas on beam and quarter. Only some such interpretation can explain the difference between the emphasis by Aeschylus on the Greek right wing and the insistence of Herodotus that the decisive action was fought on the Greek left.

Xerxes, when the Greek navy did not give chase, his ships routed and cut to pieces by the Athenians, feared chiefly that the

Greeks would sail for the Hellespont and destroy the bridge of boats, leaving him isolated in Europe from Asia. He accordingly pretended to restart the sea-battle by feinting the construction of a causeway toward Salamis. (The Great King admittedly also despatched couriers to Persia with the news of defeat.) On the advice of his military deputy Mardonius, and of Artemisia, the woman sea-captain, he finally left Mardonius with 300,000 men under command in Greece, while himself returning to the Hellespont with the rest of the army, his navy leaving through the eastern Aegean.

Themistocles, who had intended to destroy Xerxes' bridges, was dissuaded by the argument that Xerxes, if isolated in Greece, would either starve the Greeks or beat them in the field, either way living off the country. Cornered rats were dangerous. 'The great force which seemed, like a cloud, to darken the sea was now in flight. . . . Let it go. The Persians are gone . . . flung out, once and for all: so repair your homes, every one of you and attend to the sowing of your land. Let us sail for Hellespont . . . next year.' Themistocles sent another secret message to Xerxes, again via his favourite slave, Sicinnus, asserting that it was he, Themistocles, who had dissuaded the Greeks from pursuing the Persian fleet and destroying the Hellespont bridges. A lie, one intended to enhance his value to the Great King in yet unpredicted circumstances.

After Salamis and the consequent land defeat of Mardonius' army by Athenian and Spartan forces at Plataea under Pausanius and the then king of Macedon, the first great struggle between Asia and Europe ended. The separate, brilliant military administrations of both sides – Xerxes in his strategy of setting Carthage against the Greeks of Sicily, and Themistocles' appeal to the Greek Geio in Syracuse, although unsuccessful – and the Greek combination of land and sea forces were evident marks of advanced military thought, not different in kind from today.

It was not Marathon but Salamis which, by ending Persian naval control of the Aegean, also ended Xerxes' ability to maintain a dominant army in Greece. Not only had Persia endured tactical defeat, but her invincibility had been undermined. The military prestige of the Greeks had overthrown the structure of the wretched, rotten Persian Empire and, *à la longue*, ruined it. Music, sculpture, poetry, theatre, the law, all triumphed.

In Creasy's peroration, albeit on Marathon, not Salamis, 'the intellectual treasures of Athens, the growth of free institutions, the liberal enlightenment of the Western world and the gradual ascendancy for many ages of the great principles of European civilisation' prevailed.

Or, as 'Boney' Fuller said, 'with these battles [Salamis and Plataea] we stand on the threshold of the western world to be, in which Greek intellect was to conquer and to lay the foundations for centuries to come. No battles in history are therefore more portentous than Salamis and Plataea: they stand like the pillars of the temple of ages, supporting the architecture of western history' and the coming collapse of eastern tyranny.

'Alas for Persia's honoured name / Alas for all that noble host / The flower of manhood, Asia's boast . . . / Slaughtered for Xerxes who had fed / Hell's hungry jaws with Persian dead; / Lords of the bow, their country's pride / they followed the dark road and died.'

SYNOPSIS OF EVENTS BETWEEN
SALAMIS AND GAUGAMELA

After defeat at Salamis Xerxes returned to Asia, leaving an army in Greece under Mardonius, which was destroyed by the Greeks at Plataea. After 478 BC the Persians lost most of their conquests in Europe and on the coast of Asia.

In 457 BC, Athens battled against several Peloponnesian states, employing between 60,000 and 70,000 men in her fleets against Egypt and in the Aegean. A truce was concluded in 443 BC between Athens and Sparta but, in 431 BC, Sparta, assisted by the Boeotians and other Greek states beyond the Isthmus of Corinth, began the great Peloponnesian War. Plague took many Athenians, while Sparta conquered much of Thrace, where, however, fighting continued despite another truce between the combatants.

In 418 BC, Athens unsuccessfully attempted the conquest of Sicily.

In 404 BC, the Peloponnesian War ended in the surrender of Athens, Sparta triumphant.

Xenophon's Ten Thousand ('Thalassa! Thalassa!') reached the Mediterranean, while Sparta maintained its assaults against the Persian satraps in Asia: Dionysius defended Syracuse against Carthage; Rome took Veii. A combined Athenian and Persian naval victory led to the refortification of Athens. Sparta came under attack from former allies: the city of Thebes rose at Leuctra, and fell at Mantinea, under Epaminondas.

In 359 BC, Philip became king of Macedon. In 356, his son, Alexander the Great, was born. By 338, Macedonia had become supreme among the Greeks.

Philip was assassinated in 336, succeeded by Alexander, who defeated 'the northern barbarians' and Thebes. In 334 BC, he crossed the Hellespont into Asia.

CHAPTER TWO

GAUGAMELA/ARBELA, 331 BC

I n 418 BC the Spartans routed a combined Argive–Athenian force at Mantinea. Alcibiades, that corrupt, arrogant, handsome general, reared in Pericles' household, now sought to reduce Sicily and, eventually, Carthage. In 419 BC, Athens' repressive empire, freed from Periclean restraint, sought extension. The battle fleet carrying Alcibiades, Nicias and Lamachus included 134 triremes, the expedition framed, because of inadequate Athenian manpower, to deprive Sparta and Corinth of the oil, war matériel and corn accessible from Syracuse, which Athens required to pursue the war and enforce Athenian leadership in Greece.

Once at Syracuse, Lamachus' proposal for an immediate attack was foolishly rejected in favour of political warfare and disruption advocated by Alcibiades. The latter was, however, then ordered back to Athens to stand trial for destroying all the busts of Hermes in that city. He defected to the Spartans en route, betraying Athenian plans to them. In later unsuccessful naval and military actions under Nicias and Demosthenes, the Athenians suffered conclusive defeat of their vessels at sea from enemy prows, and on land thereafter.

The crews of the triremes refused to re-embark. The 7,000 survivors of the 45–50,000 sailors and soldiers whom Athens had sent to Syracuse were thrown into the quarries in circumstances of hideous brutality. Nicias and Demosthenes were butchered. 'The Athenians were destroyed with total destruction, their fleet, their army – everything was destroyed and few out of many returned.'

Had Lamachas' advice been followed, Syracuse might have fallen. The Athenian Empire thus enlarged and heading for an even greater hegemony, Sparta, Corinth, Euboea, Chios and Lesbos would have been unable to maintain a successful war against Athens. But this 'what if?' ignores the reality of a hopelessly divided Hellas, a Peloponnesian League as vicious as before and the appointment of Lysander to command by Darius II of Persia. That admiral in 405 BC captured 170 Athenian vessels, not even at sea, beached at Aegospotami. In the tumult, 'the embarrassed and receding Athenians' could only assail each other: all the prisoners, 3–4,000, were slaughtered.

'All danger from Athens to the independent nations of the West was at an end. Nor among the rival Greek republics, whom her own rashness aided to crush her, was there any capable of reorganising her Empire or resuming her schemes of conquest.' But however severe a defeat, it is still wrong to speak of Syracuse as a decisive battle, only a progressive and unstoppable decline in integrity, courage and professional skill, without which no empire could have endured. 'The dominion of Western Europe was left for Rome and Carthage to dispute two centuries later in conflict still more terrible and with higher displays of military genius than Athens had witnessed, either in her rise, her meridian or her fall.'

In the years that followed, the Peloponnesian War ended in 404 BC with the triumph of Sparta and the surrender of Athens. But the Lacedaemonians, as well as assaulting the Persian satraps in Asia Minor – leading to the retreat of Xenophon's Ten Thousand – restored democracy in Athens. The Athenians returned the compliment by defeating Sparta on the ocean and restoring Athens' fortifications.

Rome, by its capture of Veii, began its career of conquest. The Gauls overran Italy which, however, fell under Roman dominion by 290 BC. In Greece, Thebes under Epaminondas became temporarily dominant until that great leader's death. Athens was incompetent to re-establish her empire. In 356 Alexander the Great was born and, by 338 BC, his father Philip had secured Macedonian supremacy throughout Greece.

In Sicily, meanwhile, it was rumoured that 'Philip had boasted that since no other kings ruled in Hellas, none could dispute his supremacy.' Within the violet and gold vault of the temple of Zeus, Timoleon of Syracuse, among his followers in their 'roseate shawls and tunics, yellow and white robes, with jewelled ceremonial swords', rejected the crown of Dionysius in a Greater Sicily, a royal Syracuse, overlordship of Hellas, mastery of the world. 'The strength', said Timo, 'of the King of Macedon owes nothing to his adornments.'

But Timo, 'the old fellow with a dusty robe, blind, led by a dog escorted not by guards, but merry children; the Liberator', died at almost the same hour as Philip was assassinated.

At the age of twenty, Alexander became king of Macedon.

Philip's assassination on the occasion of the marriage of his daughter to her own uncle was probably the work of his queen, Olympias, enraged at the birth of a son to her husband from his latest young wife, the seventh such, Eurydice. The assassin, a bodyguard named Pausanius, fell while trying to escape and was either killed on the spot or clamped to a board to starve to death in public. At all events, Olympias' son, Alexander, could now succeed to the throne, pre-empting all pretenders, including Eurydice's baby son, and rehabilitating his mother. On the other hand, Alexander, in a letter to King Darius III, accused the Persians of causing the crime in an attempt to disintegrate Philip's expeditionary army in Asia.

The scarred, one-eyed, black-bearded Philip of Macedon, forged by years of brutal warfare, gave place to a handsome, beardless son who, dying at the age of thirty-two, had nevertheless become at twenty-five the ruler of two million square miles. Julius Caesar himself wept at the thought of Alexander, dead so young, yet 'King of many peoples' when he, Caesar, 'had not yet achieved any brilliant success'. For Arrian, 'he was a king and the undisputed lord of the two continents . . . his name renowned throughout the whole earth'.

Macedonian royalty claimed Zeus among their ancestors who, in legend, included Hercules, and Dionysus, god-king, and far away and long ago, invader of India, linked in the nineteenth century by Kipling and others with the fair-skinned Kafirs of Nuristan, aquiline noses and European features. (And red-haired, freckled Mongolians – Hoton – were seen by this writer near Lake Uvs in 1972.) Olympias, Alexander's mother, claimed descent from both Achilles and Helen of Troy. Portraits of Alexander are unreliable, but show him with a ruddy facial complexion, Caucasian skin colour, brown, streaked hair, a long, magnificent, straight nose, large brown eyes. There is a faint look of Tom Conti, the actor, in a portrait from the Alexander Mosaic in the National Museum at Naples, a face crowded with energy, humour and calculation, the head said by Plutarch to have habitually inclined to the left.

Plutarch added that he was a hunter, a scholar with a passion for Homer implanted by his tutor, none other than Aristotle. (Alexander carried with him a text of the *Iliad* throughout his campaigns.) Arrian quoted Ptolemy, king of Egypt, on Alexander, as

of much shrewdness, most courageous, zealous for honour and danger, careful of religion . . . most brilliant to seize on the right course of action, even when all was obscure, and where all was clear, most happy in his conjecture of likelihood; most masterly in marshalling an army and in arming and equipping it; and in uplifting his soldiers' spirits and filling them with good hope, and brushing away anything fearful in dangers by his own want of fear – in all this most noble. And all that had to be done in uncertainty, he did with the utmost daring: he was most skilled in swift anticipation and in gripping of his enemy before anyone had time to fear the event.

Alexander was planner, administrator, great captain, yet compassionate, bearing without arrogance the culture of Greece to the wide world while respecting Orientals as equals and permitting their religious beliefs. He differed from his predecessors in this respect, in protection for women, and in sympathy for the downtrodden, innocent and vulnerable; he differed from few in the ferocity of his reaction to insult, insubordination or treachery. He loved boys, and he loved women somewhat less.

At Siwa, the Berbers, sturdy, independent, honest, intellectual and trustworthy, were compared by him with the cringing, venal Arab, 'degenerate offspring of a race which only from its history', as the travelling Dr Randall-MacIvor's Libyan notes observed, 'can claim any title to respect'.

Achilles, Hercules, Perseus, Zeus filled his spirit. After his mysterious, solitary audience with the 'god' Ammon at the desert oasis of Siwa, where the priest addressed him as 'Son of Zeus', he took with him the concept of the god-king, incarnate victory and dominion, a concept identified in sculpture by Ammon's ram's horns, not always by the insignia of his father, Philip. At Siwa, a Berber shrine to Jupiter Ammon, among thousands of date-palms, its houses built on two great rocks and over arches spanning narrow, irregular streets, 'Alexander had taken his divine father to heart' in a reflection, much desired by him, of those sons of god who fight for ever in Homer's *Iliad*.

But divinity did not lie in conquest alone. As a result of his visit to the shrine at Siwa, he was seized with the concept of unity in concord (*homonoia*), the brotherhood of man, the City of God, a universal empire under a divine ruler without distinction of race, 'good' not confined to the Greeks, nor 'evil' to barbarians. The world should be of one mind, at peace, guided by the god Ammon Zeus, through Alexander, missionary and son, so proclaimed by the priest of Siwa.

Be that as it may, Alexander's triumphs rested on the army, Philip's model army, although Alexander's *hero* was Achilles, his legendary ancestor, against whom, all his life, he measured his struggle for glory.

The strength of that army lay in its infantry, the modified Greek phalanx, in Macedonia sixteen rather than eight or twelve men deep, their main weapon the sarissa, thirteen to twenty feet long, projecting in front of the line. These, although not by Alexander's men in India, were carried by the Foot Companions, and the Royal Shield-Bearers. The hoplites or ordinary soldiers also carried shields as large as their own bodies, and sometimes swords: they wore helmets, breastplates, greaves. The Hypaspist elite, as the hinge on the right flank between cavalry and sarissas, bore shorter spears. Light pikemen (peltasts) in eight ranks were deployed behind the hoplites, skirmishers (psiloi) ahead bearing slings, javelins and bows. The armoured (both men and horse) cavalry, 4,000 Companions on the left, wore flowing cloaks, metal kilts, fluted helmets, Thessalians on the right, both groups armed with pikes thrown or used as lances, delivered the first shattering blow, followed by the phalanx at the double. The infantrymen were joined by light cavalrymen for reconnaissance and flank protection, these usually with no armour except helmets. The horsemen had no stirrups and only exiguous saddles.

There were four phalanxes to a grand phalanx, the latter organised like modern armies in platoons, companies, battalions, regiments and divisions, an army of 32,000 men, comparable with a small field army today. Portable catapults were transported in wagons or on animals, as were siege weapons, assembled at the scene of battle by engineer units.

H. A. L. Fisher, in his *History of Europe*, asserted that 'The Macedonian phalanx changed the history of the world ... the spearmen of Macedonia marched into action in open assay and held the enemy, while the cavalry charged in upon the wings in wedge-like squadrons and decided the issue.' But, at the beginning of Philip's reign, that phalanx was directed not toward the establishment in Asia Minor of Greek settlements to feed hungry colonial mouths, but against those in Thebes and Athens, aroused by Demosthenes, who declared Philip to be a threat to the liberties of the Greek confederacy.

Macedon had been a wild and semi-barbarous region when Philip had begun in 359 BC to reconstruct its economy and to expand its frontiers. Learning from Epaminondas of Thebes, when a hostage there, the principles of coordination between infantry and cavalry, and of concentration of force at the point of tactical weakness, he defeated rebels in Illyria and, conquering the tribes, founded considerable new settlements in the Balkans up to the Danube river; in Bulgaria; and on the Black Sea where the Greek diaspora began, along and within the frontiers of Russia.

After the 'Social War' in 358 BC, Philip took territory in Thrace, hitherto the property of Athenians, a policy of conquest which he continued three years later, then defeating similar opposition in Thessaly, Epirus – the home of Queen Olympias – Illyria and Thrace again, the Danube once more, defeated once at Byzantium. It was now, 339 BC, that Demosthenes' oratory raised Thebes and Athens against Macedon. At the battle of Chaeronea, Philip, his son Alexander commanding the cavalry, defeated those powers with heavy casualties, achieving primacy for Macedonia in all Greece.

At Corinth in the following year, out of all the Greek states except Sparta, Philip founded the Hellenic League 'in perpetual alliance with Macedonia'. The king persuaded his fellow members to participate in war against Persia. His formal purposes were the liberation of the Greek cities of Asia Minor and the punishment of barbarians, Persia and her allies, in and out of Greece, for lawless treatment of Greek temples, a reference to Xerxes' destruction of Athens before Themistocles' victory at Salamis.

King Philip, chairman of the Hellenic League and commander-in-chief, sent an expeditionary force of Thespians, Corinthians, Illyrians, Thracians and only 700 Athenians, under the elderly General Parmenion, to Asia, initially as an armed reconnaissance. (The proportion of barbarians in this force was high enough to cast doubt on its designation as 'Greek crusade'.) As we have seen, before the king could leave to join his troops, he was murdered, his son Alexander elected captain-general of the Hellenic League in his stead.

The first action of Alexander the Great on accession to the throne was in Thessaly, where he avoided the narrow mountain pass at Tempe by cutting steps in the rock of Mount Ossa, descending from the heights to force bloody defeat on the Thessalians. Then, after repeating his father's chastisement of the Illyrians and northern tribes, he put down a further Theban and Athenian rising, this time inspired and financed by the Persian King of Kings, Darius III. The Thebans, supposing Alexander to have been killed in Illyria, had advanced on a Macedonian town before discovering that he was alive and only fifteen miles away. Within hours he had stormed the city, annihilated 6,000 citizens, and taken it. With the agreement of Greece's smaller cities, Thebes was then destroyed: Athens, which surrendered to Alexander, and had not openly sent troops to support the enemy, was spared.

His Greek base thus secured, Alexander was ready to march on Asia, leaving Antipater behind to command in Greece and Europe, with a second front mounted in Italy by his uncle, King Alexander of Epirus, brother of the Queen Mother, Olympias. The bid for world empire was plain, but not approved unanimously by his advisors, or not immediately. Nevertheless, in May 334 BC, leading some 30,000 infantry and 5,000 cavalry, he marched through barbarian Thrace to the Dardanelles, where he took the helm of his own royal trireme, flagship of his combined fleet of sixty vessels.

Next day he landed for the first time in Asia, marking the leap by a spear's thrust into Persian soil, the beach where Ajax, Achilles and the heroes of the *Iliad* had begun the quest for Helen. Here he sacrificed at their graves and danced naked round the tomb of Achilles: his lover, Hephaistion, similarly laid garlands at the tomb of Patroclus, Achilles' lover in the Trojan War, hammering home the parallel with the contemporary god-king. From the priests of the little town that Troy had become, gifts came of

26

Trojan armour and a shield which Alexander was to carry on to Hamadan, Merv, Meshed, the Oxus, Bactria, Kandahar, Balkh, the Hindu Kush, Swat, Lahore, Mooltan, Amritsar, the Indus, Beas, Chenab and the ill-fated Jhelum river. Then back from furthest Asia to death on the Euphrates, leaving behind eighteen cities called Alexandria; his immortal name; and the culture of Greece.

Alexander's infantry, on joining Parmenion and the advance guard, consisted of Foot Companions, Shield-Bearers and barbarians, the cavalry composed of Companions, Thessalians, Mounted Scouts, allied Greeks in cavalry and infantry, raising the Macedonians' total from 35,000 to nearly 50,000. At first, not only because of Persian scorched earth and starvation by crop destruction, Alexander had been unable to bring the Persians to open combat. After a week of unsuccessful search, the Mounted Scouts reported the enemy in a strong defensive position on the banks of the Granicus river, heavily armoured cavalry and hired Greeks under Memnon, a Rhodian Greek in Darius' employ, a smaller force than Alexander's, less able, less fit and less well trained.

Mounted on his black horse, Bucephalus, his own age, broken and trained by him to kneel in full caparison, Alexander that afternoon led the Mounted Scouts and Companions in a charge against the Persian mass, whose cavalry 'gave'. The Foot Companions, entering the breach to surround those Greeks in Persian service, killed them in conflict, captured them for despatch to servitude in Macedonia, or – the majority – massacred them. His lieutenant, Cleitus, later murdered by his king in a drunken brawl, on this occasion saved his life.

This first engagement won on the river, Alexander moved on to Sardis, which yielded Lydia, and to Ephesus, where the garrison had already fled and where, by substituting democracy for oligarchy, his actions won peaceful cooperation across the Meander from cities further south.

At Miletus he had to fight, using his siege weapons to smash down walls and outworks, forcing Milesian surrender, refusing battle against the huge Persian fleet of 400 triremes. Having seen, indeed, that his policy, with no ocean warfare whatever, had succeeded in blocking Persian naval access to the supplies and recruiting ports of the Aegean, he disbanded his entire fleet. Successful in depriving the enemy fleet of any significant land-based supplies in Asia, this policy was nevertheless one of considerable risk, revised on occasion as finance improved. It led, in the end, not only to virtual Persian maritime impotence, but to the defection of the Phoenician and Cypriot fleets.

In Caria, Queen Ada offered surrender of her fortress, Alinda, in exchange for adopting Alexander as her son. 'She kept sending him meats and delicacies every day, finally offering . . . cooks and bakers.' Golden crowns, symbols of obeisance, followed, and so did Carian complaisance in the siege of Halicarnassus, temporarily occupied by Memnon, a process involving battering rams, cata-pults and siege towers, which began in a fiery August and endured for two months, ending in savage battle. Caria had fallen. Yet another seaport, columned Halicarnassus, was therefore almost closed to the enemy fleet. Alexander moved southeast to Pamphylia and Lycia, further to deny the coast to the Persians, implanting Greek culture in Asia Minor and forbidding Persian naval access to Phoenicia and the Levant.

The army then changed direction over flat arable land through Phrygia to Gordium, his rendezvous with Parmenion and with some 4,000 reinforcements from the north, delayed because of the absence of a fleet and the consequent need to march 500 miles. These troops, when they eventually arrived in May, had been joined by those Greeks, returning from their wives, whom Alexander had sent home to winter the previous year.

Meanwhile, Darius III in his capital at Susa had appointed his Rhodian general Memnon, now at Cos with 300 warships, as supreme commander-in-chief. Memnon's overall plan was to burn the crops ahead of the Macedonian advance and cut Alexander's lines of retreat and communications, particularly at the Dardanelles. At sea, he was to undertake maximum interference with merchant shipping, particularly the corn supply; by subversion, he planned not only to raise such rebellion in Sparta and Athens as would oblige Alexander to return to Greece but also to overthrow the new democracies created by the Macedonians. The latter, alarmed, raised a new fleet but, in June, by dying at Mytilene, Memnon greatly disturbed the imperial cause.

Alexander, after Gordium, took Paphlagonia, then farmed out Cappadocia to a local satrap. He moved next in a night attack through the Cilician Gates over rich, well-irrigated grape and grain country to Tarsus, perhaps deliberately unopposed by the Persians at the pass who, in fleeing, burned crops ahead. The Great King now decided that without Memnon, Memnon's strategy would not do. The Persian fleet was ordered to beach in Syria. Their crews joined Darius on land, leaving only 100 seagoing vessels and 3,000 sailors.

The golden chariot of the sun, the treasures, the royal and holy chariots of family and entourage, an escort of Immortals, the painted portraits of the gods, moved under the burning sun to Babylon towards confrontation, hitherto rejected, with Alexander the Great, at last.

But the Persian *army* was already at Babylon. The procession, including wagons and portable bathrooms, contained only the Household, the Ten Thousand Immortals in jewelled helmets, Sons of the Kindred in their purple, the Magi with their silver altars, concubines, eunuchs, royal children, slaves, servants, cooks, artisans, all ancillaries to the waiting armed might. And while the convoy moved on painfully, Alexander – unknown to Darius – had been wounded by a bolt from a catapult while besieging Gaza, had destroyed the remaining defences at Halicarnassus, and had sent Parmenion to Syria and Phoenicia. Since, recovered from grave illness, he was unaware that the Persian was on the way, he then made south for Egypt to be proclaimed as pharaoh at Memphis, thence to the mysterious encounter at Siwa.

Through rice and cornfields, Darius III at last entered Babylon through great bronze gates in black walls twenty-five yards high, each side of the square fifteen miles of brick and bitumen, lined by banners and trumpeters. Ebony, blue and white tiles, scarlet and saffron hangings, jasmine, the cool darkness of the pools, lilies, couches clothed in linen, eased the king's spirit after the long journey from Susa. Bactrians too, with their two-humped camels, under Bessos in felt and furs, Scythians, fair-haired bowmen in lynx skins, bearing black tents, came in under the shade trees.

At Issos, the king now chose the wrong terrain, the Persian cavalry charge failed because of his flight, constrained by lack of space, and spotted earlier by Parmenion two days from the Pillar of Jonah and the Syrian Gates. In terrible heat, Alexander in forty-eight hours had marched seventy-five miles to reach the enemy, turning to meet Darius in line, the cavalry behind – Companions, supported by the foot Shield-Bearers on the right, Parmenion and Thessalians on the left – Foot Companions in the centre and Greek mercenaries on the left. The front was narrow, depriving Darius of the advantage of numbers. Alexander was faced with a swollen river and slippery banks, constrained within close surrounding mountains. The Macedonian infantry, their cry of *alalalalai* echoing off the hills, went forward, the two cavalry arms meeting in the river to throw up great plumes of water. Elsewhere, the Greek phalanx shuddered under assault from Darius' infantry. The Companions, however, encircled the Persian infantry from the rear; Parmenion held fast on the left. The Thessalian horsemen raced to help pierce the centre, where Darius' chariot was placed, the Great King forced to flee until abandoning it for a horse, leaving robe and shield behind for Alexander to find, his queen and family also captive.

One of the Naples mosaics shows the two kings in the heat of battle, eye to eye, before the rout and slaughter of Persians for which Darius' commanders, especially Bessos, blamed him (but a dagger wound in Alexander's thigh was probably the Persian's work). Alexander talked to his men after battle, rewarded them, buried them, congratulated them: the victory lay with him and the Companions whom he had trained. Like Slim, to 'talk to the men' is what makes the commander a great captain. King Darius could not encompass that.

But Darius had escaped. And although the capture of Persian baggage at Damascus made it impossible for Darius to finance the navy, the residue of which had anyway been destroyed on the beach, Alexander still had to conquer or reduce Byblos, Sidon and Tyre. The first two were taken by peaceful coup. Tyre had been a *much* tougher nut, requiring blockade and siege, arrow-shooting catapults, stone throwers with a 400-yard range, siege towers 180 feet high, battering rams, grappling irons, laborious construction, under fire, of a long mole. Before surrender, Tyre poured red-hot sand on the attackers, flaying them, and killed Alexander's envoys. Arad, Byblos and Sidon gave Alexander 100 ships between them. The Cypriots added the same. Four thousand Greek reinforcements arrived who had already, under Antigonus, routed Persian troops escaped from the Issos battle. In July, Tyre fell to Macedonian troops on scaling ladders, Alexander himself leading from the battlements.

After the victory, he took as mistress Barsine, daughter of a Persian general and satrap. Gaza had been next, taken in two months by a combination of an artificial mound from which to bombard, and of tunnelling under the walls. Alexander, as we know, was wounded again before going on to Egypt to become, after Siwa, both pharaoh and god-king. In Samaria, he destroyed a rebellion and its rebel leaders, handing part of the territory as present to the Jews. With 11,000 fresh troops, after Gaugamela, the Spartan revolt behind him under King Agis in Greece was crushed at Megalopolis.

Alexander, organising festivals, games and entertainment at Tyre for 47,000 infantry and cavalry, waited to cross the Euphrates and mount the direct attack on Darius and his armies at Babylon 700 miles away eastward for which he had waited so long. While expecting reinforcements, who arrived in time neither for Gaugamela nor for the war with Sparta, Alexander sent Hephaistion to bridge the Euphrates. Hephaistion, at Thapsacus, finding Darius' governor of Babylon, General Mazaeus, on the opposite bank, could not safely complete his bridging. The two may have exchanged messages before Alexander himself arrived. It is certain that, after burning crops in the Euphrates valley according to his instructions, Mazaeus fled without explanation when battle was finally joined, curiously reinstated by Alexander as governor, perhaps a treasonable bargain concluded on the river itself.

Equally inexplicable, when Alexander then crossed that river by sinking piles and lashing rafts with iron chains, he was not impeded on the 'unburned route', which Mazaeus had been instructed by Darius to leave open for ambush, northwards through Armenia to the Tigris 300 miles on. Captured Persian spies had earlier told him that Darius was on the Tigris with a much larger army than at Issos. When he crossed unopposed, however, breasting a fierce channel at Abu Dahir, no one was there and no crops had been destroyed. Perhaps Darius, with his estimated million men against the little army of 47,000, suffered from hubris: 'why burn valuable land when this time, scythed chariots and cavalry could be fully employed on ground levelled by slaves beforehand?'

So at Gaugamela Darius and his combat troops waited, the Household and support troops at Arbela some tens of miles south, an old grey Assyrian city, worshipping the hideous Ishtar.

In late September, 1,000 Persian horsemen were routed in a skirmish by Mountain Scouts. Prisoners reported that Darius' main force was not far away and in vast strength, up to a quarter of a million men. Alexander, in turn, had been observed by the enemy where he lay encamped on a ridge above a tell or mound beside the village of Gaugamela. Parmenion had advised delaying the attack to provide for closer reconnaissance. Indeed, an instant assault on the huge, formed Persian army below would not have had surprise and, furthermore, the innumerable camp fires below had caused panic in the little force. (Alexander, oddly, for the first time, sacrificed in honour of Fear.) Stakes and obstacles had been identified in position to disrupt a cavalry charge, while the ground in front of the Persian scythed chariots had been levelled. When, however, his generals, including Parmenion, advised him to attack that night, the Macedonian replied: 'Alexander does not steal his victories.' Disingenuous, given likely confusion in darkness against an enemy of that immensity.

Alexander had stopped Darius' policy of retreat while scorching the earth which the Macedonian had planned to conquer, and on which he had meanwhile to subsist. He intended to engage Darius in terminal pitched battle. The odds against success were substantial, not only in the total numbers of cavalry, a ratio of at least four to one, but in armour, weapons and mounted archers, on a wide plain suitable for mounted encirclement of a smaller foe, already overlapped by Darius' long lines. Among the Persians, only the infantry, although superior in numbers, lacked the incomparable drill and experience of the Foot Companions and Shield-Bearers, Alexander's own trained men. But behind Darius lay the mountains of Media where the king had served and could expect personal loyalty and a refuge in need.

Alexander's army rested for four days and nights. When he brought them down to the plain as dawn came on the final morning, the Persians were tired, short of sleep and without their edge, this gigantic force, now of 250,000 men, against Alexander's 47,000.

Darius' throne was in the centre of the front line, preceded by 200 chariots, fifteen elephants, the Royal Persian squadron with gold apples on their spears, to the left the Mardian archers, Scythian and Bactrian cavalry, with the Armenians and Cappadocian cavalry on his right hand. Immediately to the rear stood the great mass of Greek mercenaries and the Kinsmen. Beside and behind them, Indians, Albanians, more Greeks, Babylonians, Parthians, more Scythians, Red Sea troops,

Hyrcassians, Persians, meagre, avian Carians, many other ethnic and Persian troops, the whole in two main lines of which the cavalry on the flanks numbered perhaps 30,000, opposing 7,000 Macedonians.

When Alexander descended before first light, his right wing was formed by the Royal Horse Guards under Philotas. The Macedonian king, as was his practice, commanded from the extreme right of the front line, then the Royal Foot Guard, the Hypaspists under Nicanor, with six brigades of the phalanx to the left, nearest to the Shield-Bearers. Next to the infantry were the allied and Thessalian cavalry. Two flying columns, one on either wing, were unusually posted as reserves, angled to the main line in order to attack Darius' flanks if encirclement were attempted, or to act as reinforcements, wheeling inward. The columns comprised light cavalry, Macedonian archers, javelin troops under Philotas on the right and, under Parmenion's left wing, Thracian infantry, Greek cavalry and Andromachus' Greek mercenaries. This order of battle, said to be the first occasion in history to embody a reserve line, enabled Alexander to face both front and flanks.

Since he was outflanked on either wing by sheer Persian numbers, he swung his march to the right in order to concentrate the assault at one point of the enemy line, thus also avoiding Darius' racing chariot attack over smooth levelled ground. The Great King in response threw forward the Thracian and Bactrian cavalry to take Alexander in the right flank, checking his advance. Alexander, then, having called up infantry and further cavalry, began a furious cavalry battle amid the clashing of armour, shouts and cries, the wild neighing of horses, at the end of which the Hellenes had driven the Persian cavalry from the field, there and for the moment.

The chariots, supported by cavalry, were now stopped by javelins and arrows from the Agrianians and other light troops before the Companions on the right wing, wounding the horses and charioteers and slowing or stopping their progress, other than a

34

few easily captured in the rear. Darius' cavalry on his left wing again failed to outflank Alexander on his right, themselves held on *their* flank by Alexander's second line, including Aretes' light cavalry, and by the Companions led by Alexander himself. The king went straight for a gap in the Persian line, briefly revealing Darius. The Persian king, terrified by the charge and by the hedgehog spikes of the phalanx's sarissas, reversed his chariot and escaped in blinding dust-clouds.

Mazaeus, commanding the Persian right wing, outflanked Parmenion on the Hellenic left wing. Parmenion was over-whelmingly outnumbered until rescued by the phalanx who, in so doing, unfortunately opened a gap in their own Macedonian order of battle through which poured enemy cavalry who, initially unhindered, tried first to free the Persian Queen Mother from the baggage camp where she was held after capture, and then to loot and plunder, at last prevented by the second-line phalanx. In escaping, the Persian and Indian marauders, who would have done better to attack the Companions in the flank, were cut down, after killing sixty of Alexander's Royal Horse Guards and three generals. Alexander set off in pursuit of Darius, whether ignoring Parmenion's request for help or not receiving it, that general saving himself with the aid of Thessalian cavalry and Simmias' brigade of the phalanx. By this time, the defeat of the Persian army was complete.

Alexander had won a brilliant victory. Because he had not caught Darius, however, the fact that Persian casualties were much larger than his own army had suffered made him a great general, but not yet the king of Asia. That title had to await the discovery of the Great King's body, bound in gold chains, murdered by his own commanders, in a common cart with a hide roof. Alexander went on to take Susa, Babylon, Pasargadae and Persepolis, together with its palace, much of which he put to the torch in revenge for Xerxes' deprivations. (Some walls still, nevertheless, retain carved reliefs of servants bearing dishes, the king under the parasol, eunuchs, Arabs in the burnous, horses, chariots, warriors bearing the royal throne, the king on his throne.) By that time, Antipater had defeated the Spartans at Megalopolis, assuring Alexander's western bases and hinterland.

'By right of the sword, he had become King of Asia' and, by 323 BC, was so acknowledged, founding 'Alexandrias' wherever he conquered: Herat, Ghazin, Kabul. He crossed the Hindu Kush, the rivers Oxus and Jaxartes, allying with the Scythians, and with the Bactrians by marriage with their leader's daughter, Roxana. One of his armies, under his old friend and lover Hephaistion, crossed into India over the Khyber Pass. Another, under his own command, fought through Swat to the Indus, magnificently defeated King Porus on the Jhelum river, secured victory near Lahore at Sangala and crossed the Chenab.

He halted on the Sutlej only in preparation for advance to the Ganges and to 'the Encircling Sea, earth's utmost boundary' (in fact the Bay of Bengal), where he could seal an omnipotent empire within frontiers impervious to attack. But the army refused to go on, although leaving him with the Indus river as frontier, linked by sea with Persia and Euphrates, the route to India confirmed by the voyage of Admiral Nearchus.

But on 2 June, in Babylon, Nebuchadnezzar's capital, Alexander the Great died.

The triumph at Gaugamela had not been military alone. It established his passion for harmony (*homonoia*), his own mission as intermediary and missionary between man and god. It realised the brotherhood of man in the common Hellenistic culture which victory imposed and which scientific Alexandrian enquiry symbolised. It led to intermarriage between races, unity of heart and mind. The Greek world permeated both the world of the east which he had transformed and the Roman world which followed, a trading world, to flower under the Romans, but of Greek inspiration. It created another world, that of the god-king, the worship of emperors as god-kings. Later followed, in direct line, Christianity, and the change from rule by emperors to the rule of popes. It led, above all, directly to the Roman

36

Empire while, on the other side of the world, Greece has been echoed from Urumchi to the Taklamakan desert on the edge of China itself.

> Asia beheld with astonishment and awe, the uninterrupted progress of a hero, the sweep of whose conquests was as wide and rapid as that of her own barbaric kings, or the Scythian or Chaldean hordes; but far unlike the transient whirlwinds of Asiatic warfare, the advance of the Macedonian leader was no less deliberate than rapid: at every step the Greek power that took root, and the language and the civilisation of Greece were planted from the shores of the Aegean to the banks of the Indus, from the Caspian and the great Hyrcanian plain to the cataracts of the Nile: to exist actually for nearly a thousand years and in their effects to endure for ever.

SYNOPSIS OF EVENTS BETWEEN
GAUGAMELA AND THE METAURUS

Alexander had taken Balkh, capital of Bactriana, Samarkand, Sogd and Transoxiana as far as Ferghana. After reaching Akora on the right bank of the Indus, marching parallel with the Kabul river, he conquered Afghanistan and the Punjab, defeating, as we have seen, the Indian King Porus in major battle. It was at the river called Hyphasis that his troops refused to go further towards the Ganges.

Alexander thereafter began the descent of the Indus, leading his army back to Europe through modern Sindh and Baluchistan, while despatching his admiral, Nearchus, on a successful voyage to find a maritime path to the Persian Gulf. In 324 BC, ten years after crossing the Hellespont, Alexander the Great returned to Babylon. Here, in 323 BC, at the age of thirty-two, he died.

Attempts were made then by Greek states, which were defeated by Antipater, to overthrow the dominance of Macedon. But by 280 BC the last of Alexander's captains, Seleucus, had been assassinated; Bactria and Parthia receded, only Syria, Palestine and Asia Minor surviving, although Alexander's general, Ptolemy, established rule in Egypt. Macedonia fell to the dynasty of Antigonus; the other Greek states were in tumult.

Rome now, after defeating Etruscans and Cisalpine Gauls, was also victorious over King Pyrrhus of Epirus in 275 BC, and ruled all Italy from the Rubicon to the Strait of Messina. Sicily became a Roman province, despite the genius of the Carthaginian Hamilcar Barca, at the conclusion of the First Punic War. Sardinia too was lost to Rome.

Hamilcar, in compensation, won southern Spain for Carthage, thus resuming the struggle with Rome. He was followed in this course by his brother, Hasdrubal, and by his son Hannibal, who by attacking Saguntum on the Ebro opened the Second Punic War at a time when Rome was once more violently engaged with the Cisalpine Gauls. Rome's forces and those of its allies have been estimated at 700,000 infantry and 70,000 cavalrymen.

In 218 BC, Hannibal crossed the Alps and invaded Italy.

CHAPTER THREE

THE METAURUS, 207 BC, AND ZAMA, 202 BC

Although Darius fled the scene, Alexander and Darius are legendarily portrayed in the Naples mosaics as having fought in single combat at the Issos river. So is Scipio Africanus said to have struggled eye-to-eye with Hannibal at Zama, and also to have emulated at Cartagena (New Carthage) Alexander's siege of Tyre and his conduct on the battlements. The magnanimity of both commanders to the families of the defeated Darius and the Spanish Indibilis has been remarked, as has the parallel between Scipio and Jupiter, Hannibal and Melkarth, Alexander and Zeus Ammon at Siwa. These generals were 'the sons of gods', their conception achieved by means of serpents in their mothers' beds. But although at Zama in 202 BC Hannibal and the authority of Carthage were finally brought down, it was at the Metaurus river, some years earlier in 207 BC, that that power was fundamentally destroyed.

A thousand years before that battle the Phoenicians, an (Asian) Semitic people, even today distinguished by markedly flat backs to their heads, came out of the Levant to found settlements in North Africa. The most important of these became Carthage, maritime power, great city and seat of empire, now a heap of ruined stone near Tunis. Before obliteration by Rome in 146 BC, this nation of seafaring traders had visited Europe, the Baltic states for amber, Cornwall for tin. They had landed in Morocco and Senegal, had conquered Sardinia, the Balearics and much of Sicily, and compensated for eventual naval defeats at Rome's hand by invading Spain and, under great Hannibal, Italy.

Carthage was, however, racially divided, without a unifying principle, bearing self-inflicted wounds from oppressed races, Libyans and nomadic Numidians, dependent on mercenaries, a weakness which only the genius of Hannibal could overcome, and that only while he lived.

In Italy, on the other hand, the small city-state of the Roman Republic had so re-stabilised her institutions, in particular her army, as to defeat the Latin tribes in the plains south of the Tiber, the mysterious Etruscans, creators of Tuscany, and the war-like northern Gauls, after a war lasting six years. The Greek King Pyrrhus of Epirus, descendant of Alexander the Great's kinsman and ally, although twice defeating the rising power of Rome before the latter's victory at Beneventum, had long given up the struggle, as had gradually the cities in Italy of the Greek diaspora. Where the Athenians had supplanted the Phoenicians, so now did Rome supplant the children of the great Macedonian, on Rome's triumphant way to the annihilation of Carthage. In Italy itself, under Roman rule, unity, communications, law and order began to prevail.

Carthage had failed to capture all Sicily. In 264 BC, an appeal for aid from Syracuse addressed to both Rome and Carthage led to the First Punic War between these two powers. Rome had no fleet worth the name. Superior Carthaginian oar-power, particularly in carrying reinforcements to Sicily from North Africa, was initially successful. Rome's first attempt at naval construction at Messina having failed, she invented a combined grapple and bridge called the corvus (raven) which, lowered on to the enemy's deck from a pole in the galley's prow, permitted the legions to pass from one vessel to the other.

Victory followed, at Mylae and at Heracles, achieving naval command for the Romans in the Mediterranean, allowing them to land troops in Tunis. But ashore in North Africa, the Spartan

Xanthippus, supporting Carthaginian cavalry, then defeated the Roman general Regulus. In 255 and 249 BC, two storms brought naval losses, maritime catastrophe for Rome which, despairing, did not recreate its navy until 242 when, in a major sea engagement, Carthage was again the loser. Weakened by mutiny on land, the latter abandoned Sardinia to Rome, and, although the Carthaginians had sent Hannibal's father, Hamilcar Barca, to Sicily, her peace treaty with Rome included evacuation in 241 BC of that island, a concession arousing 'the wrath of the House of Barca'. Before that, the Carthaginians had bloodily crucified their own unsuccessful admiral, Hanno.

That atrocity was among the least of the horrors that followed when Carthage's troops, unpaid for months, sometimes years, came home from Sicily to find an empty treasury and corrupt administration. Hamilcar also returned to Africa but, at first away on his estates, was unable to prevent the terrible bloodshed of the ensuing mutiny, the Mutineers War, among his own men. These mercenaries, bear-skinned Libyans, Spartans, Gauls in wolf-skin, plumed legions, Negroes, slingers from the Balearics, Ligurians in skin tents, seized the chairman of the council (Safet) and his unarmed staff, these shackled at the neck, legs and arms broken by rocks, slashed, limbs amputated or torn off, pissed upon, left to rot or die in pits. Hamilcar, once back in Carthage, combined his elephants, cavalry and lance to break the military revolt, disembowelling the mutineers and defeating those still surviving in formal battle. Their bodies, alive or dying mutilated, were covered with pitch, lit and catapulted into a Tunis of cypresses and cedar, palm trees, pomegranate and figs, a trunk here, there a thigh, now a head . . .

Hamilcar had cut off the nose of the Roman Regulus and then cut out his tongue before returning him to Rome. In further revenge, to create a base for the continued war which he intended and, no doubt, to compensate for the loss of Malta, Sardinia and Sicily, Hamilcar decided to transfer the Carthaginian power to Spain, largely without the financial support of the Carthaginian authorities. In Spain he established and funded a loyal army of exiles and native soldiers, within a state controlled almost entirely by himself, albeit under the democracy of Carthage. Before dying, and the accession of his son-in-law, Hasdrubal Barca, he had taken all Spain below the Ebro and Tagus rivers. Rome in Hasdrubal's time recognised Carthaginian sovereignty over much of this territory, except for Saguntum, a Greek city and Rome's ally, in a treaty which also established the Ebro as the common frontier. At Hasdrubal's assassination, Hannibal, the successor, almost at once broke the treaty and took Saguntum in 219 BC after an eight-month siege.

At the age of eight, Hannibal, son of Hamilcar, had, on Baal's altar under his father's eye, already taken 'the oath of seven hates to Rome', no truce or mercy, the curse of Queen Dido upon the Romans: 'let them fight, they and their sons' sons, forever'. If his father had already decided on war, while Hasdrubal tactically pursued the subjection of Rome through diplomatic measures, it was Hannibal who, after his brother-in-law's persuasion of the Iberian and Celtic tribes, executed his father's military will.

Not much is known of Hannibal. His contemporaries wrote little about him and sculpted or drew even less. Livy said that 'his body could neither be exhausted nor his mind subdued by any task. He could endure both extreme heat and cold . . . his food and drink were determined by nature, not pleasure.' He could, like Napoleon, sleep at will, anywhere. He was probably dark, well built and agile: he had a straight nose, an open regard and a smiling eye. He ran well. He had charm, intelligence, courage and authority. He spoke fluent Greek and was educated in Alexandrine military thought. Livy ascribes to him reckless courage but, agreed by Polybius, alleges cruelty, lack of truth and an absence of fear of the gods.

Appianus noted that, while wintering in Lucania, Hannibal 'abandoned himself to unaccustomed luxury and the delights of love'. This does not seem unusual in a soldier seventeen years from home, and his chivalry towards women has also been remarked. He married and had a son by his wife, a woman possibly of Greek ancestry from Castulo in Spain, who sought to cross the Alps into Italy with him. But Hannibal would not permit it.

Livy commented further that 'the veterans seeing Hannibal at twenty-nine as a young commander imagined that Hamilcar in his youth was restored to them – the same vigour in his looks and animation in the eye'. When he served under his father, 'there never was a genius more fitted for the two most opposite duties of obeying and commanding . . . nor did the soldiers feel more confidence and boldness under any other leader. You could not easily decide whether he was dearer to the general or the army.' But, with all his gifts, 'the father of strategy' could not in a generation build one nation of Roman proportions from the raw material then available to him in North Africa and the Levant.

Still, according to Publius, 'of all that befell the Romans and Carthaginians, good and bad, the cause was one man and one mind, Hannibal . . . For sixteen continuous years, he maintained the war in Italy, though he had troops in his service who were not even of the same race . . . these differences, so manifold and so wide, did not disturb the obedience to one word of command and to a single will.' And Mommsen commented that 'he was particularly marked by that inventive craftiness which forms one of the leading traits of the Phoenician character . . . stratagems of all sorts, an unrivalled system of espionage . . . as a general and a statesman, he was a great man'.

The Second Punic War had begun with the Carthaginian assault on Saguntum. That deliberate provocation of Rome was also a response to Roman political intervention in the city, but was primarily part of the development of rich Spain as a base for war against Rome. This task, under Hasdrubal, had taken the form of the subjugation of tribes in small, brilliant military operations. Rome had demanded the surrender of Hannibal, an ultimatum which, when refused by Carthage, provoked Rome to declare war, thereby breaching the treaty of peace or, at least, making herself vulnerable to accusation.

The Romans, as Hannibal knew, held command of the sea, and never even imagined that Carthage would attack Italy overland across two great mountain ranges, Alps and Pyrenees, and over huge rivers, Ebro and Rhône. But Gaul, through which an enemy would have to move, was, as the Romans also knew, resentful of Roman victories. The occupation of Piacenza, Cremona, Modena, Como and Milan and the hostility of Greece presented further weaknesses. And, as the Carthaginians had planned, a developed Spain was a source, virtually inaccessible to Roman eyes, of manpower for Hannibal's army.

In 220 BC the forces available to Rome had been, according to a muster roll referred to by the historian Publius, 700,000 foot-soldiers and 70,000 cavalrymen. These formed a free, professional, citizen army based on the legion, well trained, patriotic and highly disciplined, aggressive and anchored in a system of more or less liberal, voluntary colonialism with their subjects.

The legion consisted of veterans or *triarii* who formed the third heavy infantry line; the *principes*, in their thirties, the second line; the *hastati*, a little younger, in the first line; while the youngest of all, and new recruits, were called *velites*.

The *maniples* were the approximate equivalent of a British army company, some 150 men, divided into two centuries or platoons. The *cohort* was the equivalent of our battalion, numbering about 500 men, with *velites, hastati, triarii* and *principes*. The legion itself mustered around 5,000 men, including 300 cavalry; each legion was accompanied by an 'allied' legion. One Roman and one allied legion together were the equivalent of an army corps, whereas two Roman and two allied legions comprised a field army. A consular army was 18–20,000 strong, two such armies varying in command daily between two elected – and, therefore, often incompetent – consuls.

The *maniples*, structured like a small phalanx, six men deep, in a twenty-man front, staggered or checkerboard – and therefore flexible – closed up to form a conventional phalanx in battle. Weapons carried by the Roman infantry included pikes and javelins (*pilum*) whose iron heads detached on impact, rendering them useless to the enemy, whose shields or armour they had probably penetrated. The sword was called a *gladius*; the bowmen were mostly Greek, the slingers from the Balearic Islands.

In 218 BC, Hannibal, according to Livy, left Saguntum, then the hill and magnificent harbour of Cartagena, its quinqueremes, triremes and surrounding wall, for the road into northern Spain and the Ebro, on towards the Pyrenees, leading 90,000 men, 12,000 cavalry and 37 elephants, leaving behind over 20,000 men. His precise route is unknown, but he did pass through Ampurias, a Greek colony on the coast described in 1960 by Leonard Cottrell in his magical *Enemy of Rome*:

> You approach Ampurias along a dusty road which wanders through the pines beside the restless sea: on the right are sand, sun-baked rocks, blue water and white wave crests. On the left, beside the road, stands the sea-wall of the city, broken at one point by a gateway, through which one enters and begins to climb the gentle slope towards the main square. Between lie a crescent of beach and groves of umbrella pines which sweep down almost to the water. And all around, under the clear sky, stretches the flat fertile plain where Hannibal's army must have camped.

Thence, he moved to a new base in the Pyrenees and thereafter to the north of Avignon. Meanwhile, Sempronius was forming an army in Sicily against Carthage, and Scipio's father (also Publius Cornelius Scipio), unaware that Hannibal was moving into Italy, was in Marseille, fifty miles south of Hannibal marching north up the Rhône valley to his crossing point in the Alps. Scipio therefore sent his own army under his brother Gnaeus to Spain, where Gnaeus regained eventually territory earlier taken by Carthage north of the Ebro. With their backs to the Trebbia river, three-quarters of Sempronius' troops from Sicily, redirected through the Adriatic sea to the Po valley, were slaughtered by

Hannibal in the first of three classic battles, Trebbia, Trasimene and Cannae.

It was near Trebbia, on the Ticino, that the son of Publius Cornelius Scipio, identically named, later to become 'Scipio Africanus', disciple and conqueror of Hannibal, saved his own father's life. He it was who later became, in 210 BC and at the age of twenty-four, commander-in-chief of Roman forces in Spain, seizing Cartagena, defeating at Baecula Hannibal's brother, Hasdrubal, who then escaped into Italy, and, at Ilipa, the victor against Mago and Hasdrubal Gisco. (That latter battle may have owed its brilliance to Hannibal at Cannae.) Ilipa forced Spain's total submission to Rome in 206 BC, after which Scipio sailed from Italy to meet the great Carthaginian in the final confrontation at Zama in 202 BC.

Meanwhile, Hannibal had commanded 50,000 foot soldiers and 9,000 horsemen after he had crossed the Pyrenees and forded the Rhône, compared with 90,000 infantry and 12,000 cavalry at the Ebro, after he had left 22,000 infantrymen behind to guard northern Spain. Casualties, dismissals and deserters, the result of fighting tribes in the north and at the foot of the Pyrenees, amounted to 20,000, a figure surprising in the light of Hannibal's subsequent victories. And when he entered Gaul proper after the crossing of the Alps in 218 BC, his complement was only 20,000 foot soldiers and 6,000 horsemen, the others lost to sickness, wounds and hostile mountain men. And the actual crossing of the Rhône had been opposed by wild, Celtic Gauls, although rafts of various sizes – inflated skins, coracles, canoes, tree-trunks – got the army across safely, including elephants, aided by terrifying attacks on the tribesmen from Numidian cavalry, shouting war cries.

The landscape of much of the country east of the Rhône is of sunlight, tiles, bridges, columns, red roofs and golden houses, among sunflowers, olive trees, vineyards. Its colours are purple, yellow, scarlet, green and lavender, under deep blue skies over gorges, crags, limestone peaks, blue mountains, sometimes gentle, more often sheer, towering and guarded by the watching eyes of the Allobroges. On narrow paths, already under thick November snow, abyss at one hand, vertical cliff the other, ambush after ambush fell upon the Carthaginian infantrymen, upon their pack animals and their elephants in the long column which stumbled its way through the gorges. Hurled avalanches of rock fell upon the field train and its exhausted men, desperately fighting off the Allobroges, whose cousins were the chosen guides betraying for loot the soldiers who hired them. In this vicious, bloody hand-to-hand fighting for plunder, Hannibal had lost nearly 40,000 of the men with whom he had swum the Rhône.

The descent on the other side, from the highest ridge into Italy thousands of feet below, was steep, narrower even than the climb, broken, slippery with ice and snow on slopes without roots, shrubs or other handholds. Gigantic rocks obstructed their downward passage. Hannibal himself admitted, after fifteen days in the Alps, to only 23,000 survivors in the fair, green country below.

Scipio, now in the Po valley, harangued his troops on Carthaginian treachery, also adding that after the Alpine passage, Hannibal's formation could only be a rabble. The first skirmish, however, near the Ticino river, led, as we have seen, to a defeat for the Roman cavalry, the wounding of Scipio and his rescue by his young son. Two thousand armed Gauls came over to Hannibal, and the Roman grain store at Casteggio was betrayed to him in exchange for gold coin.

The Trebbia river, flowing out of the Apennines, was the site of the first major engagement with the Romans. It resulted in the heavy defeat of Sempronius already referred to. Hannibal had placed his brother, Mago, in cover among scrubby hills, while the Numidian cavalry attacked frontally, then withdrew, over and over, to drag the enemy forward into the icy waters of the Trebbia, where they were assaulted from the rear by Mago's men thundering down the hill.

Only 10,000 Romans escaped. After the struggle, 60,000 Gauls, many of them cavalrymen with their horses, came over to the Carthaginians.

All the elephants except one died during the winter, and the horses did not do well either, although improved after bathing in vinegar (which commodity, incidentally, caused the movement and break-up, after fire had been applied to them, of the huge stones obstructing Hannibal in the Alps).

In the spring of 217 BC Hannibal crossed the Apennines through cornfields, olives, vines and cypresses, among carts drawn by white oxen, but also through the mud and filth of the marshes, to the Arno south of Florence. Tuscany with its little walled hill towns is rich, fertile country. The combined Carthaginian–Gaulish force devastated it, partly in a deliberate bid to lift the burden of supply from exclusively Gaulish acres, and partly to frighten other Roman allies, such as Etrurians in the Confederation of Italian States, thus to weaken Rome.

The blue Lake Trasimene resembles a small sea rather than a lake. It was approached from Arezzo on Hannibal's road to Rome via Cortona and Perugia. The general chose a valley or defile, under cliffs and surrounded by hills, as the point where his whole army would ambush the Romans under the impatient general Flaminius. On an April morning in 217 BC, thick mist filled the valley as the Romans climbed into the hills where the Spanish and African veterans of the Carthaginian army lay hidden beside their less experienced Gaulish allies.

Suddenly, out of the fog, 30,000 savage Numidians, half-naked barbarian Gauls, rusé Spaniards in scarlet and white burst down the slopes, the legions beset by javelin, sword, pike and spear. Although fighting gallantly in the charge, the Romans were caught between the hills and the Carthaginians. Flaminius fell dead from his saddle. Fifteen thousand died, the remainder slaughtered in full armour by Numidian cavalry at the water's edge. Hannibal kept Romans openly in chains, but released 'allied' (non-Roman) prisoners in order to encourage further defection from the allies, whose liberty he claimed as his principal aim. In

Rome itself, the people trembled: another, if smaller, military defeat occurred immediately after Trasimene, when cavalry under Maharbal successfully attacked 4,000 Roman cavalry.

Hannibal marched yet further south. The Romans elected a dictator, Fabius Maximus, Cunctator or Delayer, who raised sixteen legions, 87,000 men, Roman and allied, for service in Apulia under Varro and Paulus, with whom Hannibal sought battle. He continued by threat, example and persuasion to encourage defection among Rome's allies, while ravaging the countryside in Campania and avoiding the traps set by Fabius, whose term as dictator ended. Hannibal had captured a Roman store at Cannae and was in control of south Apulian grain; he had earlier put Spoleto under siege but, without the towers and battering rams which he had left behind in Spain, his siege train was too slight for the purpose. His troops had moved into Umbria and Apulia, killing or abducting farmers, officials and their families, requisitioning oxen, wine, wheat and olives. At sea the small Carthaginian navy had waylaid Roman grain-ships destined for Spain. Fabius continued to avoid battle despite Hannibal's depredations, until the Carthaginians provoked his men into a night attack on a herd of cows whose horns Hannibal had illuminated with flaming faggots. The 'attack' over, the disgruntled Romans were cut down in ambush by the drovers . . .

By August 216, Hannibal had contrived that his army of 50,000 men, and the Roman army of over 90,000, should occupy fortified positions six miles from one another at Cannae, on the banks of the Ofanto river. The days of prosperous, if violent foraging – 'reiving' like the Scottish Borderers – were gone. The excitable and ambitious Terentius Varro, alternate Roman commander, was anxious for action, but not more so than Hannibal in his address to troops: 'What greater gift could you want than to fight the decisive battle on such ground as this . . . by your former battles, you have gained possession of the country and all its wealth as I promised you . . . this coming battle for the cities and their wealth will make you at once master of all Italy.'

And when Gisgo, a more junior officer, remarked on the disparity in numbers, Hannibal told him that he had ignored one factor.

'What is that, sir?'

'Among those opposite, there is no one called Gisgo.'

An initial clash between the cavalry of Hasdrubal and Aemilius Paulus led to the literal crushing of Paulus' horsemen, releasing Hasdrubal for the relief of the Numidians. The Roman infantry under Varro had driven in ('rendered concave') the Gauls and Spaniards in Hannibal's centre, squeezing the legions, unable to manoeuvre or fight, between two parallel lines of African infantry. At this point, Maharbal's heavy cavalry butchered the enclosed legions where they stood compressed, and destroyed two panic-stricken consular armies, eight legions. Hannibal lost at least 6,000 men, but the Roman losses were probably 70,000 men. Varro escaped. Hannibal sent to Carthage three bushels of gold rings, torn from the dead hands of Roman knights. Non-Roman towns in Apulia, Lucania, Bruttium, the Picentes, Hirpini and the Samnites, Capua in Campania, came over to Carthage. But although Hannibal now held most of south Italy, there had been very few, if any, Latin or Greek defections.

After Cannae, Maharbal urged Hannibal to take Rome: 'In very truth, the Gods bestow not on the same man all their gifts. You know how to gain a victory, Hannibal: you do not know how to use one.' But Hannibal's strategy was not to destroy Rome in direct assault which, with a small, aging army, no fleet, aging horses and, especially, no siege train, was impossible. It was rather to encircle Italy by detaching city after city in a war of stratagem and movement, while the government at Carthage was to drive the Romans out of Spain and retake Sardinia and Sicily.

These objectives, like Hannibal's in Italy which failed for lack of a siege train, became less and less practical over the next ten of his sixteen years in Italy. By 206, Carthaginian rule had ended in Spain; Hasdrubal was defeated in 207 on the Metaurus river without being able to join his brother; and the siege of Syracuse (213–211) had ended in victory for Marcellus, described by

Hannibal, who beat him at Asculum, as 'the only general who, when victorious, allows us no rest, and when we beat him takes none himself'. Hannibal, far from 'detaching city after city', lost even those he had gained, fighting with remarkable skill and gallantry, nevertheless doing little more than march and counter march, all for the lack of the siege train which would have dealt with Italian walled cities, the obstacle to victory.

And from 209 BC, the man later to become Scipio Africanus was destroying, at Cartagena, Baecula and Ilipa, all that the Barcas had built in Spain. He had, however, failed to prevent Hasdrubal Barca from marching out of Spain in 207, like Hannibal across the Alps into the Po valley, in order to join his brother now at Bruttium in the extreme south. To oppose him was an army under Claudius Nero at Venusia facing Hannibal, Livius' army waiting for Hasdrubal, Fulvius' army in Bruttium, and three others under Porcius, Varro and Quintus Claudius.

Hasdrubal, having failed to take Placentia, raised the siege and sent an uncoded Punic language message by hand of horseman to his brother, arranging a rendezvous on the Adriatic or in Umbria, naming the route, the Via Flaminia. This unwise communication was intercepted at Tarentum by the Romans, unknown to either Hasdrubal or Hannibal. Hannibal marched north to meet his brother, but was headed off by Nero, who left most of his army to confront him while himself covering 400 miles in seven days with 6,000 foot soldiers and 1,000 cavalrymen to meet Livius. Their junction was at first unknown to Hasdrubal, revealed only when two trumpets, not one, sounded in the Roman camp. Panic had meanwhile broken out in Rome: 'two Punic wars, two mighty armies, two Hannibals, as it were, in Italy'.

Hasdrubal accordingly refused battle for the time being but, attempting to withdraw to the Via Flaminia up the thickly wooded Metaurus river, he was deserted by his guides, losing time, battle forced upon him. The Ligurians found his centre, covered by his elephants, the Spanish on the right and the Gauls on the left, his line 'long rather than deep', the Gauls, many of whom were drunk, facing Nero on the Roman right, while Porcius and Livius faced the Ligurians and Spanish respectively. The elephants, after the first charge which cracked the Roman front line, roamed aimlessly about the battlefield. Many had to be killed, in the spinal cord, by the knives and mallets of the mahouts. Meanwhile, Nero took several cohorts away from the Gaulish front and led them, unseen by Hasdrubal, round the back of the Carthaginian force to attack the right flank of the Spaniards from the rear, pushing them on to the Ligurians. (Marlborough acted similarly at Ramillies in 1706.) Hasdrubal, witnessing inevitable defeat, drove his horse into a Roman cohort and died, sword in hand, in a gesture of extreme uselessness.

The Romans, who had lost only 2,000 of their men against 10,000 Carthaginians, cut off Hasdrubal's head and threw it into Hannibal's camp. When Hannibal saw it, he exclaimed sadly: 'I see there the fate of Carthage.' It was now that the general realised that it was not Italy that was encircled but Carthage, with Sicily and Spain lost, himself isolated without a fleet, and without the troops to defend Africa against the invasion which Rome was certain soon to mount.

Scipio indeed invaded Africa near Utica in 204 BC and, in 203, heavily defeated the Carthaginians on two separate and bloody occasions. Carthage recalled Hannibal who, after killing his horses, returned to Africa with Mago, who died on board, and some 20,000 men, a force which he increased to 45,000 infantry and 3,000 cavalry of variable quality. Scipio's strength was 34,000 foot soldiers and 9,000 horsemen, much better trained and of high quality, reinforced by Numidians. Hannibal was well aware of his army's inferiority, and sought negotiation.

Scipio, having taken by surprise the Megreda valley, the bread-basket of Carthage, starved out that city. The two armies met at Zama, five days on foot southwest of Carthage. First, both commanders rode out, accompanied only by interpreters and a few horsemen. The generals, with awe, for a few moments gazed at one another. But Scipio rejected his opponent's proposals, including even cession to Rome of Spain, Sicily and Sardinia, obviously based on Hannibal's knowledge of his military weakness already illustrated by the Metaurus battle. Scipio, pointing to Carthaginian bad faith, declared: 'Put your country at our mercy or fight and conquer us.' Polybius went on: 'After this conversation, which held out no hope of reconciliation, the two generals parted from each other. On the following morning, they led out their armies and opened the battle, the Carthaginians fighting for their own safety and the Romans for the Empire of the World.'

Thereafter, the dead and wounded lay 'piled up in bloody heaps'. Livy, earlier describing Cannae, where more men died in a day than in four months at Passchendaele in 1917, spoke of some soldiers 'found lying alive with their thighs and hams cut, who laying bare their necks and throats, bid them drain the blood that remained within. Some now found with their heads plunged in the earth . . . having made pits for themselves . . . and having suffocated themselves . . . a living Numidian, with lacerated nose and ear, stretched beneath a lifeless Roman who lay upon him, and who had died in the act of tearing his antagonist with his teeth.' Zama was little different. Cottrell believed that 'even Hannibal's iron nerves were shaken by the slaughter', his rear shattered by the return of the Roman cavalry.

The Romans at Zama took 15,000 Carthaginian prisoners, and left 20,000 dead. In the treaty which followed, all Scipio's terms were conceded, but it was not until 183 BC that, too successful in rejuvenating Carthage and pursued by the Romans, Hannibal took poison in Bithynia. He reflected bitterly as he died: 'Let us now put an end to the great anxiety of the Romans, who have thought it too lengthy, and too heavy a task, to wait for the death of a hated old man.' A year later, Scipio also died, outside Rome, ordering the words 'My ungrateful country should not have my bones' for his tomb.

But, despite Livy and Polybius, it was the Metaurus, not Zama, which was the fulcrum of history. It was the conflict at that river which, as Creasy observed, 'witnessed the ruin of the scheme by which alone Carthage could organise decisive success, the scheme of enveloping Rome at once from the north and the south of Italy, led by the sons of Hamilcar . . . it not only determined the event of the strife between Rome and Carthage, but ensured to Rome two centuries of almost unchallenged conquest'. Contrary to Fuller, it was Metaurus, not Zama, that 'led the Roman people across the threshold of a united Italy to the high-road of world domination'.

SYNOPSIS OF EVENTS BETWEEN
ZAMA AND THE TEUTOBURG FOREST

The Second Punic War left Rome in possession of Italy, Sicily, Sardinia, Corsica, a great part of Spain and North Africa.

In 200 BC, she defeated Philip of Macedon, destroying that country's influence in Greece, Rome established in its stead, albeit giving nominal independence for the Greek cities. In 192, Rome secured victory at Magnesia over Syria, thus earning the title of 'arbitress of the world from the Atlantic to the Euphrates', twenty-four years later, at Pydna, destroying the Macedonian monarchy as well, thus confirming Roman control of the Greek world.

Carthage, in the Third Punic War, was wiped out by Scipio Aemilianus, adopted grandson of Scipio Africanus, in 146. In the same year, Consul Lucius Mummius stormed Corinth, most of southern Greece becoming a Roman province. War against Spain was pursued from 200 to 133 BC when Scipio put an end to it, leaving Spain tranquil, but with parts of the north still unsubdued. From 134, in 'the Revolutionary Century', Rome fought foreign wars, resulting in many accessions such as Mumidia to her territories.

From 113 to 64 BC, northern warriors such as the Cimbri and Teutons, the Italian allies, Mithridates, king of Pontus, eventually imprisoned by his own son, were all defeated by Marius or Sulla – the latter becoming dictator and waging civil war against Marius – Lucullus and Pompeius. After the last Mithridatic Wars, the Romans formed from their Asian conquests the provinces of Bithynia, Cilicia and Syria, allocating Great Armenia, the Bosphorus, Judaea and other small states to petty princes dependent on Rome.

Between 58 and 50 BC, Julius Caesar conquered Gaul.

In the civil war between Caesar and Pompeius, Caesar conquered Pompey in Spain, drove his forces out of Italy and defeated him and the aristocrats at Pharsalia in Greece. Caesar next won a war with the Egyptians, after which he made his lover, Cleopatra, queen of Egypt, then defeated the son of Mithridates in Pontus, overthrew the Pompeian leaders in Africa, and overwhelmed the remaining sons of Pompeius in Spain at the battle of Munda.

'Under the title of Dictator, Caesar was sole master of the Roman world.'

CHAPTER FOUR

THE TEUTOBURG FOREST, AD 9

By 45 BC, Julius Caesar had defeated all his enemies. As dictator for life and consul, he nevertheless maintained the forms of those republican institutions which he despised, indeed giving priority to civil over military powers, all of which were embodied in his rule. Uncrowned but undisputed monarch of a republican state, he had, in the few short months left to him, begun the foundation of the Roman Empire and the reorganisation of the condition of Italy.

In eight campaigns in Gaul he had driven the frontiers of Rome to the Rhine and, in the west, to the Atlantic. Pompey, his son-in-law, had sought his downfall, but Caesar, crossing the Rubicon with inferior forces, had driven him out of Italy at Pharsalus. Pompey's triumphs over Mithridates in Asia had already brought Syria and Palestine, Turkey between Taurus and the Iskanderum Gulf and between the Black Sea and Sakarya, to Rome. Under Caesar, the legions had been sighted on the Euphrates and the Black Sea, to which he added victories in France, Britain, Spain, Greece and North Africa.

But, on the Ides, 15 March, 45 BC, Caesar was stabbed to death on the steps of the Senate by a ring of conspirators among whom Brutus and Cassius were most prominent. The pretext, sincere or otherwise, that he had grown intolerably despotic, was almost irrelevant. Caesar, to remedy the incompetence, evil and sickening corruption of the capital, at a time when national pride did not exist, and democracy was either suppressed or unborn, had had little alternative. He could only ensure, conscious of his own real capacities, that, as well as defence, the economy, law and politics were all accountable, if not subordinate, to himself and his able attendants.

At his death, Mark Antony was surviving consul and Caesar's heir apparent. The emperor's eighteen-year-old nephew, Gaius Julius Caesar Octavianus, also claimed to be the civil heir, raising a force from among the dictator's veterans, ostensibly to oppose Mark Antony's failure to punish the conspirators. He and Mark Antony, however, later joined to fight the two land battles of Philippi, leading to the deaths of Cassius and Brutus by suicide.

In Cilicia, Antony met voluptuous Cleopatra and, like Caesar himself, besotted, fell deeply in love with her. Unlike Caesar, he remained chiefly in Egypt, for nine years, sunk in desire, lethargy and illusion. At the great sea-battle at Actium in 31 BC, against Octavian's commander, Agrippa, while Mark Antony commanded the fleet as a whole, the incomparable Cleopatra led a reserve of sixty vessels. Beaten, he and the queen escaped to Egypt. In 30 BC, after Octavian's invasion of Egypt, he killed himself, in the false belief that Cleopatra had already predeceased him by her own hand. The queen surrendered to Octavian, but learning that she would be led, like a slave, in his Roman triumph, put to her sweet, round, swelling breast a deadly snake, brought to her concealed in fig leaves. She feared, said Shakespeare, that:

> Mechanic slaves
> With greasy aprons, rules and hammers, shall
> Uplift us to the view; in their thick breaths,
> Rank of gross diet, shall we be enclouded
> And forced to drink their vapours.
> . . . Saucy lictors
> Will catch at us like strumpets.

Egypt became a Roman province.

Octavian, supreme and unchallenged in city and empire, now undertook the reorganisation of the whole polity, creating a bureaucracy, treasury and accounting systems, a standing army, decent public service, attempting also no less than the rejuvenation of morality and religion. In 27 BC he was accorded divine honours, in the name and status of Augustus, first emperor of Rome.

The Roman Empire, although including the Balkans, much of western Europe as it is today, the Levant, North Africa and Asia Minor, was, nevertheless, permanently threatened by considerable numbers of brave, aggressive, violent German tribesmen on the eastern shore and hinterland of the Rhine. Had Augustus succeeded in the conquest of these determined warriors, incorporating them within short frontiers from Baltic Sea to Danube river, by Elbe and Morava, the face of Europe would have been changed for ever, Germany in permanent subservience to Rome, the English nation unborn, descendants of Germanic ancestors enslaved or exterminated in the forests of Westphalia and the wastes of Lippe.

Mark Antony always alleged that Augustus' father, Balbus, had been born in Africa, where he had kept a scent business and a bakery, others that he was born by a baker out of a moneychanger. No recorded comment has been found from Augustus on these impeachments. We know, firstly, that he commanded the army and empire with Mark Antony for twelve years, and was in sole charge for forty-four years, undertaking five campaigns. According to Antony, he ran away in his first battle, leaving behind his horse and purple cloak, although he fought gallantly in his second engagement. After Philippi, he sent Brutus' head to Rome, to be cast at the feet of Julius Caesar's sacred statue: when begged by a prisoner to grant decent burial, he replied that that would be 'settled with carrion birds', conduct which caused the suppliant to praise Mark Antony, but openly to abuse Augustus, spitting obscene epithets in his face.

Antony accused him of falling asleep at a sea-battle off Sicily:

'he lay on his back and gazed up at the sky'. Antony and Augustus separated again. Augustus exposed Antony's illegitimate children by Cleopatra and, subsequently, after victory at Actium, defeated Antony at Alexandria, after which the latter killed himself. In Alexandria, after he had crowned the mummy of Alexander the Great with the golden diamond, Augustus rejected a visit to the tombs of the Ptolemies: 'I have come to see a king, not a row of mummies.' Egypt, having become a Roman province, owed its agricultural infrastructure and consequent fertility to Augustus' close attention from Rome.

He was, for several years, occupied with the suppression of revolts, including attempts at assassination, in one of which an Illyrian camp-orderly was found outside the emperor's sleeping quarters with a hunting knife. Although as commander-in-chief, or local commander, he was responsible for the conquest of Cantabria, Aquitania, Pannonia, Dalmatia and Illyricum, and for the pacification of Dacian and German tribes, most wars were conducted not personally, but by subordinates or lieutenants. He did himself command against the Dalmatians and the Cantabrians, wounded in the leg, both arms and the knee, and was awarded triumphs after Philippi, Sicily, Dalmatia, Actium and Alexandria.

As token that the empire was at peace on land and sea, Augustus closed the gates of the temple of Janus on the Quirina three times, hitherto over a long period closed only twice. Suetonius said of him that he had built firm and lasting foundations for the government of Rome, which abided secure, the author of the best possible constitution. He had 'found Rome built of sun-dried bricks' and 'left her clothed in marble', the Forum, the temples of Apollo and Jupiter. Augustus revived the ancient Roman dress, honoured all sorts of professional entertainers, and gave much encouragement to poets, historians and orators. As statesman, he made it his aim to restore conquered kingdoms to their defeated dynasties, keeping his royal allies united with him by treaty and marriage.

This remarkably handsome man lived and dressed simply, to the point of negligence. When he lay dying, he asked a circle of friends: 'Have I played my part in the face of life creditably enough?' adding: 'If I have pleased you, kindly signify / Appreciation with a warm goodbye.'

He kissed his wife, then: 'Goodbye, Lydia: never forget whose husband you have been,' dying in the same room as his father.

The Pax Romana began in 29 BC, when Augustus had returned to Rome after Actium and Alexandria, and endured until the time of Marcus Aurelius. In 13 BC, this emperor disbanded over thirty legions, reducing the strength of the army, including auxiliaries and ten cohorts of 1,000 men each from the Praetorian Guard, to twenty-five legions of 6,000 men. But German tribal pressure from Pannonia and the east bank of the Rhine raised this total by the end of the Pax Romana to about 400,000 men.

As early as 68 BC a German tribe under Ariovistus had been invited by Gauls between the Jura and the Vosges to occupy Upper Alsace. In 59 BC, Ariovistus was recognised by the Senate as 'friend of the Roman people', and as a 'king', titles regretted when yet more Germans moved even further into Gaul. Caesar, fearing the potential damage to Rome, defeated Ariovistus on the battlefield, conquered a tribal region of a size corresponding to modern Belgium and took the left bank of the Rhine, only crossing to the right bank in a temporary show of force.

The right bank and territory to the east were thus now occupied by a powerful warlike horde of fair-haired, large, blue-eyed nomads and hunters, consuming milk, cheese and meat, wagon-folk who held land, if at all, tribally, not as individuals, their borders surrounded by deterrent wilderness. Law was maintained by district leaders, one of whose principal concerns was to apply their constituents' energies to hard, conventional work and regular labour.

Their armies were tribal and family units, equipped with short spears, shields and little else except missiles. Sometimes they wore a short cloak. 'Their horses', said Tacitus, 'are conspicuous for neither speed nor beauty, but neither are they trained like our horses to run in shifting circles: they ride them forwards only or to the right, but with one turn from the straight, dressing the line so closely on the wheel that none is left behind. There is more strength in their infantry and, accordingly, the cavalry and infantry fight in one body, the swift-footed infantry . . . in front of the line . . . the battle line itself is arranged in wedges: to retire . . . is a question of tactics, not cowardice.' North of the Danube, east of the Rhine, their home was in the bogs, mountains, swamps and dark immense forests of the Teutoburg Wald.

Tiberius and Drusus, stepsons of Augustus, in 21–20 BC avenged a defeat of the army under Marcus Lollius by successful strikes and by a major victory on the Lippe river, followed by a continued Roman drive to the Elbe. Drusus reached the Upper Elbe, later making winter camps at Wesel and Mainz, winning a sea-fight on the Ems. He then invaded Germany proper, before dying from a fall from his horse at Magdeburg. In 9 BC, Tiberius succeeded him, but left for the east in 7 BC, only returning to Germany in AD 4, once again to restore Augustus' authority. In AD 6, he renounced the planned conquest of the Marcomanni in favour of a campaign which resulted in the capitulation of Pannonia, Dalmatia and Illyricum, after a rebellion which had embraced no fewer than 200,000 infantry and 9,000 cavalry. Tiberius' victory was achieved, not by set-piece battles, but by famine imposed from fixed bases by an army moving in columns.

When he returned to Italy, Tiberius and all Rome heard the news of a catastrophe in Germany, preceded, or so it was said, by lightning on the temple of Mars, mountains in the Alps tumbling upon one another. The heavens glowed, comets and meteors blazed; a statue of Victory reversed its gaze to look upon Italy rather than Germany. Dio Cassius said that 'Augustus, when he heard of the calamity, rent his garments . . . in terror for the Germans and the Gauls.' Suetonius alleged that 'the Emperor let the hair of his head and beard grow for several months, and would sometimes thump his head against the door posts, crying out "Quintilius Varus, give me back my legions" '.

Quintilius Varus had succeeded Tiberius at an epoch when today's Austria and much of Bavaria, Switzerland and Würtemburg had also fallen under the Roman heel. Roman fleets from Gaul sailed up the coasts of Germany and into her rivers: the Elbe, Rhine, Danube, Seine and Tagus bore her vessels, as the land bore her armies of occupation and her system of armed forts. She, like other imperial powers, was generally resented, often hated.

Velleius Paterculus describes Varus, who, not uniquely, had made a great deal of money as governor of Syria, as 'a man of mild character and quiet disposition, somewhat slow in mind as he was in body and more accustomed to the leisure of the camp than to actual service in war'. Married to Augustus' great-niece, his appointment was from the 'Court', the Imperial Court, an unimaginative bureaucrat, treating Germans like Syrians as if they were slaves, while also taxing them till the pips squeaked.

According to Creasy, Varus was, nevertheless, a typical, well-educated intellectual who had failed to 'humanise the old Roman spirit of cruel indifference for human feeling and human suffering, and without acting as the least check on unprincipled avarice and ambition or on habitual and gross profligacy'. Creasy goes further, without offering evidence other than lines from Macaulay inapplicable to the situation, in accusing him of unleashing his 'licentious and rapacious passion upon the high minded sons and pure spirited daughters of Germany'. But Varus seems, as a ruler, to have been feeble rather than 'tyrannical' and his establishment, in the piping days of peace, to have grown fat and idle.

The Germans in his region, although reluctant to pay taxes to finance Augustus' foreign wars, appeared gradually to accustom themselves to Rome's rule and habits, domestic, political and financial. But in Varus' entourage were German chieftains whose detestation of Rome was nationalist and personal: revolutionary, in a word. The most notable of these was Arminius (Herman), who had commanded German troops in Roman wars in Pannonia and Illyricum. Arminius had been forbidden by Segestes, a slavish German acolyte of the governor, to marry the latter's daughter. He then eloped with her, when Segestes promptly accused him before Varus of planned treason against Rome.

Arminius spoke Latin, dined at Varus' table and seemed to all intents and purposes to be a loyal convert to Rome. He was a Roman citizen and even held equestrian rank: he and his fellow dissidents had little difficulty in persuading a complacent Varus that their German followers were as united in support of Roman rule as they were themselves. This flattery was accompanied by Arminius' insistence to his tribesmen on apparent passivity, while simultaneously planning general insurrection against Roman dominion, a scheme to which peers and subordinates acceded.

Not all Varus' staff officers were convinced by this sycophancy. Their warnings, however, and those of truly Romanised Germans, were ignored by Varus, who considered the race to be too stupid, cowardly or incompetent to mount a serious threat to his authority. Precisely because Arminius was both intelligent and far seeing, there had, indeed, been no overt resistance, let alone open war, against the occupiers: Varus, after all, commanded three legions, 14,000 infantrymen and 900 cavalry with a similar number of 'allied' legions.

Arminius, now aged twenty-six and, according to Tacitus, 'a frantic spirit', 'the incendiary of Germany', recognised in the legions the virtues of Roman military discipline and training, and the absence in his own ranks of those attributes. But he had acquired little regard for Varus' own abilities as a professional soldier. He exploited the governor's negligence, according to Velleius Paterculus, 'as an opportunity for treachery, sagaciously seeing that no-one could be more quickly overpowered than the man who feared nothing, and that the most common beginning of disaster was a sense of security'. Arminius found no obstacle in his efforts to raise either his fellow leaders or their people in this cause. It was remarkable that he was able to maintain the secrecy of the project until its execution, although Segestes is said to have reported the uprising to Varus, to the governor's total disbelief.

Roman troops, through the peaceful summer of AD 9, appear mostly to have been employed in forestry and on roads and bridges. Just before Varus' return to winter quarters at Haltern (Aliso) on the Lippe, Arminius caused him to be informed of a 'tribal rising' east of Minden. Varus, encumbered by a large, unwieldy baggage train and by 20,000 women and children, the families of the XVII, XVIII and XIX legions, decided to suppress what he had been falsely persuaded was only a local rebellion, involving the murder of tax collectors, before going on to Haltern. This, in a violent and disputed area, among Rome's most ferocious enemies, was an act of military folly.

No explanation, other than ignorant conviction that the 'rebellion' was of only slight consequence, has ever been given for the presence of unarmed families in this dreadful march, not only a failure of intelligence, but counter to common military practice.

The first steps on his march lay along a plain parallel to the Lippe. Varus then moved into the wooded hills of what was later to become the principality of Lippe (capital Detmold) at the junction of the Lippe river and the Ems. Here valleys and plains intersected by fast streams, bursting their autumn banks, were surrounded by mountains and could be reached only by defiles that were little more than slits in the rocks. The forests were not well tended. Progress was broken by fallen oaks, conifers and deepish wadis. Ominous names, Knochenbahn (bone lane), Winnefeld (field of victory), Knochenleke (bone brook), Mord Kessel (death kettle), today mark the site of a huge battle.

Heavy rain had fallen, day after day. It started to fall again on earth already saturated to the tree-roots. The shivering procession of men, horses and helpless civilians began to squelch through soaking bogs and morass, over which the soldiers, to form a path for the sorry, dripping crew, made temporary duckboards of felled timber.

In the evening, amid the first woods and swamps, Arminius'

Germans slipped away from the disordered columns they had been guarding. Reports reached the governor that outsiders on the edges had been silently attacked in the mists and killed. The rain ruined the legions' bowstrings and weighed down their leather shields. Varus could not deploy his legionaries on the broken ground and forest paths. Constant felling and bridging were necessary to get the supply wagons through. Even then, the track was so foul and slippery that the carts incessantly stuck. The governor turned the line of march towards a road which led to Haltern but over the Dören Pass.

Arminius, with nothing but clumsy broadswords, had no intention of meeting the Romans in fixed battle. His guerrillas had already inflicted serious casualties, by missile, on the flanks of the fifty-mile column. Roadblocks constructed from tree-trunks and captured wagons had slowed down the legions, creating little groups vulnerable to German harassment, bunching or elongating the line, separating fighting units, causing carts to be abandoned wholesale. The soldiers 'were not proceeding in any regular order; but were mixed in helter-skelter with the wagons and the unarmed', wrote Dio in his *Roman History*.

Because of a forest fire, there were few trees on the hill which the Romans now reached. Here the first legion, as was the army's practice at night, formed camp and awaited the other two legions which had suffered greater casualties than their predecessor. All, nevertheless, retained discipline, forming rear, advance and flank guards, but under continual assault. When Varus had the roll called he had already lost, killed or missing, a third of his command.

Next day he moved into more open country, but with little transport. The Germans spent that day in plundering the wagons rather than in fighting. On the third day, although Varus continued stubbornly to advance, the rain fell even harder. German attacks on a weakening army became bolder, soon hand-to-hand. The Roman cavalry, under its commander, fled the field with its squadrons, while Varus himself again took to the woods, over high ground where Arminius had built great barricades of tree-trunks. The Roman line became less steady.

Arminius gave the order for 'general attack', his Cheruscans howling in their thousands as they fell upon heavily laden legionaries. (The Germans had concentrated their earlier assault on the cavalry, and the wounded horses, which 'slipped about in the mire and in their own blood, threw their riders and plunged among the ranks of the legions, disordering all around them'.) Retreat, on which Varus now decided, only caused more terrible attacks on the battered army. The legions held together for a little while. At the end, 'the Germans slaughtered their oppressors with deliberate ferocity; and those prisoners who were not hewn to pieces on the spot were only preserved to perish by a more cruel death in cold blood'.

Varus, wounded, committed suicide. One of his generals fell; another surrendered. Although lacking leadership of the quality that Tiberius or Germanicus would have provided, the army had at least fought well. 'It was exterminated almost to a man by the very enemy whom it had always slaughtered,' as Velleius said, 'like cattle.'

When the Emperor Germanicus, six years later, rescued Segestes and fought a successful but inconclusive battle against Arminius, he also visited Varus' old camps. In one, said Tacitus, he found 'the whitening bones of men who had fled or stood their ground, strewn everywhere or piled in heaps. Nearby lay fragments of weapons, limbs of horses, human heads, nailed to the trunks of trees . . . and the barbarous altars on which the Germans had immolated tribunes and first-rank centurions . . . gibbets for the captives, pits for the living.

'And so the Roman army, now on the spot . . . in grief and anger, began to bury the bones of the three legions. These had [at the last] in a ring on a little mound, beaten off every charge of the Germans, until the morrow, when they were either massacred or offered for sacrifice on pagan altars.'

Augustus Caesar knew now that Rome was not invincible.

Despite desultory campaigning under Tiberius and Germanicus, the Rhine was now the unalterable frontier. Augustus' dream of a frontier on the Elbe, a line from Hamburg to Vienna which would have shifted 250 miles eastwards the existing frontier, and the Roman Empire itself, had vanished.

The Rhine, not the Elbe, remained the line of control. Rome could not now hope to dominate western Europe. Had she won in the Teutoburg Wald, 'there would', as Fuller saw, 'have been no Franco/German problem, no Charlemagne, no Louis XIV, no Napoleon, no Hitler'.

As important to Britons, 'our Germanic ancestors would have been enslaved or exterminated in their original seats along the Eyder and the Elbe'. In his *Lectures on Modern History*, Arnold perceived that 'this island would then never have borne the name of England and we, this great English nation, whose race and language are now overrunning the earth from one end of it to the other, would have been utterly cut off from existence'.

British officers of the Occupation Forces after the Second World War were among those privileged to inspect a large bronze statue of Arminius, eighty feet from the base to the point of the upraised sword, facing the Rhine. This artefact, which lay about disjointed for many years, was erected (it is thought in 1911) by Kaiser Wilhelm II, and somewhat resembles at least in style the statue of King Alfred in Winchester High Street. It stands on the Osining, highest peak of the Teutoburg Wald.

SYNOPSIS OF EVENTS BETWEEN THE TEUTOBURG FOREST AND CHÂLONS-SUR-MARNE

In AD 43 the Roman conquest of Britain began. In AD 64 Christians in Rome were persecuted for the first time, by Nero. In 70 Jerusalem was destroyed by Titus. Civil wars started in the Roman world but, despite the violent deaths of four emperors, Trajan still acquired Dacia and lands in the east. Hadrian later abandoned them.

Following a long war between Rome and Germanic nations, civil wars and insurrections began again: emperors were once more murdered. In 226 the Parthians were overthrown by Artaxerxes and the Persian Kingdom was restored in Asia, taking prisoner the Emperor Valerian. After the 'general distress of the Roman Empire', order had been restored by 283.

In 285, Diocletian reorganised and divided the empire. Following his abdication, civil war again broke out until unity was restored by the first Christian emperor, Constantine, who placed the seat of empire at Constantinople, not Rome. But between 364 and 375, in a divided empire, Valentinian I became emperor of the west and Valens of the east. Later Emperor Valentinian III replaced the Alemanni and other German barbarians from Gaul.

Between 375 and 395 the Huns attacked the Goths who, having sought aid from Constantinople, passed the Danube and were permitted settlement in the Roman provinces. After they had destroyed Valens and his army, Emperor Theodosius 'reduced them to submission'. Nevertheless, under Alaric the Goths soon attacked both Roman empires, Alaric taking Rome in 410, and then invading Gaul and Spain between 412 and 414. Britain was abandoned by the Romans and Genseric's Vandals conquered Roman North Africa.

In AD 441 the Huns attacked the eastern empire.

CHAPTER FIVE

CHÂLONS-SUR-MARNE, 451

During the Völkerwanderung or Wandering of the Nations, the Goths in AD 376 were the first of the German peoples to cross the Danube, driven westward by the Huns. Other barbarians, sometimes, but not always, invited by a collapsing western empire, followed: Vandals, Franks, Alemanni, Burgundians, Huns themselves, Visigoths, Alans. All came ostensibly to 'defend' the empire and, in so doing, broke it, while the eastern empire survived, even grew, because of the gallant Isaurians from the Tauros mountains in modern Turkey.

In 258 BC, the Chinese emperor Huang-te had already built the Great Wall of China to defend his enormous country against the Huns or Hsiung-nu ('common slaves'), nomads from between the immense mountains of the Altai, Kunlun and Khingan ranges. By AD 445 Attila had murdered his brother, Bleda, and had been for twelve years king of the Huns, now paramount in central Europe. Supreme in his own kingdom of Hungary and Transylvania, he ruled virtually from Caspian to Rhine, via Black Sea and Caucasus, over the Teutonic tribes, while also bullying Constantinople and Rome or, rather, Ravenna.

Alan Massie in his *The Evening of the World* has depicted the cruelty of the Huns as 'exceeding all others as a great river exceeds a mountain stream'. 'It was their habit to slit the noses of captured children, but only as preparatory to raping them ... it was also their practice to sear the limbs of those infant captives . . . and then cut collops from the living legs and eat them before the camp fire'.

Priscus, an attendant at the embassy to Attila, despatched in 449 by the eastern emperor Theodocius the Younger, described Attila as short, with a large head already greying, a scanty beard, his eyes small and beady, snub nose and swarthy skin. Gibbon said he had 'a haughty step and demeanour: he fiercely rolled his eyes, as if to enjoy the terror he inspired'. As a race the Huns' heads were 'a sort of shapeless lump', said Ammianus Marcellinus,

> with pinholes rather than eyes, a stunted, foul and puny tribe, short, yet quick, alert horsemen, broad of body, ready with bow and arrow, cruel as wild beasts. They are so little advanced in civilisation that they make no use of fire, nor of any kind of relish, in the preparation of their food, but feed upon the roots which they find in the fields, and the half-raw flesh of any sort of animal . . . they give it a kind of cooking by placing it between their own thighs and the backs of their horses.

Ammianus continued: 'They all have compact, strong limbs and thick necks, and are so monstrously ugly and misshapen that one might take them for two-legged beasts . . . they learn from the cradle to endure cold, hunger and thirst.' The Huns had not learned to weave, and clothed themselves mainly in the sewn skins of field mice. Priscus said that although Attila's guests drank from cups of gold and silver, the king's cup was wooden; his clothes were very simple, without ornament and of one colour only.

The king received the embassy in a large wooden hut within a palisade. Seats were placed along the sides, Attila himself on a couch in the middle, opposite an ornamental couch behind which was a staircase leading to his bedroom. The first rank of guests was on Attila's right hand and the second to his left, seats being taken after the first libations had been drunk in the foyer, further 'toasts' being exchanged between Attila and, via the cup-bearers, each guest. ('Guest wives' were offered to the embassy in one village, a practice said still to endure in parts of Asia, although not enjoyed by this writer.)

The barbarians had prepared bread, meats and ragouts, served upon plates of silver, but for Attila on a simple plate of wood. (The horses and swords of the king's Scythian aides and lieutenants were richly decorated with 'plates of gold or precious stones'.) 'When the first dishes were eaten, all rose and no one again sat down until he had drunk a full cup of wine to the health and prosperity of Attila. Two Scythians advanced and sang verses on the king's victories; a buffoon, a kind of black harlequin, "made all sorts of ridiculous gesticulations and sayings, such men much sought after by the barbarians as excellent ministers of mirth". Attila alone preserved an unaltered visage; he was grave and motionless,' except in evident affection for his youngest son, whose solitary survival, out of all his children, had been predicted by a soothsayer. And in this strange encounter with an embassy that included Vigilius, an officer who, unknown to his ambassador, had agreed to kill Attila for fifty gold pounds, Attila greeted Vigilius with no more than abuse – 'shameless beast' or 'impudent animal'.

Yogurt and kumiss (fermented mares' milk) may also have been served. We cannot know the precise racial origins of these people. Most of their attributes match with those of Mongol stock, but their eyes plainly seem to lack the Mongoloid fold. Attila himself claimed only descent from Nimrod, 'that great hunter'.

The Hsiung-nu's westward odyssey was probably due to the terrible era of central Asian aridisation, the gradual drying before AD 500 of surface and subterranean water, the choked death of crops and vegetation, huge shifts of sand submerging whole cities of honourable, even noble, architecture beneath an almost impassable desert. The nomads did nothing to palliate, let alone control, this tragedy, destroying ancient irrigation works and tearing up trees for firewood, a practice, alas, of mindless self-destruction continuing further east, in China proper, at least until today.

St Jerome, cited in E. A. Thompson's *History of Attila and the Huns*, described the terror in 395 of Attila's first major excursion. The Huns crossed the Danube in the west and, in the east, burst into Armenia, Cappadocia, Syria, reaching even the Orontes and the Euphrates. 'The whole East trembled, for swarms of Huns had broken forth from the Sea of Azov between the Don and where the Gates of Alexander pen in the wild nations behind the Caucasus. They filled the whole earth with slaughter and panic alike as they flitted hither and thither on their swift horses ... they took pity, neither upon religion nor rank, nor age, nor wailing childhood.' Attila united the tribes, binding them to him in vassalage. 'He was a plunderer,' said Thomas Hodgkin in his *Italy and Her Invaders*, who 'made war on civilisation and on human nature, not on religion, for he did not understand it enough to hate it.' Huge as were the Huns' numbers, mobility and surprise were the keys to their triumph, the whole people a ready-made army, mounted archers capable of rapid concentration at the enemy's weakest points, moving with their wagons and families, 'travelling fortresses'.

The soldiers subsisted from their horses like the Mongols later who, according to Marco Polo, travelled each with eighteen horses and mares for nourishing blood and milk. Speed, cunning and persistence were their guides, running away when deception was the requirement. Amedée Thierry said: 'the nomads do not consider flight a dishonour: they evade to return'.

Ammianus declared that, although their master weapon was the horn bow with its silent bone-tipped arrow, in close-quarter fighting they relied on the sword and on cloth lassos which entangled and fettered the enemy's limbs. (The Huns, however, had little aptitude for aggressive siege warfare, an attribute which explains their successes in Asia and relative failure in 'built-up' Europe.)

When attacked, they will sometimes engage in regular battle. Then going into the fight in order of columns, they fill the air with varied discordant cries. More often, however, they fight in regular order of battle, but by being extremely swift and sudden in their movements, they disperse and then rapidly come together again in loose array, spread havoc over vast plains, and flying over the rampart, they pillage the camp of their enemy almost before he has become aware of their approach. It must be owned that they are the most terrible of warriors because they fight at a distance with missile weapons having sharpened bones admirably fastened to the shaft. When in close combat with swords, they fight without regard to their own safety, and while their enemy is intent upon parrying the thrusts of the swords, they throw a net over him and so entangle his limbs that he loses all power of walking and riding.

Attila's men believed him to be chosen by their gods. He had appeared before his troops with an ancient iron sword which, he told them, was the god of war itself, worshipped in the mists of time by Scythian warriors. This sword had been recently rediscovered by a herdsman tracking a wounded deer in the desert, the weapon found 'fixed in the ground as if it had been darted down from heaven'.

Attila's claimed descent from Nimrod validated, for him and followers, rule over the Babylonian Empire. Meanwhile, for his weakening Roman enemy, the legend of Rome's twelve founding vultures, coterminous with Rome's twelve centuries of existence, combined with the parallel between Romulus' 'murder' of Remus and Attila's killing of his own brother Belda, led the quaking Roman to a calculation of imminent extinction. Indeed, it was on the precise end date of these omens that Odoacer in 476 dealt the death blow to the Roman Empire.

In 445 Attila's planned assault on Rome had been delayed by the need to deal comprehensively with his own attempted assassination by Theodosius II, emperor at Constantinople, and also to suppress a rebellion by some of his tribes around the Black Sea. (He had crossed the Danube again in 441 in a lightning campaign of victories on the Morava river and at Belgrade, followed by other defeats for Theodosius in eastern Europe, including Sofia, and in Constantinople.) By 447 he had secured his rear, his armies reaching Thermopylae: Theodosius fell from his horse and died in 450.

In 451 Attila, encouraged by Gaiseric, king of the Vandals, decided first to dispose of Theodoric, king of the Visigoths – whose daughter had just had her ears and nose removed by her husband, Gaiseric's son – before undertaking the conquest of western Europe. This attempt, initially a diplomatic démarche to bring Theodoric over to the Huns against the Romans, failed both with Theodoric and with the Emperor Valentinian. The latter spoke to the Visigoths: '[Let us] unite against the lord of the earth, who wishes to enslave the whole world . . . he who clearly is the common foe of each, deserves the hatred of all . . . the Huns do not overthrow nations by means of war . . . but assail them by treachery.'

Against her brother Valentinian stood Honoria, who had been seduced by a chamberlain and sent in disgrace to Constantinople. In a passion of revenge and resentment she now sent a ring to Attila, offering her hand in marriage: her motives, given Attila's repellent appearance, can only have been those adduced, plus spite and ambition. Her appeal led the Hun formally, if cynically, to seek Valentinian's agreement to the marriage, and to the cession of half the empire of the west.

After the emperor's predictable refusal, Attila crossed the Rhine north of Mainz in the territory of his allies, the Franks, with a force reported at 500,000 (but more probably 100,000) Huns, Ostrogoths, either infantry or horsed with helmet and chain armour, Franks, Gepidae and other German allies, advancing north of the Moselle on a 100-mile front, sacking much of northern Gaul. Hodgkin does not regard the long list by Jacques de Guise of cities sacked and burned – Reims, Metz,

Cambrai, Trèves, Cologne, Amiens, Worms, Stuttgart and many more – as wholly improbable. Paris, a little town on an island in the Seine, nearly fell too, saved only by the prayers and exhortations to remain and fight of a young girl, Saint Geneviève, against the wish of the male population to stone her and throw her in the river.

After ravaging Belgic Gaul, Attila turned toward Aquitaine, home of the Visigoths, and to Orléans, once Caesar's own capital. (A thousand years on, this city, under the guidance of Joan of Arc, La Pucelle, was to be the graveyard of England's hopes of mastery in France.) By this time, the opposition to Attila had been strengthened, not only by Theodoric and his Visigoths, but also by Aetius, 'the Patrician', who had commanded Gaul for Valentinian. Aetius had *also* led Hun troops, later becoming himself a hostage to the Huns.

Renatus Frigeridus described Aetius thus:

Of middle height, he was manly in appearance and well made, neither too frail nor too heavy; he was quick of wit and agile of limb, a very practised horseman and skilful archer, indefatigable with the spear. A born warrior, renowned for the arts of peace, without avarice and little swayed by desire, endowed with gifts of the mind, not swerving from his purpose for any kind of evil instigation. Undaunted in danger, he was excelled by none in the endurance of hunger, thirst and vigil. From his early youth, he seemed forewarned of the great power to which he was destined by the fates.

Aetius' force was only half the strength of Attila's, mustering Franks, Burgundians, Roman cavalry and legions from Gaul, Alans the weakest link. The general had been warned by the bishop of Orléans to relieve the starving town by 24 June at the latest. After five weeks of Hunnish battering rams, the praying defenders, lamenting the fate of their city, at last saw their saviours appearing from Arles, at first 'like a cloud rising from the ground',

Aetius leading, among skin-clothed warriors, accompanied by Theodoric himself and the latter's son Thorismund.

Attila, at their arrival, had already breached the shattered walls and was within the city, but retreated then rapidly under a heavy rainstorm towards the open city of Troyes, the river Rhine his objective. Thierry said: 'Driven from street to street, beaten down by the stones hurled at them by the inhabitants from the roofs of the houses, the Huns no longer knew what was to become of them, when Attila sounded the retreat . . . Such was that famous day which, in the West, saved civilisation from total destruction,' the day of Aetius, 'last of the Romans', the last victory of imperial Rome.

During Attila's retreat a Christian hermit approached the Hun with the greeting: 'Thou art the Scourge of God for the chastisement of Christians,' an appellation in which the king thereafter gloried, and by which 'title of terror, he was most widely and fearfully known' – Flagellum Dei.

Attila concentrated his forces in the plain of Châlons-sur-Marne, most favourable for the cavalry, his principal arm. Soothsayers, probably shamanist, examining the bowels of sheep and the scratchings on animals' bones, prophesied 'ill fortune for the Huns', qualified by prediction of the death of 'the chief leader on the opposite side', whom Attila assumed to be Aetius not, as it fell out, Theodoric. The ground amid the rows of poplars and winding river Marne thrusts up mounds and ridges which witness, even after two world wars, the existence of an older conflict as terrible as any modern encounter.

Jordanes reported that, on the night before the main battle which followed, 1,500 men were lost in what was a relatively minor engagement against the Gepidae forming Attila's rearguard, Franks killed on the Roman side and Gepidae for the Huns.

The battlefield rose on one side to a hill, the right hand of which was manned by the Huns, and the left by the Romans, and by Visigoth infantry with shields, but no armour. Theodoric was on the right wing opposing the Ostrogoths, Aetius' legions on the

78

right. Sangiban, who had been caught trying to betray Orléans to Attila, had been posted with his Alans to the centre where he could be watched: 'For the man in the way of whose flight you have interposed a sufficient obstacle easily accepts the necessity of fighting.'

Attila stood in the middle of his line with his best and most personal troops. The Ostrogoths, under three brothers, the Gepidae commanded by King Alaric, and similar, smaller units formed the wings, Ostrogoths directly facing Theodoric and the Visigoths. 'As for the rest, the ruck of Kings watched each nod of Attila and, in fear and trembling, they would gather round him in submissive silence to receive his orders.' Aetius, in preliminary manoeuvring, took a slope which commanded the Huns' left flank. Attila instantly counter-attacked but unsuccessfully, significantly repulsed by the Romans and Visigoths under Thorismund. According to Jordanes:

Attila, seeing his army somewhat disturbed by this skirmish, thought the time a suitable one for confirming their courage. 'Let us go forward with cheerfulness to attack the enemy . . . The flimsy arms and weak frames of the Roman soldiers: I will not say at the first wound, at the first speck of dust on their armour, they lose heart . . . despising the Romans then, charge first at the Alans, press heavily on the Visigoths . . . Yonder motley host will never endure to look upon the faces of the Huns . . . if any one can linger inactive when Attila fights, he is a thing without a soul and ought to be buried out of hand.'

Their hearts were warmed at those words, and all rushed headlong into the fray. Hand-to-hand they clashed in battle . . . the fight grew fierce, confused, monstrous . . . a brook flowing through the plain was greatly increased by blood from the wounds of the slain, swollen from a brook into a torrent.

King Theodoric was thrown from his horse or, as others said, speared by the Ostrogoth Andag, and trampled to death by his own infantry, fulfilling the shaman's prophecy. The Visigoths, maddened by their leader's fall, in frenzied assault on the Huns would have killed Attila himself had the latter not fled into his camp, wagons serving as ramparts. Meanwhile, Theodoric's son, Thorismund, lost his horse and had to be rescued. Even Aetius had to shelter among his allies' shields after wandering among the enemy, whose language he had learned in earlier captivity.

Next day, at first light, the field was empty of Huns, but piled with bodies. The allies believed, although they knew that Attila would not flee unless quite overwhelmed, that victory was theirs. Attila's left was, however, still unbroken. Even though his right was in flight, the centre thrust back upon the camp, yet he sounded the trumpets, bringing his leading archers before the fortification of the wagons. On the summit of this gigantic cairn stood the great man himself with all his wives, ready for self-immolation.

Aetius had prepared to starve out the Scourge of God by blockade and siege, under preliminary rain of arrows; in the pyre of wooden horses' saddles, Attila had decided on an auto-da-fé should the enemy break through. Then none might 'boost himself and say, "I have wounded Attila", nor that the lord of so many nations should fall alive into the hands of his enemies'.

But when the allies had found the body of the old King Theodoric and had borne it away, after they had lamented and taken him to burial with his royal emblems and decorations, and after Thorismund had been crowned and installed at Toulouse, Attila made no further move on that battlefield, despite the Visigoths' departure for Gaul, until devastating attacks on Aquileia and the Veneto in 452. After meeting Pope Leo at the Minao, 'he quickly put aside his usual fury, turned back on the way he had advanced', and, not without menaces, 'returned to his own country'. It is possible that plague, or the threat of plague, was also a major reason to quit Italy.

Next year, he married a young girl called Ildico (Hilda), a name current in Hungary today. He drank in vast quantities at the marriage banquet. During the night, in bed with Ildico, Attila suffered a violent nosebleed during which the blood poured into his lungs, drowning him. Irresponsible sons atomised his empire, bringing the rapid extermination of the Huns themselves, overtaken by time, folly, vice and the burrowing of other tribes. Attila's death, after meeting Pope Leo, was seen by the laity as God's judgement, a further advance toward the concept of god-king or, now, pope-emperor, the legacy of Alexander and Siwa.

Châlons itself did not destroy the Roman Empire's most feared enemy. Attila had initially escaped, possibly with Aetius' connivance, as had Alaric from Stilicho in 403. No blockade was enforced, no famine imposed. Attila was permitted withdrawal in dignity. Perhaps Aetius thought simply that 'cornered rats are dangerous vermin'. Jordanes said that Aetius also feared that the empire, were the Huns to be annihilated by the Goths, would itself be overwhelmed by the Goths, the Romans in second or third position, a second Alaric in Thorismund. Disingenuously, Jordanes suggested, Aetius therefore advised the prince to return to his own capital and pre-empt any attempt by his brothers to seize the leadership of the Visigoths.

At all events, the battle allocated the palm of Europe not to Tatars, but to the German and Roman races. This was indeed, as Creasy observed, the last victory of imperial Rome. Although a mission already accomplished – not turning her fortunes, nor opening new paths, nor consolidating her power – Châlons decided that savage barbarians out of central Asia should not submerge, in 'the hopeless chaos of barbaric conquest', the classic civilisation of Greece, 'the [hard-won] community of laws, of government, and institutions', and the nascent flower of Christianity, Latin or Germanic.

J. F. C. Fuller, in *Decisive Battles of the Western World*, takes the view that Attila's cabal of terrorised states would have collapsed anyway: the importance of Châlons was not that the victory was specifically Germanic or Roman, but one of 'both peoples combined over Asiatics'. Just as Salamis and Gaugamela had been victories of Europeans over Persians, at Châlons, once again,

'Europeans set aside their private quarrels in order to face a common foe.'

At the later funeral of Attila, that 'common foe' rode round the dead man's tent seven times, mourning and slashing themselves with knives in a ceremony known as blood-weeping.

SYNOPSIS OF EVENTS BETWEEN
CHÂLONS-SUR-MARNE AND TOURS

Odoacer, part Hun, defeated Orestes, the master general of Italy, at Pavia in 476, deposed the emperor and assumed control, thus extinguishing the Roman Empire of the west. Five years later, Clovis established the Frankish monarchy in Gaul.

Elsewhere, northern Germanic tribes including Angles and Saxons conquered most of Britain. Justinian briefly annexed Italy and North Africa to the Roman Empire of the east, while the Lombards between 568 and 570 took much of Italy. Constantinople fought with Persia for over fifty years.

From 629 to 713, Mohammedans, initially under Mohammed himself, conquered Persia, Syria, Egypt and Africa, invading Spain and defeating its inhabitants. 'Within about two years, the name of Mohammed was invoked under the Pyrenees.'

CHAPTER SIX

TOURS, 732

Gibbon described the battle of Tours as the event that rescued our ancestors of Britain and our neighbours of Gaul from the civil and religious yoke of the Quran. Creasy, for his part, claimed that Charles Martel's victory over the Saracens 'gave a decisive check to the career of the Arab conquest in Western Europe, rescued Christendom from Islam, preserved the relics of ancient and the germs of modern civilisation'.

In words echoed to primly correct auditors in 2001 by Signor Berlusconi, the Italian prime minister, it 'established the old superiority of the Indo-European over the Semitic family of mankind'.

Up to the sixth century, Arabs were identified, if at all, as either traders with the Levant or as nomadic tribesmen, who worshipped an enormous black stone in Mecca called the Qaabah, 'the cube'. By the middle of the seventh century, however, Bedouin or not, those same people had conquered Egypt, Persia and Syria, seized large regions of central Asia, and of North Africa from the Berbers, menaced Spain, France, the eastern empire in Constantinople and, at sea, dominated the Mediterranean, all in the name of Allah. The black cube had become the temple of Abraham.

It may be true that these conquests were driven rather by the desire for plunder and booty than by Islam, the religious creation of Mohammed, a polygamous Qureshi trader from Medina.

Nevertheless, as a unified faith sanctioned by authority, and by the correspondence of monotheistic Islam with the monophysite Christianity already active in the Levant and Egypt, that creation aided the acceptance of Arab domination in those countries.

Meanwhile, in Asia Minor, Justinian II's anarchic empire, devastated by barbarians and by Saracens, was replaced by the regime of Leo the Isaurian, a professional soldier, perhaps a Syrian, earlier military assistant to the emperor, later commanding imperial troops against two Muslim armies of the Caliphate which were marching through Anatolia and Cappadocia preparatory to an attempt to blockade Constantinople. Leo, having defeated Theodosius II's son *and* held the Muslim troops, was crowned by the patriarch in St Sophia as Emperor Leo III, his first and urgent task to repair, fortify and replenish the Byzantine capital of Constantinople against imminent Arab blockade. That city, with a population of under a million, although powerfully built and defended, was vulnerable to seaward, from Dardanelles and Bosphorus. A great deal therefore hung on the empire's fleet, much smaller than the caliph's, lying protected by a huge chain hung across the entrance to its harbour north of the Golden Horn, possibly the same chain over which Harold Hardrada rowed in the eleventh century to escape the Byzantine Empress Zoë's attentions, before returning to Norway, via Novgorod, and marriage there to the king's daughter.

A Muslim general, Muslemah, commanded one Muslim army unreliably estimated at 80,000 men, with a navy under General Suleiman of some 1,800 vessels, carrying 80,000 foot soldiers. The caliph also disposed of a reserve army under his personal command, and a fleet of supply and transport ships in North African ports.

Muslemah crossed the Hellespont at Abydos, which will be remembered from accounts of Salamis and Gaugamela. The defeat of his immediate land attack on Constantinople, repelled by brilliant Byzantine sappers, then led him to the final, confirmed decision for blockade. This step, to be enforced by Suleiman's fleet, was to isolate the city from support from the Black Sea on the one hand, and from the Aegean on the other: moats constructed by the Caliphate separated Constantinople from the Arab military camp.

Fuller refers to 'the strong current which sweeps round Seraglio Point' as casting the first vessels of Suleiman's Black Sea squadron into disarray. It was at this juncture that Leo lowered the boom between the towers guarding the harbour and ran for the open sea. His galleys were oared, under sail as well, each with a complement of up to 300 men, including marines. All were mounted with 'war engines' in revolving turrets, and with bow-tubes throwing explosive Greek fire.

Greek fire, according to Lieutenant-Colonel Hines in *Gunpowder and Ammunition* (1904), was a mixture of 'sulphur, naphtha and quicklime, projected and ignited by applying the hose of a water engine to the breech of a siphon'. It was effective and terrifying. On this occasion, it was so deadly that Suleiman made no further attack on a Byzantine fleet whose total strength amounted to no more than 200 vessels, of which far fewer weighed anchor that day. The supply line to Constantinople kept open, famine was averted.

After a terrible winter, to which many of the Arab invaders were quite unaccustomed, thousands of their troops in the trenches died of disease or starvation. The Caliph Suleiman, on his way to join them, also died but, according to Gibbon, of indigestion. 'The Caliph had emptied two baskets of eggs and of figs, which he swallowed alternately, and the repast was concluded with marrow and sugar. On a pilgrimage to Mecca, Suleiman had eaten at a single meal seventy pomegranates, a kid, six fowls and a huge quantity of grapes.'

Others, particularly pressed Christians, seized all opportunities to defect to the Byzantines with accurate and up-to-date information on the Muslim order of battle. A large Egyptian fleet, however, managed to close the Bosphorus at Büyük-Deré, north of Constantinople. Another (African) squadron anchored in the

Black Sea off today's northwest Turkey. The reserve army, not under Suleiman's successor, the irresolute, neglectful and bigoted Caliph Omar, but under the Caliphate general Merdasan, reinforced the trenches, where they found that the besiegers' strength had been so reduced by cold and privation that cannibalism had accompanied mass death.

To exploit the intelligence afforded by the enemy's deserters, Leo once more lowered the chain across his battle-squadron's harbour. The Byzantines again attacked the listless and unprepared Islamic fleet, sinking ships with the ram and burning with missiles and Greek fire the wretched Muslim vessels which, when not unmanned, rapidly became so in the terror which the assault inspired. According to Gibbon, Greek fire was, indeed, the principal factor in this war, 'Flying through the air, like a winged long-tailed dragon, about the thickness of an hogshead, with the report of thunder and the velocity of lightning: the darkness of the light was dispelled by this deadly illumination.' The African squadron was almost totally destroyed. Leo now despatched a Byzantine land army across the Bosphorus to the Asian shore where, in this most daring coup, it ambushed Merdasan's unit and the winter's survivors with deadly effect.

It was as well that he secured these victories, and that of his allied Bulgars, who killed over 20,000 Muslims south of Adrianople. Had the straits remained closed, through incompetence, inaction or weakness, Constantinople would have fallen. As it was, the failures of the Muslim forces and a carefully circulated rumour that the Franks were arming to join this Christian cause in the eastern Mediterranean caused Caliph Omar, after thirteen months of warfare, to give General Muslemah, Caliph Suleiman's brother, permission to retreat and to raise the siege. Although the cavalry escaped on the Asian shore without further loss, the defeat of Merdasan's troops, added to earlier losses, contributed to arrival at their home base of only 30,000 of the 200,000 men originally engaged on land.

Of the vast Muslim navy of over 2,500 ships, those still afloat after the sea-fights with the Byzantines were sunk in a storm off the Hellespont. Only five vessels returned to their home ports.

Whether won by Greek fire, superior generalship or western organisation over Asian carelessness, Vasiliev, in his *History of the Byzantine Empire*, claimed that Leo's victory ensured 'the survival of the Byzantine empire, the entire eastern Christian world, but also of all western European civilisation'. There are few, if any, dissenters to that view, the consequences of which endured until the Ottoman Turks stormed Constantinople on 29 May 1453, and the Asian nomads took over.

In the west, the Berbers – referred to as Numidians in the story of the Metaurus river and Zama – under the invading Arab governor Musa bin Nusair, had taken North Africa up to the Atlantic seaboard. In 710 Musa, seeking booty, not yet territory, had next turned his Moors against Spain across the straits. To that purpose he employed four vessels provided by the Berber governor of Ceuta, in recent times the capital of Spanish Morocco.

The caliph's limited approval was obtained for a raid of some 500 men which struck Algeciras, adjacent to Gibraltar, returning immediately with the loot. But next year, knowing that the Visigoth king Roderic was distracted by internecine strife with Franks from the north, Musa sent to Spain a much larger expedition of 7,000 men.

This force was bound not on piracy, but on conquest. Thanks to treachery in the Visigoth army, the commander, Tariq ibn Zayad, defeated Roderic and seized his capital, Toledo. The empire of Islam in the west had begun and Musa, now assuming command, used alternating brutality and indifference to conquer nearly all Spain, as did Chinggis Khan 500 years later in the rest of Europe.

In the years that followed, Gaul was the next country to be assaulted by the Islamic horde, pouring first across the Pyrenees into Duke Eudes's territory of Aquitaine. The duke bore throughout the southern provinces the role and title of king, gathering under his banner Goths, Gascons and Franks, initially defeating the Muslims under al-Hurr and al-Sama at Toulouse, where al-Sama, governor of Spain, was killed. But Narbonne, which had been captured by the Muslims under al-Hurr, was retaken when they once more crossed the Pyrenees in strength, occupying the Languedoc, Gascony, Burgundy, Bordeaux and even the Vosges. 'The whole of the south of France from the mouth of the Gasconne to that of the Rhône assumed the manners and religion of Islam,' said Gibbon.

Among the cities of the south, Nîmes and Carcassonne were lost to Christianity for a little. The new Arabian commander-in-chief, Abdur Rahman, moved his cavalry in single column toward Arles, and the passage of the Rhône. En route, he defeated Duke Eudes and slew Munuza (Othman bin abi Neza), a Moor defector 'who commanded the most important passes of the Pyrenees' for Eudes: 'the Duke's beauteous daughter had been awarded to the embraces of that African misbeliever'.

'Perigord, Saintonge and Poitou had fallen to the Muslims, whose standards were planted before the gates of Tours and Sens and as far as Lyons and Besançon; at Arles, thousands of the defenders' dead bodies were carried down the rapid stream to the Mediterranean.' The churches were despoiled of the few precious jewelled ornaments, hangings and other treasures left to them: the memory of Muslim atrocity and devastation has to this day not died in France.

In a famous peroration, Gibbon concluded that, were the Arabian advance to have continued, 'the Arabian fleet might have sailed without a naval combat into the mouth of the Thames. Perhaps the interpretation of the Quran would now be taught in the schools of Oxford, and her pulpits might demonstrate to a circumcised people the sanctity and truth of the revolution of Mohammed.'

The old Roman Empire was being torn apart by the teeth and claws of the Arabs in the south and by armed dissension in the north. 'Gaul was not yet France.' The Germans, although many had converted to Christianity, had not yet replaced the unifying power of the Caesars, while the bulk of the population consisted of Gallic, Romanised Celts. Although the Teutonic Franks were superior to both the other members of their confederation, and to the conquered natives, the Frankish Merovingian dynasty was in pathetic decline, as well as in sharp opposition to Eudes of Aquitaine.

The present leader of the Franks was, however, the Merovingian Charles, son of Pepin II, Mayor of the Palace, whose dynasty had produced Clovis, but also a line so despised that its titular kings were dragged to their rubber-stamp assembly in ox carts, a sad destiny for the family which had under Aetius fought Attila at Châlons.

But Pepin II and his illegitimate son Charles were horses of a different colour, Pepin having conquered Austrasia, Neustria and Aquitaine, until Eudes broke away. Charles defeated Eudes and extended his own rule into Bavaria, Thuringia and Frisia before seizing Berri in Eudes's Aquitaine. His ambition in the eighth century did not stop there. Charles intended to conquer and unite Gaul, just as Abdur Rahman meant, at least according to Reinaud's *Invasion du Sarrazins en France,* 'to unite Italy, Germany and the Greek Empire to the already vast domains of the champions of the Quran'. Plainly, plunder had given place to empire.

Charles, before taking Berri across the Loire, had embarked on a Danubian campaign against other Germanic tribes. There in 731, learning that Abdur Rahman had moved in a series of bloody encounters from the Garonne to the Dordogne, he hurried to Paris. In Paris, after his own defeat, Eudes, hitherto Charles's enemy and a Goth, decided to bow to overall command by the Franks. The combined army, united against Islam, was directed at the Arab drive towards the supposed riches of Tours and Poitiers, in an Islamic army estimated by Arabs at 80,000 and by Christian chroniclers as 'many hundreds of thousands more'.

Southey described the infidel forces as 'a countless multitude; / Syrian, Moor, Saracen, Greek renegade / Persian and Copt, and

Tartar, in one band / of erring faith conspired – strong in the youth / and heat of zeal – a dreadful brotherhood'. Light cavalry was their principal medium, the sword and lance their main weapons. They wore little armour, neither did they much use the bow. Their attacks were unregulated, confined to frequent and uncoordinated cavalry rushes. Their aim, ultimately, was still devoted to loot which, when considerable, reduced their freedom of manoeuvre.

The horde appears to have had no administrative base, let alone a commissary. 'They came out of Spain with all their wives and their children, and their substance in such great multitude that no man could reckon or estimate them. They brought with them all their armour, and whatever they had, as if they were thenceforth always to dwell in France.'

The Franks under Charles Martel, the Hammer, after Judas Maccabaeus, were little better disciplined: an unpaid infantry force, with some heavy cavalry, dependent on piracy for wages, co-opting local militias which, according to Lavisse's *Histoire de France*, dispersed when victuals ran out. And those who today complain of absence of hierarchy or lack of respect towards superiors might consider this from Gregory of Tours: 'no-one fears his king, no-one fears his duke, no-one respects his count and if any one of us tries to improve his state of affairs and to assert his authority, forthwith sedition breaks out in the army and mutiny swells up'.

Before the battle Charles also recommended Eudes to wait until the Arabs had so grossly sated themselves with plunder that divided counsels would outweigh their undoubted valour, thus ensuring victory. But whatever Eudes thought of this advice, it is improbable that the Franks, for their part, would for long have patiently tolerated the thievish barbarities of the Muslim troops.

It is not clear whether surprise was a major factor in the ensuing battle. 'Somewhere south of Tours' Abdur Rahman was apprised of the secret, speedy approach, from behind a range of hills, of a superior force led by Eudes and Charles. The next six days were spent in desultory combat, probably in an attempt by the Arabs to protect their lines of communication, and to hustle the treasure-train to places of safety. The actual site of the battle, near the Loire at Cenon, may have therefore been closer to Poitiers than Tours, by both of which names it is known.

The Dupuys, in their *Encyclopaedia of Military History*, claim that Charles Martel, when battle was finally joined, had dismounted his heavy cavalry to form an infantry phalanx, which he knew the Muslim light cavalry would be unable to break. Arab sources imply that a Christian flanking attack enveloped a Muslim wing, driving the Arabs back on their camp. Both sides carried swords and wore chain mail. The Franks wore conical helmets. The phalanx held under incessant cavalry assault: 'The men of the north stood as motionless as a wall: they were like a belt of ice frozen together and not to be dissolved, as they slew the Arabs with the sword. The Austrasians [under Charles], vast of limb and iron of hand, hewed on bravely in the thick of the fight.' It was they who found and cut down the Saracen king, by one account with 'a multitude of spears'.

Abdur Rahman's death, and a false rumour that the Franks and Goths were pillaging the Muslim camp, caused these warriors to ride off to protect their tents, eventually abandoning the treasure in panic in order to flee southward. They did not return: 'no further serious attempts at conquest beyond the Pyrenees were made by the Saracens. All the host fled before the enemy and many died in the flight', the absurd figures of 350,000 Muslims, according to Italian monks quoted by Gibbon, and only 1,500 Christians.

The first consequence of Tours, in Creasy's view the decisive aspect of the battle, was that Islam did not make further inroads into western Europe but instead remained beyond the mountain barriers of the Pyrenees. Perhaps even more importantly for history, had Charles Martel been defeated in Gaul, the empire of the Franks, the Carolingian Holy Roman Empire, could not have been born.

The empire of Charlemagne, Pepin II's grandson, became, in H. A. L. Fisher's words, 'the strongest instrument for government and conquest which Europe had seen since the great days of the Roman Empire'. Germany, most importantly the Saxons, Bohemia, Lombardy, Croatia, Carinthia, nearly all of central Europe, entered the Christian tradition, 'a conquest for Rome greater than any single conquest since the days of Julius Caesar', the fruit of over fifty successful military campaigns, and even one failure, at the pass of Roncesvalles. Charlemagne was crowned by Leo III with the imperial crown on Christmas Day 800. Learning, currency and the law were reformed. Intellectual life was revived and preserved, no little owing to men of Ireland, York and Northumbria; even Charles the Great's death could not prevent the gradual, subsequent spread of Christianity and its culture into Poland and Hungary.

Charles Martel had consolidated in western Europe Leo the Isaurian's victory at Constantinople. The empires of east and west alike had survived continued Oriental assault. Although the 'empire of the west' did not long survive Charlemagne's death, Creasy felt confident enough to assert – admittedly in the piping, imperial days of the nineteenth century – that, from Charlemagne's accession onward, Christianity and modern Europe 'went forward in not uninterrupted but, ultimately, certain career', which was also Gibbon's verdict, as our first lines showed.

SYNOPSIS OF EVENTS BETWEEN
TOURS AND HASTINGS

Charlemagne reigned between 768 and 814.

The empire was much divided after he died. Civil war proliferated. The kingdom of France separated from Germany and Italy. From 832, the Norsemen raided Europe, including England, the latter rescued by King Alfred and his descendants by 954. The Norsemen remained, however, victorious in Neustrian France, called Normandy after them. Normans, originally bound on pilgrimage to the Holy Land, settled forcibly in Italy and Sicily.

William, son of Duke Robert of Normandy, had succeeded to the dukedom when his father died after a pilgrimage to the Holy Land in 1035.

Soon after Canute's death, the Saxons were restored to their own sovereignty in England. Edward the Confessor, son of Ethelred (then in Norman exile), became king in 1042.

CHAPTER SEVEN

HASTINGS, 1066

By command of the Duke, you rest here a King, O Harold
That you may be guardian still of the shore and sea.

S o read the legend on the gravestone to King Harold Godwinson,
overlooking the shore he had defended. According to Guy
d'Amiens' *Carmen de Hastingae Proelis*, the stone was raised by
William the Conqueror, soon after Hastings. Other suggested
destinies for the ruler's body are manifold: bought by his old
mother, Gytha, Godwin's widow, for its weight in gold; burial in
Waltham Abbey; no death at all but refuge in Denmark; a hermit
in a cave in the white cliffs of Dover; in a chapel near Chester; led
in Shropshire like a blind man. And the legend itself resembles a
sneering reference by Duke William, harsh and unforgiving, when
initially refusing Harold's cadaver to Harold's mother.

After Canute's death, he and his Anglo-Danish kingdom
had been succeeded by Edward the Confessor. The succession
thereafter lay – within the English establishment – between
another Harold, son of the mysterious Godwin, Earl of Wessex,
whose origins are still unknown, and Edgar, grandson of Edmund
Ironside. Foreign candidates included Harold Hardrada, the
lethally pugnacious king of Norway, and King Swein of Denmark.
The bastard son of Duke Robert and Arletta, a ravishing tanner's
daughter from Falaise, was an ambitious and most formidable

rival, Duke William of Normandy, later King William I.

Normandy was that country taken in about 911 by Viking Norsemen, gradually to become 'French and Christian', soon to conquer not only Maine, Anjou, Aquitaine and Gascony, but Sicily, south Italy and Antioch, braving the might of the Byzantine Empire itself, the Norman Empire in truth, 'this whole race of Northern robbers'. The historian H. A. L. Fisher said that 'Duke William could not be described as one of nature's clergymen'. But in William's polity, wisely allied to Rome, and with all power in his despot's hand, the duke, not his nobles after their defeat at Val és Dunes, governed Normandy as, indeed, he later governed England.

Although not of English royal blood, his great-aunt had been the mother of Edward the Confessor and had married Ethelred and Canute, both kings of England. Neither was Harold of Wessex himself of royal blood. The only claimant who had met that condition was the Aetheling Edward, son of Ironside, who had died on landing in England, leaving only Edgar now, at thirteen, hardly capable of prevailing over his mighty competitors.

In 1066 Harold was aged about forty. He was prudent, discreet, balanced, good tempered, well mannered, cheerful and polite. A handsome man, he may have suffered from arthritis or rheumatism, afflictions which diminished neither his energy nor his physical strength. He loved at least one woman well, Edith Swanneshals, 'Swan's Throat', by whom he had three sons. Not his 'official' wife, they were together for twenty years: it was she who identified his broken body, gashed and hacked to death by his Norman killers at Hastings.

William of Poitiers, the king's chaplain, in his idolatrous work of sycophancy to his master Duke William (*Gesta Guillelin*), described Harold as a 'proud and cruel despot . . . a hateful tyrant who had reduced [the English] to shameful slavery'. Were this true, England would not have exploded after his death in armed rebellion against the usurping William I. Although not exactly 'pious or lowly', Harold was a conciliator, patient, steady, and a man of peace, his coins stamped with the single word PAX. Before being anointed he had – as Subregulus (Under-King), Dei Gratia Dux, titles not accorded even to his father Godwin – managed the kingdom for the melancholic, repressed and neurotic Edward the Confessor as the king swung between inaction and paranoia.

That loyalty, furthermore, was to a man who had dispossessed and exiled his own wife, Edith, to a nunnery, and who had exiled all Godwin's family after Godwin's protest at the defilement of Dover in 1048 by the French Comte Eustache de Boulogne. Only armed action had secured the family's return to Britain and to the partial replacement of Norman advisors and functionaries at Edward's court. But while the English family had been in exile, William had visited the king in England.

In 1051, the duke, then aged twenty-three, arrived with a large and glittering retinue, designed to impress a population for whom he had no regard, and one already under the heel of Norman courtiers and clergy. Edward had neither the power nor the right to dispose of the crown without the agreement of his advisory assembly, the Witenagemot, or Witan. Nevertheless, he now did so, promising it to William, whether formally, which is improbable, or 'vaguely', as was his wont.

Yet only one of the English chronicles, according to David Howarth's *1066, Year of the Conquest*, spoke of the visit. Not one reported the promise. No Norman document described the visit, either, but all referred freely to the promises, and at length. This was the only occasion when King Edward is known to have met an adult William, an opportunity for England's future to be discussed with the 'successor'. The latter returned to his country, convinced wrongly and through misunderstanding of his destiny as ruler of Normandy and England upon the Confessor's death.

According to William of Poitiers, Harold travelled to William on Edward's instructions in 1064 to confirm this promise. William of Malmesbury, however, claimed that, caught in a storm while fishing, Harold had been blown on to the French coast and made the pledges only in exchange for release.

Both scribes agree that Harold promised to ensure that, after Edward's death, William would succeed to the English throne. Harold, meanwhile, would act as Duke William's representative at King Edward's court, personally garrison Dover with the duke's knights and garrison other castles on his behalf. He undertook, moreover, to marry William's daughter, Agatha, then aged eleven, and betrothed his own sister to a Norman baron. Harold was then required by William to do homage and fealty, swearing the oath over a chest covered with a cloth of gold, which – unknown to him – contained bones and other relics of saints. Harold, on being later so informed, expressed the deepest alarm: 'His hand trembled and the flesh quivered.' But Wace's *Roman de Rou* says that he then returned to England and dealt ably with Anglo/Danish skirmishing in Northumbria.

The oath was certainly taken: it is pictured in the Bayeux Tapestry. But, equally, it was taken under duress. The circumstances of the shipwreck, Harold's arrest by Comte Guy de Ponthieu, his release to William's custody and the trickery with bones all attest to that. So do the absurd promises over garrisons in England, which could not have been given by Edward, or Harold as Dux Anglorum (leader of the English), without charges of treason. And Harold knew as well as Edward that the crown, unlike continental symbols, was not his, but for Parliament or Witan to give.

The other explanation, that Harold and William had formed an immediate bond, is similarly negated by these considerations, although an 'arrangement' would have had the advantage of shutting out other contenders, whether Edgar, Hardrada or Swein.

For the English, perhaps even for any Anglicised Normans, Harold had already established his right to orb and sceptre. But Church and empire on the continent favoured William over the native line, perhaps a legacy from Charlemagne and imperial Rome. Nor should we forget, in examining the recesses of Edward's mind, that Godwin, although twice acquitted of complicity, handed over Edward's brother Alfred to be blinded and killed by Canute's son Harold I.

Godwin is supposed to have died in 1053 at the Confessor's table, in a probably mythic trial by ordeal. The Norman poet of *La Estoire de Saint Aedward Le Rei* ends his tale:

> Now cries the King
> Drag out this stinking dog.

In 1065 Harold's relatively peaceful conduct of affairs had been disturbed by the news that Northumbria had thrown out its own earl, his brother Tostig, thought in the *Vita Aedwardi Regis* to be King Edward's favourite. A personal visit to Northampton, whither the rebel thanes had marched after plundering the northern treasure and attacking York, persuaded Harold that charges of unjust government, even murder, were unfortunately true. The thanes planned to march further against the king himself at Oxford. Tostig was replaced and exiled to Flanders, believing that his brother had engineered his downfall.

News took a long time to drift down to the little villages of Sussex, whether from the great international world, from London, or even from Lewes. It had to trickle through desolate heath, marsh and woods, away from Roman roads, by obscure pony tracks, carried – often distorted in the telling – by monks, pedlars and mendicants, through to the small hamlets behind their palisades. Those tiny thatched villages – each with its little allotments for vegetables, owning a few chickens, perhaps geese, pigs outside the settlement – lay in open fields. They seldom housed more than seventy people, including the thane, in the silence of the English countryside; wolves howled, however, in the forests. Over the marshes which surrounded them rose the Sussex Downs, and the blue sea beyond to France.

The population of London itself is unlikely to have been more than 15,000, York less than 10,000 and, according to David Howarth's *1066*, not greater than 1,500 to 4,000 for some dozen other towns; most housed much fewer. The courtiers, in London and when travelling with the king on the hunt, lived much as the thanes and villeins. Although their houses were larger, they were still primitive, lacking glass in the windows, cold and uncomfortable, without efficient chimneys. The rich ate more, of course, drank more too, and were more elegantly dressed. The fare was plain, mostly grown in England; silks were imported, as were spices, these probably available to earls, bishops and the grander reaches of Church and society.

The commonalty as a whole was not one of luxury, but it was not brutal, nor savagely discontented. It was concerned with land, the animals, children. Common problems, including custom and the law, were discussed, and sometimes solved, in the Hundred, Shire and Witan moots.

The arts flourished: silver, gold, illuminated manuscripts. The people worshipped. They had many feasts, pagan as well as Christian. They drank beer in large quantities, told stories, wrote poetry. They worked very hard in their fields and gardens. They seem, in their little Anglo-Saxon world, to have lived short lives happily and simply, without resentment or rebellion against a hierarchy which, they may have thought, gave them as much as they gave to it.

There is no evidence that the general populace, at least in the south, was pained by the suggestion that one earl, Harold, might – as Tostig complained – have caused the forcible downfall of another, his own brother at that. Maybe, in turbulent and unregulated times, they would not have been as shocked as today's *bien pensants* pretend at the behaviour of their betters: the turbulence, in Tostig's case, had been in the north and, like the wars with Welsh and Scots, no doubt seemed far away.

The news which 'drifted down' to the villages on 5 January 1065 was more important than Tostig's fate. It was of the death of King Edward the Confessor. Edward, learning of his favourite's overthrow, had had a first seizure which, by that date, in 'bleak mid-winter', led to other strokes, delirium, the revelation of a crazy prophecy, and his deathbed declaration.

He addressed those gathered, Archbishop Stigand of

Canterbury, Harold, his deputy and second-in-command, Queen Edith – nursing his chilled feet in her lap as in the Bayeux Tapestry – the half-Norman Robert Fitz Wimark, whose witness at least prevented Duke William from denouncing the Confessor's legacy as an English hoax.

Indicating his wife Edith, Harold's sister, the king said to Harold, in the words of the anonymous author of the *Vita Aedwardi Regis*:

I commend this woman and all the Kingdom to your protection. Serve and honour her with faithful obedience as your lady and sister, which she is, and do not deprive her, as long as she lives, of any honour she has received from me. I also commend to you those men who have left their native land for love of me and served me faithfully [the Normans at the English court]. Take an oath of fealty from them if you wish, and protect and retain them: or send them with your safe conduct across the Channel to their own homes, with all they have acquired in my service.

The declaration, in not directly naming Harold as successor, was equivocal. It was not so seen, however, by the Witan which, on the afternoon of Edward's funeral, not only confirmed Earl Harold as king, but crowned him in Edward's camp, the chilly abbey of West Minster, on Thorney Island. The new king, bearing sword, sceptre and rod, was anointed, swearing peace, justice and mercy in the huge, sacred theatre of that coronation service whose symbols and order remain unchanged to this day. The Confessor's last words were thus understood, in England at least, in the absence of any other nomination, as naming a king, not approval for Harold's continued service as deputy to someone else unnamed, but Harold Godwinson himself.

In Normandy, Duke William had been only seven when he succeeded his father. Anarchy followed until, aged nineteen and aided by the king of France, he defeated the rebel barons in the mounted battle of knights at Caen in 1047. The further suppression now began of such independent minor 'kingdoms' as had survived Caen. Expeditions started towards the gradual expansion of Norman power outside its own frontiers. Externally and internally, William's immense personality, vision and military ability led, by central decision rather than by any careful process of law or democratic discussion, to Norman dominance in much of Europe and the eastern empire.

As for England, since the duke presumably believed that Edward had agreed in 1051 or 1064 to his peaceful possession of this island at the Confessor's death, conquest was not something he had had to consider. In any case, if William of Malmesbury's *De Gestis Regum Angolorum Vita Wulfslan* were a guide, he felt little but disgusted contempt for that nation. The writer regarded the English as wanton and luxurious, yet living in houses squalid and ill-constructed, at least in comparison with the continent; irreligious, given to gluttony and drunkenness, a sort of general bulimia. One of their foibles, he also complained, was the impregnation of servant girls for subsequent sale into slavery or prostitution. The English appearance, especially its short skirt, gold ornaments, long hair, clean-shaven faces and tattooed bodies, was also evidence – to the Norman chroniclers – of corruption and decadence, a view of our countrymen not peculiar to the eleventh century.

It may therefore have been with anger and surprise that William received the first tidings of Edward's death and of Harold's almost immediate coronation. There had been no previous communication, let alone consultation. The duke believed that he had had a need, even a right, to know.

He was momentarily encouraged by the necessity for Harold to travel to York to reverse a decision by Morcar, one of the northern earls, to refuse recognition. Recognition *was* then granted, possibly after Harold's alleged agreement to formal or official marriage with Morcar's sister, Ealdgyth, widow of the Welsh king, Gruffydd, defeated in 1063 by Harold. And a grain of comfort to William, if only as a spoiling action, might have been gathered from Tostig's unilateral and hopeless attempt at a raid against England. This foolish venture caused Harold to order a general mobilisation which, alas for him, had legally expired by the time that William was ready to sail on his own more effective voyage.

According to William of Poitiers, the duke had 'resolved to avenge the insult by force of arms, and to regain his inheritance by war'. He started off with a series of messages to Harold containing appeals, all of which were rejected. The last response – from Harold – reported that his sister had died: did the selected Norman baron want to marry a corpse? This was seen in Rouen as unusually impolite. Across the Channel, in England, the people were worried by the sudden appearance of Halley's Comet which, with its glowing tail, blazed in the dark skies for seven nights before illuminating Tostig's squadron off the Isle of Wight at the point where he, his father Godwin and the family had returned from exile nineteen years before.

King Harold's forces consisted, firstly, of 2–3,000 'professional' soldiers, house-carles, drawn from his own resources as monarch or earl of Wessex, and some hundreds of the same from his brothers. The rest of the army, the Fyrd, was, rather, a part-time militia, territorials, manned by thanes and men from the hides (120 acres) and hundreds. The house-carles, or some of them, were horsed and mailed. The arms the English bore were lances, spears, javelins, two-handed axes, great and small swords. Howarth estimated the Fyrd, country-wide, at 50,000, but the figure has been questioned. Certainly, unless the Fyrd had fought in Wales against Gruffydd they were, if not untrained, inexperienced and out of practice. Archery played a very small part among the Fyrd and cavalry little or none, unlike Duke William's cavalry knights, constantly in battle against foreign and other foes.

The total strength of Harold's army in the south may *then* have been 10–12,000 men. His navy, like all others of that epoch unable to sail except with the wind astern or on the beam, could have numbered up to 400 vessels, each carrying crews of four men and thirty marines or soldiers. Because of the limitations on manoeuvre imposed by square sails, it was very rare indeed for vessels of opposing navies actually to meet in armed combat: the ships were mainly employed as landing-craft of which, on the Norman side, William commanded some 100 for stores and so forth and about 350 for knights and horses.

William now sought to justify his claim to the English crown before the emperor and the pope in Rome, presented indirectly through the Italian Lanfranc, later archbishop of Canterbury, under the pretext of reform of the English Church. That institution was, of course, no more in need of reform than the corrupt and divided Holy See: in 1046, for example, three competing popes had had to be dismissed by Emperor Henry III, and a fourth nominated. Harold, obviously, was not represented at the conclave, and so could not make a defence.

Pope Alexander II blessed William's cause, presented him with a ring and papal standard and, according to the *Roman de Rou*, excommunicated the English faithful. 'The conquest and pillage of England by the Normans', in Fisher's phrase, 'was carried out under the banner and sanctified by the authority of the Vicar of Christ.'

As we have seen, just as mobilisation of Harold's forces legally expired, so then Tostig landed. The brother moved on from the Isle of Wight, originally in sixty small ships up the east coast and, after defeat in the northern earldoms, joined King Harold Hardrada of Norway off the Tyne. The joint force, according to the *Anglo-Saxon Chronicle*, sailed with 300 ships against England, destroying Scarborough, routing the two northern earls at Fulford on 20 September. English corpses 'paved a way across the fen for the brave Norsemen'.

Learning this disturbing news, King Harold of England made a remarkable mounted journey north via Tadcaster, by night and day, with a force which virtually destroyed Harold Hardrada's army, including Tostig and Hardrada himself, on 25 September at Stamford Bridge, and subsequently at Riccall as the Norwegians fled back to their ships. Only 24 out of 300 vessels returned to Norway.

Ordericus Vitalis in *Historia Ecclesiastica* referred to great heaps of bones still, in the twelfth century, on the battlefield as 'memorials to the prodigious number which fell on both sides'. Having failed to break the Norwegian phalanx, King Harold had ordered a pretended retreat which he then exploited by unleashing the English mass on the excited and pursuing Norwegians. Massacre ensued, from which Norway needed twenty-five years to recover. But Harold too lost many men whom he could not afford in the next four weeks to meet the looming presence of Duke William across the Channel.

It had been a great victory, preceded by a march of nearly 200 miles in four days on their English ponies. Harold's men were strengthened all the way up the Roman road, and at York by their countrymen, no longer beaten but ready to fight Hardrada's Norsemen again. The king rested, feasted and rejoiced, thinking perhaps of mill, church and home at Bosham in Chichester harbour, with Edith Swanneshals and their children. Yachts today, and dinghies, lie at moorings where the king too once kept a small boat or two for fishing and fowling.

But the message was not long in coming. Before a week had passed, word reached the camp at York that Duke William had landed at Pevensey. Before another four days were gone Harold had repeated in reverse, with his now reduced troops, the astonishing journey that he had made the month before. He arrived in London, some of his soldiers dead, some wounded, all exhausted, on 5 October. Here he waited for six days, collecting such troops as he could raise, perhaps, given the losses at Fulford and Stamford Bridge, not more than 6–7,000.

En route he had made a solitary diversion to the stone figure of Christ on the Cross, enclosed in silver, which stood on the hill by his own abbey at Waltham. He had bowed to it, and the canons had seen a miracle: the Christ seemed to return the bow, and stayed bent thereafter in acknowledgement.

William's invasion fleet had lain in the Dives river estuary, delayed by a northerly wind, from 12 August until 12 September, when a southwester blew. The duke sailed for St Valéry, to attempt thence the direct crossing of the Channel. There were losses, perhaps severe, en route. On 28 September, after further adverse weather, 'God drove the clouds from the sky and the winds from the sea, dispatched the cold and rid the heavens of rain. The earth grew warm, pervaded by great heat and the sun shone with unwonted brilliance,' as William cleared St Valéry for Pevensey. But by that date Harold had demobilised his navy and his southern military. The regulations had expired, food was running out. The winds had changed, blowing for the Normans, only two days after Stamford Bridge. Duke William's landing at Pevensey, led by his flagship *Mora* with a great leading light on the foremast, was unopposed.

Pevensey and countless villages between it and Hastings, where William made his headquarters, were casually made waste in the fashion of the time: Hailsham, Hurstmonceaux, Bexhill, Crowhurst, many others, all 'wasta', even the Norman property in England of the abbey of Fécamp. In Hastings, the duke received a message from Harold bidding him to return to his own country.

William's response proposed submission to law, even partition, or, in the last resort, single combat. The messenger, a monk of Fécamp, heard Harold say on receipt of this challenge: 'We march at once. We march to battle.' It was only now, according to the *Roman de Rou*, that Harold understood that England had suffered papal excommunication, most terrible of mediaeval judgements.

Ordericus Vitalis and William of Malmesbury concur that Harold's brother, Gyrth, now proposed a major change of plan. Because, he declared, Harold was exhausted, and because Gyrth was not bound by the oath to William, and because, if Harold were killed, the kingdom could fall to the Normans, Gyrth should command at Hastings. Harold's role, meanwhile, should be the creation of a scorched earth, which would deprive William of resources for survival northward should the battle be lost.

Harold refused, in Howarth's opinion mainly because excommunication, with its defiance of Pope Alexander as well as Duke

William, meant that the battle must be fought at once, and by him, without delay. 'It had become a private matter of conscience.' Only God could judge. To have waited for reinforcements might have been more sensible, but Harold, his brothers Gyrth and Leofwin, some clerics and Harold's army now rode out of London, down the Dover road, to 'the hoary apple tree' on Calbec Hill where he took up position. (Edith Swanneshals was not with them when they met there on 13 or 14 October.) But because Harold had preferred speed over numbers, his strength on the hill was only a third of the requirement and, of that third, many were exhausted by the two extraordinary marches.

The battle was fought near the Hastings road, where it joined the main London–Dover artery. To the east of Harold, and behind him to the northwest, was forest, marsh to the south. His standards, the Fighting Man and the Dragon of Wessex, were planted, and later fell, near the present high altar of the abbey church. It may be that Harold and his men slept in the woods, reaching the ridge and the apple tree only in the early morning of 14 October, when the enemy found them. According to the *Chronicle*, the Normans had spent the night in prayer and preparation, while the English had filled the darkness with drunken song, consequently oversleeping into daylight: 'William came upon him in surprise before his army was drawn up in the battle array.'

Among the downs and sunlit uplands of that October morning, the coverts and green hills, the English infantry began to form its customary shield-wall, shoulder to shoulder, a phalanx ten ranks deep, the house-carles and their steeds on the flanks. The Normans advanced in three divisions: on the right, Franco-Flemish under Eustache de Boulogne, the architect at Dover of Godwin's exile; Bretons on the left; and the centre, commanded by William, of Normans behind the papal standard. (The duke had started the morning badly by putting on his armour back to front.) The archers wore helmets with nasals, and, on their feet, buskins, with bows and quivers hanging from their belts. The knights, clothed in chain armour, steel boots and shining helmets, carried kite-shaped shields, lances and broadswords. They formed the rear echelon of each division, with infantry – in chain mail and leather jerkins – as the middle line and, in the very front, archers.

Before battle a Norman juggler called Taillefer, singing the songs of Roland, Oliver and Roncevalles, rode across the English line behind its shields, throwing and catching his sword in the air, before driving a lance into the body of an English soldier, and striking another before being brought down. Trumpets, bugles and horns sounded, shields and lances raised, bows bent, mace and sword readied.

The first strikes, from the Norman archers or crossbow men, arrows loosed uphill, were missing their targets. Spears, javelins, stones, missiles of every kind hurled by the English were more successful. 'Shouts were soon drowned in the clash of arms, by the cries of the dying . . . the battle raged with the utmost fury.' The defenders remained squarely behind their shield-wall while their missiles easily pierced the attackers' armour and the shields over chain mail. And 'few who came within the unerring sweep of an English axe ever lived to strike another blow'.

As the Normans slowly moved up the slope under the steady rain of arrows, their left wing of Breton knights began to break in panic and fall back. Not their archers, infantry or cavalry could dent the fenced shield-wall. The English right counter-attacked, hastening the Bretons' flight and, with it, the cavalry's. Suddenly the Norman centre too started to yield. William himself lost his horse. Before mounting another, to reassure the troops that their leader survived, he pushed back his helmet, crying, 'Look at me well. I am still alive and by the grace of God I shall yet prove victor.' This gesture, and his leadership, rallied the Normans and prevented rout, the cavalry knights now brought forward, crying 'Dex Aie', to the English 'Out! Out!' The English shouted 'Holy Cross' and 'God Almighty', transcribed by the French, as 'Olicrosse' and 'Godemite'.

An English charge drove the Normans with considerable casualties into a deep fosse. But Harold did not exploit the momentum already achieved, inexplicably failing to attack the fleeing enemy along the lines, the opportunity for a general advance lost.

William, unable still to break the shield-wall, decided then on two separate feigned retreats, both of which deceived the English into headlong and deluded pursuit, actions which may have cost Harold the victory. The Normans, on each front, like Mongol and other eastern armies before and since, stopped dead, wheeled their horses, faced their pursuers and slaughtered them.

The battle continued most of the day with great gallantry, but little advantage to either side. The mêlée was tumultuous; hatchets, lances, spears clove and pierced. An Englishman beat in the duke's helmet with his hatchet, before being lanced by the Normans. Axes, maces and bills, as well as hatchets, were the favoured weapons of Harold's army, unaccustomed yet to jousting or the use of the lance on horseback.

Archery accomplished little against the English, until the duke ordered vertical aim, the arrows in descent plunging on to the enemy's heads and faces. Unless guarded by shields, the eyes were put out. An arrow struck Harold above his right eye. In agony, he pulled it out, breaking it as he did so. Four men, according to Wace, attacked him as he lay blinded on his shield, Duke William, Eustache de Boulogne, Ponthieus's son and Walter Giffard, who not only murdered him but dissected him, hacking him to pieces. One stabbed him in the chest, another cut off his head, the third disembowelled him and the last cut off and carried away a thing euphemistically described as his 'thigh'. For this crime Giffard was, according to William of Malmesbury, condemned by the duke and dismissed from the army.

William and some 1,000 men moved in for the kill, rushing upon the English, at last breaking the shield-wall by the sheer weight and speed of their armoured assault, horses and men together. The English fled, many fell, trampled down by the cavalry, rallying when they could, for as long as they could. But, as the *Roman de Rou* declares, 'the standard was beaten down, the golden standard taken, so they left the field and those fled who could'. But William of Poitiers does not hesitate to refer to those Saxons who, from the forests after the battle, cut off pursuing Normans.

Stephen Morillo's *Battle of Hastings* concluded that the battle was lost by the English chiefly because Harold was paralysed by the huge moral weight of excommunication. And the sheer size of the battle, for those days, coupled with his inability, unlike at Stamford Bridge, to command on horseback, deprived him of the mobility to change from the defensive posture in which he found himself at dawn to the attack which he preferred thereafter.

Although their various arms differed in quality – the cavalry superior in William's army, the infantry in Harold's – the reasons for Harold's defeat were not only technical, but in leadership. William's generalship was superior. But the ultimate criterion was that in an age in which men tended to fall apart when their leaders were killed, not only did Harold and his two brothers die at crucially adverse stages of the battle, but so did a large proportion of the entire Saxon leadership.

It is only surprising that, whereas in similar circumstances unled mediaeval armies did not last longer than an hour, Harold's lasted from dawn to after dusk: in Morillo's words, 'given essentially equal armies, William simply outgeneralled Harold, and had a bit more luck', whether from Norway or the winds.

Thereafter, in government, while William's brutality, repression and cruelty were catastrophic, on an almost twentieth-century scale, Howarth's closing sentence is also true: 'The children of a beaten race never became Norman, they remained most stubbornly English, absorbed the invader and made of the mixture a new kind of Englishness.' Creasy believed, in greater depth, that Guizot also was correct in his view that England owed her liberties to having been conquered by the Normans, 'planting far and wide as a dominant class [Pitt's *Iron Barons*] a martial nobility of the

A first century BC carved stone tablet depicting a trireme, of the type used by both the Greek and Persian fleets at the battle of Salamis (*Museo Archeologico Nazionale, Naples/Bridgeman Art Library*)

Alexander the Great, who defeated Darius, king of the Persians, in 331 BC, and took Greek culture into Asia (*AKG London/ Erich Lessing*)

Hannibal, the great Carthaginian general and statesman. The eventual defeat of Carthage, at Zama in 202 BC, led to Roman hegemony in Europe (*AKG London*)

The survival of the Germanic races hinged upon their victory over the Romans in AD 9. This bronze statue of Arminius stands on the highest peak of the Teutoburg Wald, facing the Rhine (*AKG London*)

Attila the Hun, as depicted in the fifteenth century. The Huns rampaged west through Europe until they were finally halted by an allied force at Châlons-sur-Marne in 451 (*AKG London*)

Charles Martel's victory over the Moors at Tours in 732 stemmed their progress into western Europe. Moorish influence remained south of the Pyrenees until they were eventually expelled from Spain in 1492. The Alhambra palace in Granada is a lasting legacy of Islamic culture on the Iberian peninsula (*The Art Archive/Dagli Orti*)

King Harold is fatally wounded at the battle of Hastings, as depicted in the Bayeux Tapestry. William the Conqueror's victory was the last successful invasion of the British Isles (*AKG London/Erich Lessing*)

Saladin, the Saracen leader who masterminded a great 'victory for Allah' by overwhelming the Crusaders in 1187 (*British Library, London/ Bridgeman Art Library*)

Chinggis Khan's Mongol armies were a ruthlessly effective mounted fighting force that swept through most of Europe in the thirteenth century. Here their arms and armour are depicted in a Persian manuscript from the same era (*The Art Archive/Edinburgh University Library*)

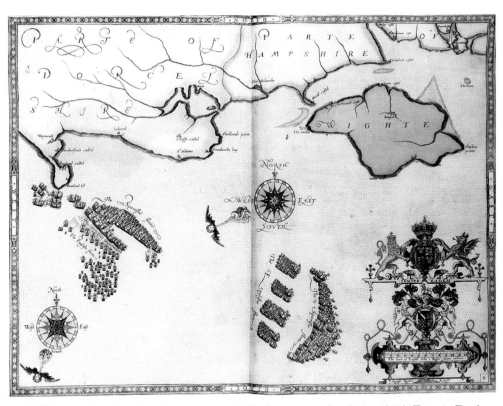

A 1588 engraving showing the progress of the famous sea battle in which Francis Drake defeated Medina Sidonia's Armada. In the grouping on the left the Spanish fleet is being attacked from the south and northwest, and is then pursued across the Channel by the English ships (*Private Collection/Bridgeman Art Library*)

A contemporaneous painting by Franz Geffels entitled *The Relief of Vienna*. In the foreground, Jan Sobieski can be seen storming Kara Mustapha's tent (*AKG London*)

Robert Clive's defeat of a combined French and Bengali force at Plassey in 1757 ensured the establishment of the British Empire in the east (*The Art Archive/India Office Library*)

Britain's colonial superiority in Canada was sealed by the capture of Quebec in 1759. This engraving shows how the British managed to take the stronghold by using landing craft to penetrate the enemy's defences (*The Art Archive/ General Wolfe Museum, Quebec House/ Eileen Tweedy*)

View of the Taking of QUEBECK by the English Forces Commanded by Genl. Wolfe Sep: 13th 1759.

bravest and most energetic race that ever existed . . . Saxon institutions were the primitive cradle of English liberty, but by their own intrinsic force, they could never have founded the enduring free English constitution' institutionalised through the Magna Carta by barons, yeomen and citizens of England in 1215.

England owed much to the Conqueror, odious though he was: loyal armed forces, just systems of revenue, eventually the common law. To William also was owed a unified country, one which by its adherence to western Europe helped to consolidate that concept, rather than existing as an insecure component of a Scandinavian mini-state.

William himself, without the power of prophecy, might not have agreed. Ordericus Vitalis in *Historia Ecclesiastica* purports to quote him: 'I persecuted the native inhabitants of England beyond all reason: whether nobles or commons, I cruelly oppressed them: many I unjustly disinherited: innumerable multitudes, especially in the county of York, perished through me by famine and sword. I stained with the rivers of blood I have shed.' But Vitalis was 'pro-British'. At least, according to the *Anglo-Saxon Chronicle*, we may say that 'we must not forget the good order [William] kept in the land, so that a man of any substance could travel unmolested throughout the country with his bosom full of gold'. Most men of substance were not English.

Fuller's view was that 'in the place of a loosely knit and undisciplined country was substituted a unified and compact Kingdom under a firm and hereditary central authority'. Ernest and Trevor Dupuy described the battle as 'the initiation of a series of events which would lead a revitalised Anglo-Saxon–Norman people to a world leadership more extensive even than that of ancient Rome'.

SYNOPSIS OF EVENTS BETWEEN
HASTINGS AND HATTIN

William the Conqueror, duke of Normandy, reigned over England from 1066 to 1087, establishing complete internal dominion over that country. It was a Francophone state wracked by almost continuous civil war yet, particularly under Henry II, was well governed.

In 1096 the Byzantine emperor, Alexius Comnenus, at Constantinople, successfully sought the agreement of the pope to join the First Crusade in order to retake his Asian dominions. This and further Crusades mounted by Greeks, Franks, English, Germans and other nobles to recover the Holy Places failed in their objectives, leaving great religious, trade and cultural legacies, but only Levantine sea ports headed by Acre in terms of territorial conquest of Muslim land.

Barbarossa, who could have defeated the Muslim leader Saladin, was drowned, and the Holy Sepulchre was lost to Christianity for over 700 years.

CHAPTER EIGHT

THE HORNS OF HATTIN, 1187

In September 1176 the Seljuk Turks, under Sultan Kilij Arslan II of Rum, virtually destroyed the Byzantine army, under its emperor Manuel Comnenus, in a pass of the Taurus mountains near Myriocephalum in Konya province. 'This battle', according to Kugler in *Studien zur Geschichte des Zweiten Kreuzzuges*, 'decided for ever the destiny of the whole East.' Other 'Middle-Eastern' battles in the eleventh and twelfth centuries have been so described: this one mingled cowardice and incompetence in equal measure.

As early as the eighth century Islamic unity under the Ummayud Caliphate collapsed after massacre by the Abbasids, only Abdur Rahman in 732 escaping to Spain and to his eventual defeat by Martel at Tours. Widespread civil war then followed the death of Haroun al Raschid, hero of the *Arabian Nights*, who had taken globalism so far as to put even the Holy Sepulchre under Charlemagne's authority. Turks, and then Persians, succeeded to the Arab Caliphate.

As for the Byzantine Empire in Constantinople, its anarchy was relieved by Basil I, a powerfully seductive peasant youth who had so aroused Emperor Michael III as to induce that monarch to appoint him chief groom. When the emperor's passion later moved in the direction of a handsome boatman, to ensure his own succession Basil caused the assassination of both the royal lover and – to make doubly sure – his uncle, thus founding the Macedonian dynasty.

After his death in 886, successive rulers struggled with the Bulgarian Empire, and with the Northmen under Rurik of Novgorod, whose men were to form the Varangian Guard of the Byzantine emperors (this duty later performed by English Varangians, including Edgar Aetheling, once a potential successor to Edward the Confessor, at the capture of Lattakia). To these rulers fell Crete, Cyprus, southern Italy, Caesarea, Antioch, Damascus, Tiberias, Nazareth, Homs, Tripoli, Biblos, most of Armenia and, under 'the Bulgar-slayer', Basil II, the entire Bulgarian Empire from the Mediterranean to the Black Sea, from Russia to the Pindus mountains.

The succession to these triumphs fell then, alas, into the hands of eunuchs, priests and sycophants. The empire's military and diplomatic genius, its knowledge of the wide world, the rich splendour of the Orthodox Church were not enough to balance the blindings, amputations, corruption and mindless superficiality of mobs and leaders alike. Even Basil II, under whom the power and grandeur of Byzantium reached its material zenith, in his dotage married off his daughter Zoë, no more than a high-class, stylish prostitute, to a worthless noble. After the marriage she adopted her lover, a money-changer called Michael, as her 'son' and, after murdering her husband, raised the money-changer to the purple as Michael IV. This emperor lasted only four months before being blinded and incarcerated in a monastery. Zoë's last coup was marriage to an old lover who refused to part with his mistress: on state occasions, this emperor was to be seen seated between whore *en titre* and wife.

Bussell's *The Roman Empire from AD 81 to 1081* refers to the empire as

a brilliant unreality, sovereigns who are play-actors, ministers who are the viziers of 'Hamlet or of a pantomime'. Matthew of Edessa, admittedly himself an Armenian, claimed that

Armenia, his 'country' was delivered up to the Turks by that sterile, effeminate and ignoble nation, the Greeks ... As guardians of our country, they placed over it generals who were eunuchs ... when they discovered an illustrious warrior, they either blinded or drowned him ... they made eunuchs of our sons and, instead of furnishing them with armour, they dressed them like women.

The Byzantine army, guided by manuals dating from 579 and 900, was still, theoretically, a stable strategic entity based on a defensive system demanding fortresses, concentration of force and the annihilation, after long unsuccessful siege, of enemy foragers. In its steel and chain mail, it continued to practise conventional, if rigid, generalship, employing conventional weaponry too: bow, sword, axe, mace and lance. But because of a shortage of Frankish volunteers, with consequent excess of foreign mercenaries, and because, above all, of crippling parsimony, the force had become, in Fuller's bitter phrase, 'a highly organised vacuum – the shell of a blown egg'. This was an army once contemptuous enough of its foe to throw a dead pig into the Turkish camp, while the citizens shouted: 'O sultan, take this sow to wife and we will present you with her dowry.'

But from about 1034 the Seljuks crossed the Oxus westward, bent on plunder, destruction of settlements and seizure of grazing land, deploying light, mobile cavalry against Byzantine cavalry and heavy infantry. At Manzikert, in the baking August of 1071, Sultan Alp Arslan instructed his army commander to 'win or be beheaded'. With that he plaited his horse's tail, assumed a white gown, scented himself and exchanged his bow for a mace. In the subsequent confrontation, treason – including actual desertion – on the part of Emperor Romanus's allies and mercenaries reduced the vast Byzantine army to a handful of men: Romanus himself, although well treated by Arslan, was later blinded by Michael VII, another usurping emperor, so viciously as to bring about his horrid death.

Gibbon said that, as a result of Turkish arrows and the closure of the horns of the Turkish crescent on the rear of the fleeing Byzantines, 'the Asiatic provinces of Rome were irretrievably sacrificed'. A vast Muslim ransom was inflicted, huge transfers of men and land undertaken. Laurent's *Byzance et les Turcs seldjoucides* claimed that, after the ruin the Turks had left Asia Minor by 1072, 'nothing there was left alive . . . devastated fields, trees cut down, mutilated corpses, towns driven mad by fear or in flames . . . as they [the fields] fell fallow, the Turks with their tents and flocks wandered over them contentedly, as they had done in the deserts out of which they had come,' fulfilling the principal aim for which they had fought.

The empire, after Manzikert, could no longer defend itself. The lands from which it drew its defenders no longer lay beneath its hand. The eastern frontier had gone, while in the same year in the west the Normans under Robert Guiscard took Bari, followed by later Norman conquests of Corfu and Durazzo, and the defeat of Alexius I Comnenus in Thessaly.

To the appeal of Alexius for western help in reconquering Asian territories of the empire, Pope Urban II responded with a First Crusade, designed not so much for that purpose but to recover Jerusalem and the Holy Places, the eastern frontier thus remaining unprotected from the Turk. It should, furthermore, not be forgotten that the churches of Rome and of the East were in formal dispute, having severed relations with each other. Constantinople regarded Charlemagne's empire, with its German, Frankish and Norman accretions, as a barbaric usurpation condoned by a papacy whose authority therefore could not be recognised by a Greek Church regarding itself as autonomous.

Alexius, in other words, did not greatly welcome a crusade, many of whose members were as opposed to those forming a schismatic, if still Christian, Church as they were to the Muslim despoilers of the Holy Land. But Urban's response, with its reward of land, riches, liberty and even eternal life, was hungrily welcomed, particularly in France, by between 25,000 and 30,000 men among a host of missionaries including Peter the Hermit, many being persuaded by Urban himself.

The Crusaders set off for Constantinople in August 1096 from four different starting points. Apart from the majority of brutal and undisciplined illiterates, they included at least a nucleus of veterans under Godfrey de Bouillon, his brother Baldwin commanding the Lorraine contingent, Bohemond and Tancred of Taranto and Robert of Normandy. Badly depleted by the climate and the natives, only Godfrey would give the oath of allegiance rightly demanded from his other rapacious allies by Emperor Alexius.

Nicaea was taken in May 1097 before this rabble, in heavy leather and chain mail, determined on land piracy and the creation of principalities, moved on to Antioch, Bohemond becoming its prince. On 15 July 1099, Jerusalem yielded. Hideous massacre ensued. Godfrey was appointed as the first Defender of the Holy Sepulchre, Baldwin I eventually overlord of Antioch, Edessa and Raymond's Tripoli. Ignorant of custom or geography, inappropriately clothed and equipped, with a hopeless commissariat, slowed by hordes of women, children and other camp followers, devoted to rape and plunder, the Crusaders of the First Crusade yet achieved triumphs unrealised by their successors. And the capture of Jaffa in 1097 provided a port through which the fleets and ships' chandlers of Genoa, Pisa and Venice supplied their customers ashore.

On Christmas Day 1144 the Muslims reconquered Edessa, causing not only alarm and distress in Europe but, under the messianic appeal of St Bernard of Clairvaux, the despatch of the Second Crusade led by Louis VII of France and Conrad III of Germany. The True Cross accompanied them. Much wasted en route through Asia Minor, the Crusade failed in an attempt to take Damascus and returned to Europe. Attacks on the settlers then increased, mainly under the direction of Nur ed-Din of Mosul, squired by the young Saladin in Damascus, Edessa and Antioch.

Saladin (Salah ed-Din Yusuf) was born at Tikrit in today's Iraq (the birthplace, incidentally, of Saddam Hussein). He began his military career in Egypt, fighting under Nur ed-Din, including success against the Crusader and Byzantine siege of Damietta. In 1169 'he renounced pleasure' on succeeding as vizier to the Fattimid Caliph of Egypt, whom he then deposed to found the Ayyubid dynasty. As ruler of Egypt, he claimed all of Nur ed-Din's (Zangid) lands, enforcing his intentions on his rivals and on the Crusaders through Mameluke (slave) archers and lancers.

Baldwin IV, a leper who, in the end, lost his toes and fingers and went blind, reigned as king of Jerusalem until his death in 1185. His son's suspicious death after one year on the throne led to his sister's marriage to the handsome Guy de Lusignan, a weak, indecisive man, lacking ruthlessness, of whom his own brother remarked: 'If they made him a King, they would have made me a God.' This family's major claim was in descent from Melusine, the water-fairy. All that distinguished Guy in the Levant, however, was his enmity to Raymond of Tripoli, an able soldier and administrator, whose refusal to pay homage to the new King Guy deepened the many rifts in the kingdom, from which Saladin, by continual harassment, was able to profit.

When, however, the headstrong and violent Reynaud de Châtillon broke a truce by murderously attacking a vast convoy out of Egypt from his castle at Kerak des Chevaliers, Saladin planned war, not harassment. As the first step, in April his young son sought the approval of Raymond at Tiberias to cross the latter's land in Galilee. Raymond reluctantly agreed, adding only the condition that the armed Saracen party should cross the frontier at first light and return before dusk, and should do no damage to any settlement. At dawn on 1 May he watched an emir and 7,000 Mameluke cavalrymen pass the castle. Before darkness fell, he saw it pass again, in the other direction. This time, and it was several hours before the light failed, each lance in the vanguard bore the bleeding head of a Templar Knight, killed by the Muslims in the Springs of Cresson, between Jenin and Nazareth. There could be no immediate reaction. The Saracen agreement with the Latins had not been breached. No *buildings* in the settlements had been harmed.

Sharply conscious that Saladin was on the edge now of a major assault, Guy and Raymond hastily negotiated a mutual reconciliation, the other Christian leaders also bringing up reinforcements. As to numbers, a wide choice is offered, Steven Runciman estimating 18,000 Saracens and 15,000 Crusaders, of whom about 1,000 were knights with an additional 120 subsidised by King Henry II in expiation for the murder of Thomas à Becket; perhaps 10,000 infantrymen and 4,000 Turcopoles (non-Muslim Turks). Runciman's *A History of the Crusades* believes that neither side was greatly superior in weaponry, the Christian knights better equipped than the Saracens, but the Muslim light cavalry better than the Turcopoles. There was probably no substantial difference between the infantry on either side. Christian armour was superior, evidenced by an earlier victory by 300 knights over a vastly greater number of Mamelukes. Unsatisfactory cooperation between Crusader infantry and cavalry was probably a more significant factor.

After the massacre of Latins in Constantinople (1182) by Emperor Andronicus Comnenus, Andronicus had signed a treaty with Saladin which, the emperor hoped, would protect his eastern frontier and, for Saladin, remove any threat from the north. In fact, by 1185 the repressive emperor had already fallen, dragged on an old unhealthy camel through the streets of Constantinople and then torn to pieces by the mob. When Saladin reviewed his men at Ashtera, it was thus in the knowledge that the Crusaders had lost their imperial ally. This cautious, scholarly general, possibly even knighted earlier in Egypt by Constable Humphrey, had many contacts among the Franks; his reputation stands not alone on his military record, defeated only at Montgisard, but − despite his hatred of Christianity − on his relative chivalry toward the Franks.

Saladin's army waited five days near the Sea of Galilee reconnoitring the Christian positions before crossing the Jordan to attack Tiberias, while the rest of his army camped in the hills at Kafr Sebt, west of Galilee. Raymond's wife, Countess Eschiva, held out in her husband's castle at Tiberias, while Raymond was with King Guy at Acre; but the *town* of Tiberias was rapidly taken by the Saracens.

At Acre, Raymond recommended to the king that, in the searing heat of a Levantine summer, the defending Crusaders should maintain their defensive advantage, allowing the attackers to wear themselves out in the arid countryside. Reinforcements from the Franks in Antioch would soon arrive. Saladin would have to withdraw. Muslims always retreated if they did not win quickly. The Crusaders' strategy was to avoid battle in unfavourable conditions. The vacillating king agreed. But, convinced by the Grand Master of the Temple, Gerard de Ridford, significantly one of the few angry and terrified survivors of the Springs of Cresson, and by the unbalanced Reynaud de Chatillon that Raymond was a treacherous coward, Guy ordered the army to advance towards Tiberias.

They bivouacked next day, 1 July, at Sephoria (Saffuriyah), an excellent defensive position. In council there, a moving appeal for help was received from Countess Eschiva at Tiberias, heard amid the tears of her sons. The town was walled, with a church, St Anne's, and overlooked gardens, a mill stream and golden wheat fields. Yet Raymond, often categorised by a minority as Saladin's paid agent, strongly repeated his opposition to an aggressive advance by the Christians over waterless territory in the terrible Asian July: although his wife was endangered in Tiberias, he declared that he would rather that she and everyone in his castle should be lost than lose the kingdom.

The indecisive Guy initially agreed to Raymond's plan for a defensive stance at Sephoria; then, yielding to the Grand Master's midnight visit to the king's tent ('Sire, are you going to trust a traitor?'), countermanded the previous day's decision, again

120

ordering the march on Tiberias, Raymond in the van as was his territorial prerogative.

The knight's uniform, a cloth overcoat, a chain-mail hauberk to the knees, then a leather jerkin, a mail neck and face piece, a pot-shaped helmet with nose-piece, could hardly have been less suitable for the climate. The True Cross, in a case adorned with precious stones, a piece of the Crucifix, was borne by the bishop of Acre in the king's own central division, the Hospitallers and Templars in the rear.

This jealous, divided army left the pleasant, green, well-watered town of Sephoria for the bare, stony hills of the Jebel Turan, Tiberias twenty miles away. Raymond had warned them that in this desert wilderness there was only one small spring before the Sea of Galilee. Thirst and the incessant arrows of the fast-mounted Saracen bowmen struck almost at once at the parched and desperate Crusaders. On the limitless, brown plateau, the castles on which they could have depended lay empty, their garrisons ironically recruited to add numbers to Guy's force.

Saladin, through reconnaissance or Christian spies, had been warned that the Franks were taking the road to Tiberias through Lubia, the Galilean hills and Hattin. Ahead of the Franks, now at Marescalia, was a rocky hill with two projections, the Horns of Hattin, said to be the site of the Sermon on the Mount. The Saracen troops were drawn up in a crescent, the wings forward, so as better to encircle the enemy. 'Not an ant could have escaped' from that pretty village, with its spring and olive and fruit trees. The shining water of the Sea of Galilee lay below to the east, Mount Hermon snow-capped across the valley.

Raymond, seeing the enemy on the Tiberian hills, had urged the king to hurry on to the sea or to the Jordan, before all the Franks' water was used and they died of thirst, or the army suffocated in the dust, or was slaughtered by the bowmen. But the rearguard of Templars and Hospitallers said that they could go no further that day, under the murderous fire and the heat.

The king halted just beyond Lubia, toward the Horns, near a well which was found to be quite dry after the army had laagered round it. Raymond, when he saw it, cried, 'Ah, Lord God, the war is over. We are dead men: the Kingdom is finished.'

There was no sleep for them that night. Saladin took advantage of a changing wind to fire the bush and scrub round them. The Crusaders feverishly tried to shelter from the smoke and missiles. Behind them the Saracens moved into the morrow's position for attack. The Crusaders were totally encircled.

The Muslim assault, with cries of 'God is good' and 'There is no other god but God', began at first light, supported by a train of seventy pack camels bearing arrows which, once in flight, were 'thick as clouds of locusts'. The Christian infantry, obsessed by the need for water, strove mostly to run down the hill towards the lake below and were killed, wounded or captured as they fled. Raymond's knights, it is said, tried to persuade some of Saladin's men to put the wounded out of their misery where they lay bleeding, tongues swollen, in agony. In the mêlée, a terrified soldier on the hill cried, 'Sauvons-nous, sauvons-nous', and caused a greater panic.

The Frankish horsemen nevertheless fought with great courage, driving back with heavy loss the repeated charges of the Muslim light cavalry. Guy ordered Raymond to save the day. But when he and other knights drove at the chain of Saracens, commanded by Taki ed-Din, bursting through it, the enemy soldiers closed up behind him, an action described by some as 'aiding their escape', and used by Raymond's enemies further to diminish his name as he and his companions rode away to Tripoli.

At last the king withdrew with his red tent to the peaks of the hills, his knights around him, joined – because of the known presence of the True Cross – by archers, infantry and the Templars. Saladin's young son saw the confused mass. 'The knights made a gallant charge and drove the Muslims back upon my father. My father changed colour, pulled at his beard, then rushed forward, crying, "Give the devil the lie." ' Twice more his son said to him, 'We have routed them', but it was not until the red tent was overturned that his father 'dismounted, bowed to the ground, giving thanks to God, with tears of joy'.

The knights lay upon the ground, beaten and exhausted, handing over their swords in surrender. A single Saracen dragged thirty Christians tied together with a tent-rope. The king, Constable Amalric, Gerard the Grand Master, Reynaud de Chatillon, Humphrey of Toron and other barons were taken to Saladin's tent. Saladin seated the king next to him, passing him 'rose-water, iced with the snows of Hermon' or, some say, sherbet. When he had drunk from it, Guy handed the cup to Reynaud. Saladin instantly reminded the king that, in the Arab custom, to make that gesture to a prisoner meant that his life was safe; Guy, in his situation, could not exercise that authority.

He upbraided Reynaud for previous crimes. De Chatillon replied with careless indifference. Saladin either had him decapitated by a guard or despatched him himself with his own scimitar. 'A king does not kill a king, but that man's perfidy and insolence went too far.' All the other barons were unharmed during their imprisonment. But Saladin's name for kindness and honour was either undeserved or radically besmirched by the murder at his command of the 200 bound knights of the Military Order, an action conducted with pleasure at the bloody hands of a troop of fanatical sufis, men in whom the Taleban would have rejoiced.

Saladin then occupied the Crusader castles, also releasing the brave Countess Eschiva, soon to be widowed at royal Byzantine hands. Almost the whole order of Christian chivalry had been destroyed, the True Cross taken by the Saracens. Quoting Steven Runciman, Fuller remarked: 'the greatest army that the Kingdom had ever assembled was annihilated. And the victor was lord of the whole Muslim world.'

Failure to take Syria and the desert road from Aleppo to Aqaba led to the loss of Jerusalem, of the Fertile Crescent, of the crucial junction between Mesopotamia and Egypt, of the great land barrier of the Byzantine Empire, which guarded Europe from

Asia. It was, more significantly, a victory for Allah, a blow to the papacy so grave that it was approached in magnitude only by the death blow delivered to the Byzantine Empire in 1204 by the Fourth Crusade.

At Hattin, a year afterwards, the heaps of bleaching bones could still be seen. 'On the day of the battle,' said Imad ed-Din, Saladin's secretary, 'the dead lay in heaps, like stones upon stones, among broken crosses, severed hands and feet while mutilated heads strewed the ground like melons.'

The War Song of the Saracens

We are they who come faster than fate,
We are they who ride early or late.
We storm at your ivory gate;
Pale kings of the sunset, beware.
Not in silk nor in samet we lie,
Nor in contained solemnity die . . .
But we sleep by the ropes of our camp
And we rise with a shout and we tramp,
With the wind and the sun in our hair.

James Elroy Flecker

SYNOPSIS OF EVENTS BETWEEN
HATTIN AND LIEGNITZ

In 1189 Richard Coeur de Lion became king of England and, with the king of France, joined the Third Crusade. At his death, his brother John took the throne of England and of the Plantagenet lands. A series of defeats by the French king, Philip Augustus, in Normandy, Brittany, Anjou, Maine and Poitiers followed. Within the lands of England, the signature of the Magna Carta at Runnymede established unity between Anglo-Saxon and Anglo-Norman – one language and one system of laws, equality without distinction of race. It also brought an end, enforced by barons, citizens and yeomen, to the royal tyranny of King John, and its replacement, far away in the future, by the tyranny of the common man.

CHAPTER NINE

LIEGNITZ AND MOHI, 1241

The Mongols claim descent from the union of a wolf and a doe at Burkhan Kaldun, the Holy Mountain, home of Tengri, Sky God and Protector. They spring from the Taiga, the Siberian region of mountains and conifers.

Kutula, one of the first Mongol khans, is represented in Arthur Whaley's *Secret History of the Mongols* as 'the Mongol Hercules with hands like bear-paws, a voice that rolled like thunder through the mountain gorges . . . capable of devouring a whole sheep, and drinking an enormous jar of Kumiss (fermented mares' milk) at a single draught'. His nephew, Yesugei, a minor clan chief, kidnapped and married the wife of a Merkit chief. The son, born holding a clot of blood 'large as a knuckle-bone' in his clenched hand, was named Temujin after a captured Tatar chief recently abducted by Yesugei.

At the age of nine, that son was promised by his father to Börte, of the Ongirrat clan, famous for the beauty of its women. On his journey home, Yesugei was murdered by Tatars with a slow poison, in probable revenge for the earlier capture of their chief. Temujin accordingly returned to his mother, and the little group, now with seven children, and their Taijiat allies, on that bleak, bitter steppe, treeless and harsh, subsisted on moles, larks, nuts, roots, berries and fish taken from fast, wide rivers. Even then, seeing Temujin as a potential rival, the Taijiats seized him, placed him in a *cangue*, or wooden collar like the stocks, and dragged the boy from place to place until he escaped to join his family.

Soon he acquired adult male status by formally marrying Börte. At the same time, he made alliance with Toghrul, an old Keriat friend (*anda*) of his father. When Börte was kidnapped by the Merkits, perhaps in revenge for Yesugei's kidnap of Temujin's mother, Toghrul with 20,000 Keraits and a group of Jadrans led by Jamukha, an equivocal, not to say ambiguous 'blood brother' of Temujin, beat down 40,000 horsemen of the Merkit and recovered Börte. 'I will unite your scattered people,' said Toghrul to Temujiin, 'I will bring back your straying children.' Jamukha, later jealously to oppose him, cried, 'We will take this [enemy] by surprise. We will overturn the shrine of his ancestors and destroy his people until the place is an emptiness.'

The tribesmen thenceforward started to pour in to follow this new great leader. 'We will make you Khan. You shall ride at our head, against our enemies. We will fling ourselves like the lightning upon your foes. If we disobey you on the day of battle, take our flocks from us, our wives and children, throw our worthless heads out on the steppe,' they shouted, in more or less sincerity, at the *huraltai* or assembly which ensued. Temujin was carried on a great carpet for nine circuits of the assembly, raised to the title of 'universal leader', Chinggis Khan, known to the world as Genghis Khan.

Under the nominal leadership of Toghrul, newly ennobled by the Chinese as Wang Khan, Chinggis mounted a series of campaigns against all those who disputed his nomadic mastery, Tatars, Naiman, Merkit, Taijiat, Ongirrat and those subject to the now dissident Jamukha. Even the defection of Wang Khan and a close-run engagement at Baljuna, when Chinggis took refuge under water, failed to halt the defeat of those clans opposed to his hegemony. Jamukha, when taken, either had his back broken or was pressed to death in a carpet, methods preferred by aristocratic Mongols to the actual shedding of blood; although his own measures, such as boiling seventy of his enemies to death, had not excited emulation. At *huraltai* in 1206, Chinggis was proclaimed 'supreme ruler of all who live in felt tents'.

For Mongols, survival was the imperative. Sometimes, in necessity, they would drink the blood of their own horses, themselves the only guarantee of survival. They ate meat; milk with its products of kumiss, curds and cheese; a little garlic, otherwise no vegetables at all, or very few; cereals as flour for mutton pancakes and dumplings. Meat not immediately consumed was smoked for consumption in their round felt tents (*ger*), out of the whirling snow and wind. They were, in their red, blue and green sashed robes – the *deel* – silk and fox-fur hats and high boots, a solid four-square people, dirty, short, frequently evil-smelling, with slit cats' eyes, bow-legged, cheerful, but not greatly given to laughter. They were, and remain in the mind's eye, one with their horses, perhaps the origin indeed of the centaur.

The Supreme Ruler himself was described by Juvaini, the great Persian historian, as tall, robust, white bearded, with eyes like a cat's, flat, yellow countenance, resolute, just, bloody and cruel. Guided by a Liao scholar-mandarin, Yeh-Lu ('Khan') Chu-tsai, and by an Uighur bureaucrat, Chinggis codified the legal system in a code called Yasak and rendered Mongol documentation into the Uighur script. Similarly guided in matters of trade, both internal and foreign, and in the civil administration of captured territory, Mongol policy substituted land-tax, customs and local industry for the alternative, the extermination of local peoples and the consequent conversion of their lands to pasture, although that course may have been more congenial personally to Chinggis himself. New measures included protection for roads and for travellers, alone or in convoy, and, in general, defence of the interests of merchants dealing on the Silk Road and other Asian highways. There must have been many who, despite the almost unspeakable horrors of the Conquest – live evisceration, death by ingestion of molten gold, disembowelment – may have had cause to enjoy the financial benefits of the Pax Mongolica in a peace which embraced tolerance of other faiths.

It was in war, however, that Chinggis's genius was both pre-eminent and most vile. His armies were based on units of ten, platoons of ten men the smallest, rising through companies, brigades and divisions of 100, 1,000 and 10,000 (*tumen*) mixed tribe units, a departure from the old Turkish and, indeed, old Mongol clan formations. Since a nomad without a horse was almost a contradiction in terms, infantry was rare. Engineer units grew, often drawn from appropriately qualified Chinese and other prisoners, to meet the increasing demand for siege warfare, rams, engines, slings, catapults, stones, bolts, arrows, flaming pots of naphtha. Cavalry weapons included lances, spears, javelins, scimitars and, above all, the bow.

Two ranks of heavy cavalry in armour, carrying curved sword and lance, led the Mongol advance, followed by three ranks of mounted archers, the latter armed with heavy Mongol bows, each with ranges of 200 or 300 yards. Quivers of arrows hung at the belt with equipment designed to pierce armour. The archers wore stirrups, permitting shorter saddles. These enabled the rider to twist and turn in the saddle, firing at the gallop with deadly accuracy, the Parthian shot among them, released when the archers were in apparent full retreat, volleys of arrows then exploited by heavy cavalry in howling charge, with thunderous light cavalry in support with javelin and bow.

Apart from his brilliant system of 'post houses' with food and fresh horses to ensure rapid communications over the vast distances of central Asia, Chinggis developed an intelligence service against the enemy, based mostly on *de visu* agents in trading caravans, and created, more cruelly, a pattern of terror intended to paralyse his victims before battle even began. Disinformation was practised on a major scale: dummies on riderless horses, smokescreens, incessant false retreats and their consequent bloody reversals.

'Terror' was intended to spread such fear of Mongol brutality that entire countries would surrender without the trouble of actual warfare. It took many forms and was well publicised by word of panicked mouth. Cold murder of the populations of entire cities, selected killings of helpless women and children by the axe, pretended releases of captives followed, however, by their instant, gleeful execution, the slicing out from a living woman's stomach of a hidden pearl, all those horrors channelled in disciplined, icy organisation.

J. J. Saunders observed in *The History of the Mongol Conquests* that Chinggis's aim was conquest rather than plunder. As soon as he had united the peoples of Mongolia under his rule, he attacked China herself, firstly her smallest and weakest component, the (Tibetan) Tangut Hsi-Hsia. Although initially without a siege component, he forced acknowledgement of his sovereignty on the Hsi-Hsia before assaulting the mighty Chin.

Here, he first deliberately insulted their new king: 'Is such an imbecile worthy of the throne and shall I abase myself before him?' Onguts, a Turkish people, and the Mongol Chi Tan, joined the crusade in 1211 which ended only in 1234, after Chinggis was dead, but not before he had created a corps of engineers, carried out the first terrible massacres of civil society by barbarian nomads and at last, by Ögedei, caused the total collapse of the Chin.

In the meanwhile, the Mongols conquered the Kara-Khitaj or Black Cathay, a Sinicised Mongol state and, eventually, the great Khwarismian Empire (Turkestan, Persia and North India) under Mohammed Shah. In this first war against Islam, Chinggis and his sons Ögedei, Chagatai, Tolui and Jochi took Otrar, Bukhara and Samarkand: at Bukhara, Chinggis announced from the pulpit of the main mosque that he was 'the flail of God sent to punish the people for their sins'. Palaces and mosques were destroyed, prisoners driven in battle by the Mongols before them to impress Samarkand with a false size of their enemy's army.

Ögedei took over command from the quarrelling Jochi and Chagatai. The Mongols smashed the dams of Urganj, flooding the town, diverting the Oxus to the Caspian for 300 years; Merv held out for three weeks, Nishapur for three days. After Tolui had spared the population at Herat in Afghanistan, the enraged Chinggis sent another army, with orders: 'Since the dead have come to life, I command you to strike their heads from their bodies.' Juvaini said of one burned city: 'The stench of death hung over the stricken land.'

Mohammed Shah had died in 1220 on an island on the Caspian Sea. His son, Jalal ad-Din, after a legendary horsed leap at Parwan near Kabul, escaped into the heat of the Punjab plains where, after a preliminary encounter, the men of the steppes disdained to follow him, the victor of the only Mongol reverse of the campaign. Otherwise, the fighting took its usual path of destruction, and of massacre to deter resistance further on, rebuilding often, in order to create economic development but, at the same time, compelling the emigration of many local craftsmen to Karakoram, the imperial capital.

Jochi, whom Chinggis may have thought illegitimate (by a Merkit khan), died in 1227, the year that Chinggis died, his *yurt* divided between his sons Orde and Batu, founders of the White and Golden Hordes. Ögedei succeeded Chinggis as Supreme Khan in 1229, while Tolui acted as regent, accompanying his brother against the Chin. Tolui died of drink in 1232 having fathered, by a Kerait Nestorian Christian princess, Hülagü and Kubilai, khans of the Middle East and of China. Ögedei's triumphs were against the northern Chin, against what was left of the Khwarismian Empire and then, via Russia, to the legendary Mongol victories in western Europe.

Ögedei against the Chin, under his general, Subatei, succeeded in taking the capital Kai Feng in 1233. This coup triggered the emperor's suicide, the end of the Chin Empire and the start in 1235 of the war against the southern dynasty of the Sung, which ended only forty-five years later under Kubilai, emperor and Great Khan. The wise method of Chu-Tsai – 'The Empire was won on horseback, but won't be governed on horseback' – led to the continuation in China of traditional government and, therefore, to relative Chinese support for their nomad masters, 'a regime which grew progressively sinicised and which, under Kubilai, could almost pass for a Chinese dynasty'. The conquest of Korea – later reversed by rebels, but retaken – followed. Even today, the Korean physiognomy bears an uncanny resemblance to its progenitors and their descendants.

The return from India of Jalal ad-Din, Mohammed Shah's gallant son, did not lead to reunification of the Khwarismian state under Islam, rather to serious disputes with other Muslim leaders of Rum and Damascus and to attacks on Christian administrations in Georgia and Armenia, in 1221 also invaded by Mongols. The Mongols returned in 1230, with an army under Choragan, again ravaging – this time from Azerbaijan – these Christian states.

But later hopes, aroused by Nestorian influence in the Great Khan's court at Karakoram, of a Mongol–Christian alliance against Islam through Persia into modern Iraq and Turkey (Anatolia) were soon deflated. Although Baiju, Choragan's successor, sought to absorb the lands of the Seljuk Turks, neither the latter, nor Baghdad and Cairo, the great cities of the Caliphate, remained under threat, at least until the time of Hülagü.

Instead, after the *huraltai* at Karakoram to commemorate the fall of Chin, a vast army of 150,000 men under Subatei, Batu and his brothers, and the sons of Ögedei, Tolui and Chagatai, started on the bloody campaign which led them to Albania, Poland, Germany and Hungary. And had it not been for the anachronistic decision for legalised democratic choice among these savage peoples, the nine yak tails and other appurtenances of wild and alien warriors would have carried the mark of Mongol rule to Paris, Rome, even London. The consequences for the civilised world are imaginable, but unbearable.

In 1237 this mass, after long planning and the securing of supplies and communications, moved against the Bulghars of the Volga and the Bashkirs of Greater Hungary, home of the Magyars. Subatei took and sacked Bulghar, a civilised fur-trading city with sumptuous buildings, followed under Möngke, son of Tolui and later Great Khan, by the subjugation of the Bashkir. Möngke went on to conquer the Kipchaks of the eponymous steppe, north of the Caspian, their title of khanate later awarded to Batu's Golden Horde.

When captured, the Kipchak leader, ordered to prostrate himself, replied: 'I have been myself a king and do not fear death. I am not a camel that I should kneel.' Möngke ordered cleanly that he be cleft in two.

As for the Russian cities to the west, their princes were too divided to offer effective resistance except at Novgorod: Kiev, according to John of Plano Carpini, was ruined, but many cities had been bypassed or even restored after original destruction before the chroniclers saw them. In Kiev, 'dense clouds of Tatars', their horses' hooves, the thunder of the wagons and their bellowing cattle drowned speech within the city walls; 'the arrows obscured the light so that it became impossible to see the sky'. The staging point was ready for the next assault, on Hungary.

The Mongols were not ignorant about the complexities of European politics, in particular the hostility between the Holy Roman Empire under Frederick II and the papacy. That tension would, the Mongols calculated, prevent these two mighty powers forming a united front in support of European kings and nobles, Hungarians, Poles, Bohemians, Germans, whom it was the Great Khan's urgent intention to destroy. Before mounting the main attack, nevertheless, against King Bela IV of Hungary, the Mongols saw the need to block other potential supporters: Wenceslas of Bohemia, Boleslav of Sandomir, Duke Henry von Schlesien. An army under Kaidu was sent to deal with these nobles and another, commanded by Kadan, against the southern provinces, while Subatei and Batu prepared the central thrust against Gran, where Bela IV waited with 10,000 horse. Unfortunately, that king neglected and persecuted the Kipchak refugees who could have saved him.

In 1241, the Mongols attacked Poland toward today's eastern Germany. At Liegnitz (Legnica), near Breslau, they were confronted by Duke Henry von Schlesien, Henry the Bearded. At this place, now Wahlstadt, the duke commanded a force of 30,000 Silesians, Polish nobles, Hospitallers, Teutonic knights, a glittering contingent heavy with polished armour and bearing bright, armorial pennants. Their rank and file, however, peasants and miners, lacked unity and the fierce, controlled horsemanship of the Mongols. Nor could they be saved by the nearby presence of 50,000 men under Wenceslas of Bohemia. Mongol mounted mobility, training and archery again won the day. Nine sacks of Christian ears were sent to Batu after his victory. Henry's wife, St Hedwiga, who brought both monasteries and civilised Tyroleans to Silesia, recognised the cadaver of her husband only by the six toes on one of his feet. (Seven centuries later, Colonel Hyacinth von Strachwitz, descendant of a von Strachwitz present at Legnica, commanded the first Panzer regiment to reach the Volga at Stalingrad.) The portal of the baroque church at Wahlstadt is still supported by two enormous Mongols.

Cracow and Breslaw were burned to the ground, Sandomir vanquished, before the terrors of Mongol cavalry moved on to Moldavia, Transylvania and the Bukovina. At Cracow today, the hourly trumpet-call from St Mary's breaks in mid-note to mask the Mongol arrow which interrupted it some 750 years ago. In a frightened West these actions lost nothing in the telling: cannibalism – virgins' breasts a speciality – enjoyed by devils incarnate, Tatarus their dwelling place, and Tatars their sobriquet. But, panic apart, there is no doubting their mindless, joyful brutality.

Subatei, meanwhile, in a three-day battle at Mohi, based on the familiar tactic of the feigned retreat – followed by subsequent attack launched from little ponies at high speed against vainglorious and deceived pursuers – destroyed 70,000 of Bela's Hungarian cavalry. 'Their bodies lay everywhere, like stones in a quarry,' said an eyewitness, 'in those blood-blackened marshes, plains and river banks.' Neither pope nor emperor replied to anguished cries for help from the tatters of European chivalry.

The continent lay in the gnarled hands of Subatei and Batu. Nothing except a few days' ride, easy for Mongols, stood between these two – bristling in their encampments at today's Pesth, Scutari, Dubrovnik, the Adriatic, at Breslau in the north – and their target westwards, the golden treasuries of Paris, Rome and, across the sea, London. The civilised world hung quivering in the balance. *Nothing*, it seemed, could stop its imminent descent into the pit.

No military obstacle did.

The Mongols triumphed because of mobility, good intelligence, drill, surprise, a rigid signal system of black and white flags which made messages and orders otiose. Nor did they close with the enemy until the latter was already weakened: Plano Carpini said that they 'wounded and killed men and horses, and only when the men and horses were worn down by the arrows, do they come to close quarters'. 'Their opponents', said a chronicler, 'fell to the right and left like leaves of winter.' They were, in this epoch, invincible.

But on 11 December 1241, the Great Khan, Ögedei, died at Karakoram. The Yasak of Chinggis Khan demanded election of a successor in the capital itself. Batu knew that his prospects were not improved by the enmity of Ögedei's wife and of his son, Güyük. Accordingly, he moved with his armies and supporters to Sarai on the Volga, on the Kipchak steppes. In thus founding the Golden Horde, he forsook the campaign for central Europe, his own quest for supreme rule and the Mongol conquest of the west, a Tatar chieftain abandoning the ambition of world domination. What remained to him was large enough: the Balkans, the Russian principalities, the Bulghar Empire, the Carpathians and the Transylvanian Alps.

Without him as candidate, the rest of them rode slowly and bloodily home, slaughtering released prisoners from the beaten foe like game. Güyük *was* elected, but as late as 1246 and surviving only two years. His successors in no way declared a loss of interest in Mongol conquest, but conquest of China and the Middle East, not Europe, defeated only by the Mamelukes at Ain Jalut. One authority has recorded that the cause of the sudden, precipitate withdrawal did not lie with Batu's doubts about the future, or the stern electoral requirements of the Yasak, but in a sudden Mongol realisation that, large and bountiful as was the Hungarian *puszta* (Great Hungarian Plain), it could not support enough horses to mount a permanent Mongol force in western Europe.

These battles were not in themselves 'decisive'. They did not change the history of the world. But, if a royal heart had not simultaneously stopped in central Asia, their course would have so changed the world in which we exist today that our consequent lives and cultures could not have been other than different in kind, not degree, and probably horrid beyond imagination. Under Kubilai and Hülagü, the Mongols may have created the largest empire the world had ever seen; we should therefore wonder at what nightmare might have been, had some unknown consideration in the thirteenth century not diverted them from universal dominion.

There exists today, no less than before, the Gothic horror of these events which subsumed the most wrenching changes in western history, and the way that it is viewed, since the birth of Christ 2,000 years ago. Even had the Mongols not 'gone home' in 1241, their legacy had already dispersed Turkic peoples to the corners of the earth, with all that implies for the military history of China, India and the Middle East. 'Certainly, Genghis Khan, by displacing westward the then insignificant tribe of Ottomans, initiated a sequence of events that devastated the established order in the Near East, replaced it with another that survived into [the twentieth] century, and held Europe under threat of an Islamic offensive that persisted from the fall of Constantinople in 1453 until the raising of the siege of Vienna 230 years later.'

SYNOPSIS OF EVENTS BETWEEN THE MONGOL WITHDRAWAL FROM EUROPE AND THE ARMADA

In 1346 Edward III, king of England, defeated France at the battle of Crécy, and at the battle of Poitiers the French were again defeated by the Black Prince. In 1415 Henry V, claiming the crown of France, invaded and conquered that kingdom, winning Normandy and, in 1420, concluding the Treaty of Troyes with Charles VI and Philip of Burgundy. After winning further victories in 1421, Henry V died in 1422, the same year as Charles VI. Henry VI became king of France and England, but the Dauphin was proclaimed Charles VII of France. In 1428 the Duke of Bedford defeated French supporters of the Dauphin and their Scottish auxiliaries: the English began the siege of Orléans, although by 1452 the legacy of Joan of Arc had secured the expulsion of the English from France.

Immense activity took place over the next hundred and more years: Sultan Mohammed destroyed the Byzantine Empire, taking Constantinople in 1453; in England the Wars of the Roses began (1455); Spain achieved unity under Ferdinand and Isabella (1479); in 1492, Columbus discovered America when, coincidentally, the Moors were expelled from Spain; while Vasco da Gama reached the Indies via the Cape of Good Hope in 1497. In Europe, dispute over indulgences in 1517 initiated the Reformation; in 1519 Charles V was elected emperor of Germany; Henry VIII renounced papal supremacy in 1533; Charles V abdicated in 1556; Philip II became king of Spain, and Ferdinand I emperor of Germany; Henry VIII's daughter Elizabeth became queen of England.

The Turkish navy was defeated at Lepanto in 1571 and the St Bartholomew's Day Massacre of Protestants in France took place in 1572. In 1579 the colonised Netherlands revolted against Spain and in 1580 Philip II conquered Portugal.

CHAPTER TEN

THE ARMADA, 1588

Never earth nor sea beheld so great a stake before them set,
Save when Athens hurled back Asia from the lists wherein they met.

A. C. Swinburne

Emperor Charles V in his fifty-sixth year transferred dominion over Spain, Italy, the Netherlands and the New World to his son Philip II, king of Spain, retaining for himself Austria and her possessions, and the imperial crown. Philip, the husband of Mary Tudor, queen of England until she died, acquired no popularity in that kingdom after the Marian persecutions, the burning of Cranmer, Latimer, Ridley and hundreds more. The accession of Elizabeth at her sister's death helped further to increase the English dislike of both Rome and Spain, deepening Protestant sentiment.

But relations between England and Spain were not based on exclusively religious grounds, rather on commerce and the desire of English seamen to breach Spain's monopoly – granted by the pope – on trade and development in the Indies and the Americas. They were founded also on the dependence of English prosperity on the industries of the Spanish Netherlands which, in its turn, sought help from England, both in furtherance of the reformed religion and the establishment of the Dutch republic. In revenge for English sanctuary to Flemish refugees, Philip closed the ports of all Spanish possessions to all English shipping.

This seafaring English race, under its Protestant encouragement, had by the late sixteenth century created a Royal Navy which, if not in numbers or displacement, had become equal and often superior to the great Spanish and Portuguese fleets, the latter hitherto dominating the oceans but, since 1581, annexed by Philip to the Spanish crown.

The English quest was led by islanders who, almost until our own day, have seen their island's future as *outre mer*, across the water. Thus, by their own will as it were (their revered queen's policy, in the sixteenth century at least, almost ancillary), they focused first on the Spice Islands, barred by Arctic ice in the northern passages, and then on the South Seas monopoly. Francis Drake was the guiding star, initially with John Hawkins after Spanish treachery at San Juan de Ulloa in 1568, against de Bazán, later marquis of Santa Cruz, then at Nombre de Dios in the *Judith* ('Slung atween the round shot in Nombre Dios Bay / And dreaming arl the time o' Plymouth Hoe'). On the voyage of circumnavigation in *Pelican* from 1577 to 1580, in mid-winter, he traversed the Magellan straits without charts, overhung by mountains, heavy snow below, fresh food sometimes, from seal and penguins. *Pelican*, rechristened *Golden Hind* when they arrived at Deptford in September 1580, carried twenty tons of silver bullion, thirteen chests of silver coin, a hundredweight of gold, diamonds, pearls, silk and emeralds from the ships and depots of the Spanish Main. The loss proven by the Spanish government was far more than the published schedule, but known probably only to Drake, and to the queen. Her Majesty knighted her paragon at the dockside; 'The Master Thief of the Unknown World'; El Draque, the serpent with only two ships and seventy men.

In 1585 Drake's *Elisabeth Buonaventura* with twenty-five vessels, financed by the queen and others, had the audacity to re-equip and work up in Vigo Bay before destroying Sant Iago in the Cape Verde Islands. Yellow fever in the Americas took 300 men from his fleet, the epidemic halted by Carib roots and herbs, thus enabling the seizure by Drake's soldiers of San Domingo on Hispaniola, where the baroque and gorgeous cathedral (with its grave of Christopher Columbus) was spared, one of the few edifices left standing by the English.

In this splendid colonial city, an infuriated Spaniard ordered the murder by lance of Drake's Negro messenger. Drake hanged two of the instigators, both friars, and threatened more until the murderer should be himself executed by his own superior's hand: the governor complied. Compliance did not protect his magnificent palace, or the arms of Spain, a globe with a horse leaping upon it and, in the animal's mouth, the scutcheon 'Non sufficit orbis', or the world is not enough. England had, on this occasion, gone too far, the treasure really exhausted, only 25,000 ducats' ransom paid for the doomed and lovely city, modelled on the greatest houses of Spain.

Drake's troops under Carlile then took Cartagena, only ransomed at 30,000 ducats extorted from the Spaniards. Sickness, which limited his force to 700 men, would not permit an attack against Nombre de Dios or Panama across the isthmus. The profit from the whole expedition was as little as £20,000 which the owners and officers passed on to the common seamen, 'wishing it were so much again as would be a sufficient reward for their painful endeavours . . . Thus all were well satisfied, conscious all that they had done their duty to their Queen and country.'

Even before Cadiz itself, the king of Spain had thus been challenged in his foreign holdings. Cities had been taken with inferior force, Spanish omnipotence exposed, nothing safe from Drake, whether the Peruvian treasure, the Pacific littoral, or the Celebes in 1580 . . . And in 1587 Drake entered Cadiz harbour flying his flag in the queen's own *Buonaventura*, under the batteries in the very harbour's mouth, sinking, burning or capturing thirty-seven Spanish vessels, many bound for Lisbon and the preparations there for the Armada. King Philip claimed that the losses, which included 'the carrack *São Philipe* with a cargo valued at £140,000 after heavy looting, were not very great, but the daring of the attempt was very great indeed'. Drake's subsequent destruction of hoops and barrel-staves for 25,000 tuns at Cape St Vincent may also have had an appreciable effect on the carriage of Medina Sidonia's stores in the forthcoming battle.

He had singed the king of Spain's beard, but he knew, as he told Walsingham, that 'preparation was never heard of, or known, as the King of Spain hath and daily maketh to invade England which, if they be not impeached before they join, will be very perilous. I dare not almost write of the great forces which the King of Spain hath. Prepare in England strongly and most by sea! Look well to the coast of Sussex.' Beards grow again, but the enemies of Spain were delighted, her friends apprehensive: Philip had suffered great humiliation.

It is likely, however, that of the Protestants only Drake and his captains, Burghley, Leicester and Walsingham, had sought open war between England and Spain. Neither Philip nor Elizabeth would have attacked if they had not felt themselves mortally threatened, at sea, in the Low Countries and in their home ports. In Elizabeth's case the threat came via the sedition on the one hand of Mary Queen of Scots, revealed in Babington, Ridolfi and northern plots; in Philip's via the assaults of Drake and Hawkins on the Spanish Main and in Cadiz Bay.

Elizabeth's execution of Mary Queen of Scots at Fotheringham in 1587 was also a step towards war, not sought by Elizabeth, but finally not to be avoided. (James VI said that at the news of his mother's death, the queen 'fell into deep grief, accompanied by unfeigned weeping'.) For his part, so long as Mary was alive, Philip would try, like his father Charles V, to prevent a Franco-English alliance which his claim to the English throne might create. While Mary breathed, Spain would not mount total war against the Tudors: but a queen in London with allegiance to France?

In France itself, the stability of that country was ravaged to the point of civil war, both by the St Bartholomew's Massacre of the

Huguenots under Henry of Navarre led by Condé, and by the financial subvention from Philip II of Spain, not to the legitimate Valois king, Henry III, but to the duc de Guise and the fanatically Catholic Holy League which had the pope and Philip as patrons. Civil war in France was Philip's instrument towards suppression of French support for the Netherlands rebellion, towards intervention and invasion of England. Victory for the league would, after the assassination of William of Orange, damage the Protestant cause in France, upset the rule of Henry III, frustrate the Netherlands rebellion and deeply affect Queen Elizabeth, paymaster of the Protestant coalition.

Henry of Navarre was heir to the French throne. The Leaguers thought otherwise: 'Better a Republic than a Huguenot king.' A series of battles, sometimes favourable to Navarre (at Coutras), sometimes to Guise (at Auneau), ensued after the Day of the Barricades in May 1588. Guise then shut Henry III's troops out of Paris.

The king had Guise murdered. 'Now I am king of France,' Henry III told his mother, Catherine de' Medici, 'I have killed the king of Paris.' The Queen Mother replied: 'But have you made sure of the other towns?' The league, nevertheless, governed Paris through terror until an assassin disposed of Henry III, when Navarre succeeded as Henry IV. The brilliant reign which followed was ended in 1610 by a Catholic assassin with a knife.

Even in 1587, at the time of the Cadiz raid, Francis Drake had scarcely left Plymouth before the queen sent an order forbidding him – because she still wished to smooth over quarrels with the Spanish – to 'enter forcibly into any of the King's ports or do any act of hostility upon the land'. Drake, in fact, did not receive this message, which also contained the more stirring injunction to 'get into your possession such *shipping* of the said King or his subjects as you shall find at sea'. Mattingley points out that 'the fiction that England and Spain were not at war could thus be maintained, and the negotiations in the Netherlands [with Parma] go on'. It was after this action at Cadiz that Drake made his moving observation to Walsingham: 'There must be a beginning of any good matter, but the continuing to the end, until it be thoroughly finished, yields the true glory.'

Philip, despite English support for the Dutch rebellion and the Portuguese pretender, did not decide on the formation and despatch of the Armada until the civil war in France lifted the French threat to Spanish forces in the Netherlands. These were commanded by Alexander Farnese, duke of Parma, nephew of Philip II and the greatest soldier of the age. Conqueror already of most of the Netherlands, Parma was at the same time falsely 'negotiating' with the English his own Spanish withdrawal from the Netherlands, free admission of English ships to the ports of the Americas, guarantees of the liberties of the Seventeen Provinces, and firm Spanish denial that any invasion was planned. (One result of this protracted disinformation was that his army, in a foul winter, had shrunk through disease and malnutrition from 30,000 to 15,000 troops, though, admittedly, in England they would face only yeomen of the trained bands summoned by beacons should an enemy land in Kent or Sussex.) Parma believed, provided that it were supported on arrival by English Catholics, that a force embarked in barges from Dunkirk and Nieuwpoort could cross the Channel unobserved without a supporting fleet from Iberia – no principled difference from the plans of Bonaparte and Hitler, and equally impractical.

The king had originally asked Santa Cruz in 1586 for an estimate of forces required to take England by sea: 510 sailing ships, 86 galleys manned with 16,500 sailors, 55,000 infantry and 1,200 cavalry, was the admiral's reply; Philip proposed otherwise. His plan was to reinforce (by land from Italy) Parma's army on the Flemish coast and join the latter's 15,000 men with a smaller armada of 141 ships with 20,000 infantrymen. In the event, Parma at Dunkirk had no secure ports for his barges and inadequate protection for them when launched: no more than four shallow-draft warships (galleys) had set off from Lisbon and none of them crossed Biscay safely. As the troops could not therefore be embarked under hostile Dutch guns, the invasion could not have taken place.

Meanwhile Santa Cruz had died. The duke of Medina Sidonia, an excellent naval administrator but inexperienced in battle, succeeded him with as profound reluctance and professional distaste as Santa Cruz had for the king's ill-thought project, to find that the fleet was already consuming victuals at greater speed and quantity than could be loaded. Guns were old and often unsuitable, ships were far from adequately provisioned in water, food, powder and shot. As soon as the Armada put to sea, furthermore, it was struck by gales, and had to put into Corunna for repairs and fresh victuals. The men, soldiers and sailors, were mostly inexperienced conscripts, certainly not the Spanish *tercios* famous throughout Europe. There were only 19,000 soldiers, not Santa Cruz's 55,000. Provisions rotted and water stagnated in casks whose replacement hoops and barrel-staves had been destroyed by Drake at St Vincent. Sickness among the crews, due to long confinement on board, was already rife and spreading.

Dr Ian Thompson, lecturer in history at Keele University, said in 1988 that the Armada's order of battle in May 1588 was 141 vessels in six front-line squadrons, with 63 or 64 fighting ships, plus 4 part-oared galleasses, and the 4 galleys earlier referred to, which never turned up. They were led by the two elite squadrons of royal galleons, the flag-squadron of nine galleons of the crown of Portugal, the Castilian squadron under Diego Flores de Valdés with nine galleons of the Indies Guard, the Andalusian and Levant squadrons, a spectacular and impressive sight, together with store ships, caravels and pinnaces.

The objective of this fleet, all others now discarded, was only to cover Parma's crossing of the Channel and, in that context, to neutralise the English fleet. Santa Cruz's extraordinary plan, to employ over 500 ships to assault England directly, and another plan to create a diversionary rising in Ireland or the Isle of Wight, had been dropped because of shortages of men and matériel, grain, shot, munitions, guns and ships. And the Spanish knew that superior English gunnery would not only dictate both the subjection of the Armada to long-range battering by the largest English artillery and the abandonment of Spain's favoured strategy of close contact by boarding but also negate the dominance of the *tercio* or Spanish infantry which, anyway, numbered but one-third of the soldiers Medina Sidonia thought necessary.

The Armada was underequipped and undermanned. The chief-of-staff, Francisco de Bobadilla, reported to Philip's minister of state that

> the enemy had great advantage in ships, better than ours for battle, better designed, with better artillery, gunners and sailors, and so rigged that they could do with them what they wanted. Some vessels of our Armada fought very well . . . but the rest fled whenever they saw the enemy attack . . . We brought so few cannon balls that I hardly had a fighting ship that had anything to fire. Thus, the *San Mateo*, having run out of powder and shot, was caught and destroyed, and if the enemy had attacked us one day more after we made to the north, the same would have happened to the rest of our ships.

The English, in terms of shot, were in not much better state.

Queen Elizabeth, on her accession, acquired a fleet of only forty ships, of which she could afford to keep only twenty-four at fourteen days' notice, thus ensuring not only rapid mobilisation, but healthy crews, under the benevolent ministrations of the Navy Board, surveyor, controller and clerk of the ships.

The Navy Board was supervised by the lord admiral of England, Lord Howard of Effingham, who was also given command of the fleet against the Armada. His ships were, on the whole, faster and much better than his opponents' and, with their lower castles, more manoeuvrable. 'I have been aboard every ship that goes out with me . . . and I do thank God that they be in the estate they be in; and there is never a one of them that knows what a leak means . . . I think there were never in any place in the world worthier ships than these are, for so many. And few as we are, if the King of Spain's forces be not hundreds, we will make good sport with them.'

These optimistic comments were in sharp contrast to those of a Spanish captain, Bertendona:

It is well known that we fight in God's cause. So, when we meet the English, God will surely arrange matters so that we can grapple and board them, either by sending some strange freak of weather or, more likely, just by depriving the English of their wits. But unless God saves us by a miracle, the English, who have faster and handier ships than our own, and many more long-range guns, will knock us to pieces with their culverins, without our being able to do them serious hurt. So we are sailing against England in the confident hope of a miracle.

Howard's original intention, to defeat the Armada before it had sailed from its harbours, was frustrated on several occasions by adverse winds. But on 19 July the pinnace *Golden Hind* entered Plymouth Sound to report that she had sighted the Spanish fleet off the Scillies. By morning of the next day the English had beaten out of the Sound and, by the following morning, had worked to windward of the Armada. The Spaniards had lost the weather gauge and the chance to force hand-to-hand fighting on their numerically weaker military opponents; the seamanship of the English surprised and alarmed the enemy.

The English, for their part, were awed by the remarkable discipline of Medina Sidonia's huge fleet in its crescent formation, heavy galleons ahead and trailing on the quarter and astern in two great horns, the transports almost invulnerable in the centre. Untrained in this kind of convoy manoeuvre, continual attempts by the English to break the 'excellent good order' of the Spanish by cannonade over the next few days were all unsuccessful: 'We durst not put in among them, their fleet being so strong,' wrote Howard after the battle.

In the drizzling rain, Howard had opened hostilities, as in a mediaeval joust, by sending in the pinnace *Disdain* to fire a single shot, his opposite number Medina Sidonia hoisting the sacred standard. Soon both fleets, although the English fired one and a half rounds an hour per gun and the Spanish the same rate *per day*, were running out of powder and shot. This was a lack more easily mended by the home team than by the Armada, miles from their bases and unable to expect anything other than incessant attacks astern from windward by guns bowed or quartered or bow chasers or broadside.

Damage was undoubtedly caused to the Spanish fleet, but not so much as either side had anticipated: the Spaniards were not, as they had feared, 'knocked to pieces', although there were many casualties, and spars, masts and rigging needed repair. The only losses were the *Nuestra Señora del Rosario*, which lost her foremast and bowsprit in accidental collision, and the *San Salvador*, which blew up. (Later gossip had it that the cause was sabotage by a Flemish master gunner cuckolded by a Spanish officer, who threatened the same to the gunner's daughter, both ladies allegedly on board.) Medina Sidonia abandoned the *Rosario* with its captain; to Frobisher's rage, Drake took the vessel as a prize. But nothing, despite their best efforts, would permit the Spaniards to bring the English within boarding range or to take the weather gauge again.

That night, Monday, 31 July, near Start Point, Lord Howard ordered station to be kept on the stern light of *Revenge*, Drake's flagship. At dawn, however, he found himself alone and in great danger in the middle of the Spanish fleet. The *Ark* had been following the stern light not of *Revenge* but of *San Martin*, Medina's flagship. Sir Francis, irresponsibly unable to resist the benefits of piracy, had extinguished his own stern light in pursuit of prizes, either *Rosario* or some harmless German merchantmen in the vicinity. No mention of this peculiar incident was recorded from Howard: rich prizes were the objective of most captains of that time, naval discipline was otherwise almost non-existent.

From Wednesday to Friday the Spaniards failed to seize Frobisher's *Triumph* and the English similarly did not manage to take the *Gran Grifon* which, aided by its fellows, escaped. Howard now put his fleet, for better concentration and use of broadside, into four divisions under himself, Drake, Frobisher and Hawkins, superseding the previous line abreast, a procedure best designed for deployment of forward-firing armament. But he did not adopt any other change in fleet organisation, tactics or coordination, which remained rudimentary.

Heavy fighting took place on Saturday off the Isle of Wight, where Medina Sidonia had intended to anchor awaiting instructions from Parma about a rendezvous. But when both the tide and an attack by Drake appeared to be driving the Armada on to shoals, the Owers, near Selsey Bill, the Spaniards abandoned the idea of Spithead and the Solent for the open sea. This, although not an English victory and hardly reason for the investiture as knights by Howard of Frobisher, Hawkins and other captains, had 'coursed the enemy so that they shall have not leisure to land'. Howard followed them but, short of ammunition, said he would defer bombardment until Dover.

It was now, off 'the Cape of Margate', the Downs or North Foreland, that Medina Sidonia understood that there was no possibility of landing an invasion force in England. Parma, as we have seen, had no secure port of adequate size. His landing barges were too large to cross the Flanders Bank, nor could they navigate the shoal water by the bank without being sunk by the Dutch rebel shallow-draft warships, of which neither he nor the Armada had any. Since the king's orders were clear – no independent landing, only the embarkation of Parma's army, which was not feasible – there seemed nothing for the Armada to do except to anchor in the open roads off Calais. The English, under Howard and with Lord Henry Seymour's squadron, a total of 140 sail, anchored near by, directly to windward.

Eight English fire ships loosed on the Spaniards did little or no damage to a well-prepared enemy, but did cause the Armada to stand out to sea, for the first time in at least temporary disorder. The English weighed anchor next morning and went into the attack, Howard wasting time in selecting a damaged galleon inshore, which he looted.

The English, faced with a gallant, disciplined foe, but one so short of round shot as almost to be confined to small arms, sank two Spanish ships before the Armada, in bad visibility and heavy seas, restored its formation. Two more were then driven on to the Zeeland shoals which looked, until the 'miracle' of a sudden wind change to the south, to be the graveyard of the entire fleet.

The Spaniards, damaged, lacking food, water, powder and shot, and unable to beat into the southerly, now had no choice except the awful voyage round Scotland and Ireland, 'those boisterous and uncouth Northern seas', in Drake's words. It was as well for them that English stocks of ammunition were little better: Howard gave up the chase after the Firth of Forth.

After the terrible gales of that early autumn, only sixty-seven Spanish ships reached their own country, many sorely damaged and with only a third of their troops and ships' companies, surely one of the greatest maritime disasters in history, on a par with the Mongolian *kamikaze* catastrophe against Japan in the thirteenth century.

Interrogation of Spanish prisoners revealed that some vessels had 'no water but what they brought out of Spain which stinketh marvellously and their flesh meat they cannot eat, their drouth is so great. It is a common bruit among the soldiers that if they may once get home, they will not meddle again with the English.'

England 'won', according to Michael Lewis's *Armada Guns*, because of several factors. The first was the superior sailing power of their ships and the second that, although the Spanish had many ship-killers – 'smashing-guns' – they were too short range to fight the better sailors in the English fleet, who held their ships at long range with the weather gauge. (The longer-range English guns, nevertheless, did little *ship* damage, no doubt because many were light shotted.) The Spanish defeat lay in the impossibility, as both Santa Cruz and Medina Sidonia had protested, of carrying out the orders of King Philip II: the venture was not, in itself, a practical proposition, and the king's obstinacy over the responsibility for and nature of the landing, as well as in myriad details like the shallow-draft warship contribution, doomed the expedition from the start.

Garrett Mattingley believed that the battle was decisive in ensuring that 'religious unity was not to be imposed by force on the heirs of mediaeval Christendom'. After 1588, Spain was no longer invincible. The momentum of Spanish conquest slackened. States began to develop their own national attributes without deference to another's command. Men everywhere responded to 'the eternal myth', as Nicholas Rogers described it, of 'the defence of freedom against tyranny, the victory of the weak over the strong, of the triumph of David over Goliath'.

Fisher said that, after the Armada, 'the haunting fear of Spanish tyranny passed out of Europe', above all in France, Ireland and the Netherlands. And 'the Armada completed the process which the Marian persecutions had begun of making England a Protestant country'. Nor was any serious attempt ever made thereafter to invade England, although that was perhaps also to be credited to Nelson, and to 'The Few'.

SYNOPSIS OF EVENTS BETWEEN
THE ARMADA AND THE SIEGE OF VIENNA

Henry IV conformed to the Catholic Church, thus ending the civil war in France. Philip II of Spain died in 1598 and Queen Elizabeth of England in 1603. In 1618 the Thirty Years War began, while in 1630 Gustavus Adolphus marched to the aid of the German Protestants, Sweden continuing her remarkable – given her size and geography – role in Europe.

In 1642 the English Civil War began; regicide followed and, in 1653, Oliver Cromwell became lord-protector. But in 1660 Charles II took the throne and the Stuart line was restored in England. From 1661 Louis XIV was engaged militarily in Spain, in the Spanish Netherlands, in Franche Comté and Alsace, while Peter the Great ascended to the throne of Russia in 1682.

CHAPTER ELEVEN

THE SIEGE OF VIENNA, 1683

Jan Sobieski, son of the Castellan of Cracow, and of the granddaughter of the Hetman Zolkiewski, served against Chimielnicki and the Cossacks at Borestecko in 1651 and at Batoka. (The Cossacks were originally Tatars, the word itself denoting a 'free soldier', but their hero, Chimielnicki, was a Lithuanian Jesuit member of the gentry or *szlachta*.) His equivocal, even treasonable record during the Swedish invasion in the 1650s was eased by the expulsion from the Central Provinces by him and Czarniecki in 1656 of Charles X of Sweden. For services to King John-Casimir, he succeeded Czarniecki as commander-in-chief in 1668, but earned later opprobrium for conspiring with Louis XIV and the elector of Brandenburg against his own king, Michael Wisnoiwiecki. These intrigues led to the shameful Treaty of Buczacz under which the Ukraine, Podolia and Kamieniec were yielded to the Porte.

Sobieski's name was rehabilitated by his defeat of a Tatar army at Podhajce and by a brilliant action, as King Michael lay dying in 1674, against Turkish janissaries commanded at Chocim by the Grand Vizir. At the elective Sejm on 21 May 1674 he was, in clouds of consequent glory, elected Jan III, king of Poland, despite the candidature of the duke of York, later James II of England, and the Bourbon prince de Conti. His campaign in the electoral field was openly supported by 6,000 of the armed veterans of Chocim: 'Let a Pole rule over Poland'.

Fighting in the Ukraine with Cossack help, accompanied by skilful negotiation through the varying channels of Louis XIV and the Tatar khan caused postponement of his coronation until February 1676, the siege of Trembowla under his Jewish lieutenant, Jan Samuel Crhzanowski and 3,000 men holding off the Turkish horde for eleven days. In October of the same year Sobieski and 13,000 men in his entrenched camp at Zaravno resisted 80,000 Turks for three weeks. The treaty which followed could not restore Kamieniec to Poland, but did recover two-thirds of the lost Ukraine.

Count Adam Zamoyski, in his scintillating and comprehensive *The Polish Way*, has described Sobieski at the age of forty-five in 1674: 'From his close-cropped head and his jewelled fur cap to his soft yellow boots with their silver heels, he was every inch the Sarmatian magnate.' (Sarmatians were warriors from the Black Sea steppe, invading Europe in the sixth century.) 'He spoke Tatar and Turkish' and loved 'banners, tents, carpets, horse-cloths and weapons, whose aesthetic value he appraised like a Turk'. Gold, silver and jewels covered these artefacts and the bridles and saddles of his armies' steeds, his officers' breastplates studded with gold and set with precious stones. The Husaria, the 'winged cavalry', wore jewelled armour, bows and arrows, their horses' trappings in gold thread. Fur lined their cloaks, scarlet were their breeches. The front line carried huge wings made of black eagle feathers which, 'planted' in two arcs from shoulder or saddle, rose menacingly over their heads. 'The long lance was painted like a stick of rock . . . with a five-foot-long silk pennant which made a frightful noise at the charge.'

At least throughout the seventeenth century, the Husaria was the decisive feature of Polish cavalry and, greatly outnumbering the infantry, the victors in most engagements. The curved sabre, lance, sword, pistol, bow and arrow, and a 'long steel hammer which could go through heads and helmets like butter' were all employed. The infantry, firing much quicker than even the Spanish *tercio*, carried pikes and hatchets as well as muskets.

Self-sufficiency and mobility, in terrain varying from marsh to savannah to forest, were the essential qualities of Polish armies in that era.

Sobieski lived at a time when Poland had already become the granary of Europe. The freedom of the peasantry had accordingly declined in inverse proportion to the holdings and power of both magnates and *szlachta*. Coincidentally, Lithuania and Poland had formed an Act of Union at Lublin in 1569, 'the Most Serene Commonwealth of the Two Nations', considerably increasing the authority of the *szlachta*, and of the Sejm, including election of a candidate to the throne of the commonwealth. The Sejm, the Senate and the king together represented the people, the king perhaps to be seen as their mouthpiece or executive, at least until after the departure of the Lithuanian Sagiellon dynasty.

The three orders sought participation, not dominance, in the workings of the commonwealth, but the increased riches and independence of the magnates substantially diminished the authority of the throne. When the Vasa king Zygmunt III died in 1632 he disposed of the royal crowns of Sweden and of Muscovy, but not that of Poland; what, however, lay in his gift was the appointment of senior officials of commonwealth and Senate. But Poland was weakened internationally by the loss (as an ally) of the Ukraine at the Treaty of Andrusov in 1667.

King James II's authority, restrained by the constitution, was not much advanced by the maelstrom of Swedes, Tatars, Turks, Russians, Bourbons, Habsburgs, Bohemians, Livonians, Pomeranians, dissident Vasa and other natives in which Poland had to function, or by his own turbulent marriage.

Marie-Casimir Sobieska, Marysiénka, had arrived in the country as a child (Marie d'Arquien) in the entourage of Marie de Gonzague, the French queen of Poland and consort of King Ladislas IV, remaining as a maid of honour. (Two years later, Ladislas died, the widow remarrying the brother, John-Casimir, already a cardinal.) Although at fifteen Sobieski was a suitor, her first marriage was to Zamoyski, prince of Zamosc, idle, hospitable, a good soldier, a heavy drinker and brave. (When the king of Sweden sought terms after bombarding Zamosc, the prince replied: 'Do not let his Majesty disturb himself, he has killed nothing but one pig: he can go on if he chooses without causing me the least inconvenience.')

Marysiénka was thought exquisitely beautiful. 'Her face was oval,' according to the anonymous biographer of King John-Casimir, 'the corners of her little mouth turned upwards scornfully, her nose aquiline, her eyes almond shaped, a mass of black hair, and her slight person decorated with treasures.' But as to her character, a Benedictine nun quoted in Waliszewski's *Marysienka* leaves the impression of the 'greatest solicitude for her own personal comfort without regard for others' welfare, love of society, scorn for other people's opinions, extreme freedom of deportment. In short, self-worship, exacting, imperious and a will which bore not contradiction.'

It is unsurprising that after the early deaths of all three of her children by Zamoyski, Marysiénka tired of marriage to a boor who stank of wine like an innkeeper and swore like a trooper. Sobieski, now grand marshal, stood in the wings, noted by the queen herself as having worn a ring of Marysiénka's from her last visit to Warsaw. Many meetings, perhaps a secret wedding, and much correspondence took place: the lovers parted, Zamoyski's health deteriorated, virtue returned to Sobieski and Marysiénka. But in April 1665, the prince of Zamosc died, rumoured to have been poisoned by his widow.

Only a few days after Zamoyski was buried, Celadon and Astrea, as the lovers now called one another, met near Zamosc. Next day, Sobieski's letter to her grossly said that 'he would avenge *sur son petit raisin sec, toutes ses longues impatiences*'. On 6 May, to general disapprobation, they were married. Marysiénka was barred from the castle at Zamosc, to shouts of 'Off with the Sobouka', not an epithet she was inclined to tolerate. Sobieski, although stouter than before, was after all not only a fine figure of a man, but one whose father could raise whole squadrons of cavalry, the 'Golden Hussars'. On his mother's side, Hetman Zolkiewski had brought back the tsar himself to Warsaw as his prisoner. Later, the Hetman, surrounded by Turks at Cecora, had dismounted, killed his own horse, and died on his feet: 'Stand as befits an Emperor.'

During their marriage, Marysiénka only once caught her husband in an act of infidelity. She instantly 'took most unsavoury vengeance on the offender'. (Waliszewski, maddeningly, claimed that further detail was unfit for English ears.) It was not this single incident, but the fact that she was violent in her tenderness and fierce in her jealousies – 'the Furies entered Poland in her train' – which made a misery of her husband's life. She raised, 'neither sensual nor sentimental', every occasion to complicate and torment his existence, an icy, tenacious, irritating coquette.

The couple spent little time together, Marysiénka preferring France and the company of the bishop of Béziers to that of Poland and her husband. It was in 1667, with Astrea in Paris, that he completed his great defeat of Tatars and Cossacks at Podhajce: 'Neither this victory nor the salvation of my country can give me joy, so long as I cannot see that which makes all my life, nor be where I have buried all my heart and all my thoughts . . . in the last two years we have not lived two weeks together. And I am a faithful husband . . . I have heard that you spoke of me in a letter to the Palatine of Russia, as a *gallowsbird*.' Meanwhile, his wife failed to tempt Louis XIV into any serious negotiation over the Polish crown.

'Your love indeed', he cried in his next epistle, 'always reproaches, always complains. And it is always my fault if the smallest thing happened to annoy you. In my company, you are always gloomy and morose: the moment you leave my side, your speech and merriment return. I envied your dog – you treated him far better than you treated me.' He complains that she would not kiss him on the lips. Endless political intrigues followed in and out of Poland, until Marysiénka contracted smallpox, treated by applications of milk and pig's feet. Her hair and eyebrows fell out. Celadon said that he hadn't noticed.

'Your letters are very cold,' she observed.

'Yours do not burn me either. Frost must have set in early in France.'

It was in November 1673 that Celadon had disappeared, the warrior Jan Sobieski reborn, at the vast battle of Chocim, where 10,000 Turks and Tatars were killed and another 10,000 drowned in the Dniester. A *Te Deum* was sung in Hussein Pasha's tent. On the day before the battle, the feeble Piast monarch, William, died. Sobieski returned to Warsaw and it was now that he was rapturously elected king by virtual acclamation. But turmoil continued, with further huge incursions by Turks, and Russian devastation in the Ukraine, until the battle and treaty of Zaravno in 1676.

In 1675, Sobieski wrote to Queen Marie, now temporarily reconciled to the habits of her newly regal husband: 'How I wish I could turn myself into one of those dewdrops so that with it I might traverse space and fall upon your feet.' Astrea's malign response was that, for her part, she would make every possible effort to cure herself of the unlucky affection she still had for Celadon. 'If you drive me from your bed,' he cried in rage, 'you make me a desperate man.'

Five years later, however, he told her that he loved her as he had loved her on the first day.

In 1683, Turkey turned against Austria, preparatory to an assault on Cracow. Despite all attempts by the French court to draw Poland into the anti-Habsburg league, Sobieski now signed a treaty of alliance with Emperor Leopold and prepared for war. Whatever his deficiencies as lover or husband, he was a patriot, a Catholic and a considerable soldier/statesman, a large, genial man in body and in spirit.

He sought always to drive the Turks out of Europe, unlike the aim of the French king, in permanent enmity to Austria. 'To give the barbarian', declared Sobieski of the Turk, 'conquest for conquest, to pursue him from victory to victory over the very frontiers that belched him forth upon Europe: in a word, not to conquer and curb the monster, but to hurl him back into the deserts, to exterminate him, to raise upon his ruins the Empire of Byzantine, this enterprise alone is chivalrous: this alone is noble, wise, decisive.'

In reflecting upon that statement, we might remark that the armies led by the Grand Vizir against Kamieniec, Chocim and Livow in 1672, 1673, 1679 and 1683 numbered up to 200,000 men *on each occasion*, against a very maximum of 40,000 Poles – only 20,000 at Zaravno. Although the memory of Sobieski's conspiracies still hung about him, Leopold and the German princes did not hesitate on 14 July 1683 to invite the king with his 30,000 battle-scarred troops to take supreme command of those allied forces confronting the Turkish siege of Vienna. Kara Mustapha's troops, who had left Belgrade in June, massacring and plundering en route, now numbered 180,000 men, the sharp edge of Muslim armies which infested Hungary, Serbia, Greece, the Ukraine, the Adriatic coast, Egypt, the Maghreb and Levant, all now bound through Vienna for Rome and the Rhine, the heart of Christendom.

The Imperial Corps lacked Leopold, the Habsburg monarch, who retired with his family from Vienna to Passau on 17 July. Voltaire said later that 'the battlefield of Vienna had gathered together the whole Empire except the Emperor himself': he did not mention the truancy of the elector of Brandenburg or of his friend, Frederick the Great. It had, nevertheless, a complement of 40,000 veterans, trained and tested against Condé and Turenne. Sobieski observed: 'These people are like horses: they do not know their own strength.' Although he was unconcerned about the *figura* of his hussars and cuirassiers, he was worried about the impression that might be given by his magnificent but tattered infantry.

Instead, however, of hiding or smuggling them through in darkness, he put them at the head of the whole Polish order of battle. 'Gentlemen,' he said to Eugene of Savoy, the princes of Baden, Holstein, Würtemburg, the electors of Saxony, Bavaria, Hannover, Hesse, and other princes of Germany, 'these ragged men have sworn an oath to wear nothing but garments taken from the enemy. They have cast off the Turkish clothes they were wearing before the last treaty, but you will soon see them dressed in splendid Eastern garments.'

Marysiénka, from whom he took leave, weeping, at the Tarnow Pass, was more interested in the effect produced on the allies by her husband's personal surroundings. But princes and electors alike fought one another to do him homage, his pages in rich livery, horses with gorgeous equipage, cloth of gold lining the chambers of himself and his son, 'Fanfanik'.

Deserted by the emperor and 60,000 of the capital's richer inhabitants in their carriages, Vienna was defended by Count Starhemberg and little more than 20,000 armed men, with a civilian population of 60,000. At dawn on 14 July the invaders appeared, having left garrisons on all routes behind, even beyond Linz. The Turkish camp lay in a tented crescent west of the Danube, in a great semicircle running from the river in the southeast corner at Semmering, to Fesendorf and Intzersdorf, to Schönbrunn, Preitenace, Alterkling in the north, Wahring, Dobling on the Danube again, but northeast of Vienna itself. The Grand Vizir's tent, variously described as 'scarlet' and green silk, was visible in the northwest sector from the Kahlenberg hills on which Sobieski waited, the united allied army now totalling 70,000 men.

Within, as it were, the centre of the crescent, Vienna still stood, defences much broken, great stone walls pierced or shattered, mined and counter-mined, stricken by starvation, fire and disease. From St Stephen's Cathedral the bells clamoured and Starhemberg's distress rockets rose to the skies, prayers arising too around that great church. Those besieged continued to repair such fortifications as remained. Although Kara Mustapha could probably have taken the city by storm, treason or negotiation, he had chosen – since he hoped to reign over it himself – to meet his enemy in open country. Nor, until 10 September, did he hear from his Tatar allies of Sobieski's imminent and unexpected arrival: the Turks feared the king above all men.

On the morning of 10 September 1683 Starhemberg, watching at sunrise, suddenly saw westward on the heights of the Kahlenberg a vast red standard with a white cross, the flag raised by King Jan III to mark his assault, after a mass in the open air at a convent ruined by the Turks. Below, unprotected by redoubts of any kind, lay the 100,000 tents of Kara Mustapha, his camels, mules, oxen and sheep, with a private court – according to Sobieski's letter to Marysiénka after the battle – 'as large as Warsaw'. In that court were rich embroidered tents, seraglios, 'very rich and beautiful toys', gardens, fountains, kiosks, aviaries and a decapitated ostrich.

The king knew that the Grand Vizir had blundered. Before releasing the main assault, however, he despatched a reconnaissance attack in the shape of a squadron of young hussars, all *szlachta*, including his younger son Alexander and 150 gentlemen. These wore the dress of the Husaria, in steel or mail, with the black wings of eagles, tiger-skins over their cuirasses, curved swords, fifteen-foot lances which broke on impact without unseating the bearer. Waliszewski describes their action after the king had pointed to a commotion in the left wing of the Ottoman army where Kara Mustapha was strengthening his line:

On they flew like destroying angels ... the finest cavalry in Europe. Away the squadron started [to 'the little scarlet tent which had just been pitched for the Vizir'], first at a canter, then quicker, right through the Turkish outposts, plunged like a cannon-ball into the second and far more serried line, disappeared for a moment, emerged beyond it close to the main body and the scarlet tent, bent to the right, tore at full gallop across the front of a great troop of Tatars, who moved neither hand nor foot, and back again toward the Christian camp ... one fourth of the squadron had fallen.

Then came on the allied main body, manned in the centre by Germans, mostly Bavarians and Franconians, on the left by the duke of Lorraine commanding Saxons, imperial infantry and Polish cavalry under Zubomirski, ordered to relieve the city of Vienna itself. The right wing, advancing through the Wienerwald, was composed of Poles, infantry and cavalry, under Jablonowski and Sieniawski, directed to cut off the enemy's line of retreat. The total order of battle, as has been said, was some 70,000 men, of whom a third were Polish, the rest Germans, French, Scots, Irish and Spaniards.

Sobieski led his army down the Kahlenberg, more abrupt and rugged than he had supposed, on either hand precipices, ravines and high mountains. The janissaries on the Turkish left went forward under their green standard to face the king's ensign, a falcon's wing at the tip of a long lance, against which they had fought bloodily before. (They had now, at least, the advantage of facing only a limited range of artillery – dragged by 'bare-foot Polish soldiers' – since, in the terrible heat of that September, the Germans could not get their guns over the mountain tracks.) By three or four in the afternoon, as the infidel retreated step by step, Sobieski was tempted by the heat and the men's exhaustion to postpone until the next day his full-blown assault.

But the king could see the enemy training his heavy guns away from Vienna towards his army. He had seen the erection of the little red tent, and the masts or poles with the horse and yak tails. He now sent forward Jablonowski's Husaria against the janissaries, then diagonally in a vast, heaving mass of caparisoned heavy cavalry through the formed Turkish ranks, lances lowered and the 'evil hiss' which Zamoyski attributes to the black wings, 'the ground shook with the pounding of fifteen thousand hooves'. Polish and imperial cuirassiers and dragoons, Bavarian, Saxon and imperial infantry fell like an avalanche upon the fleeing Asians.

The Pashas ran, followed by Mustapha's whole army, the Grand Vizir escaping just before the king hurtled into the Turkish camp. 'The Jihad', as Zamoyski claimed, 'had been defeated by the last Crusade . . . Yet when the fighting was over, the Poles went home, hung the captured Turkish trophies on their castle walls, and returned to their own pursuits. There was no Polish participation in negotiations between the Sultan and the Emperor, no claims, no compensation, no diplomatic victory.' The Turks lost 10,000 men and the whole of their baggage train, vast quantities of booty including jewelled girdles, no doubt for Viennese houris, Kara Mustapha's charger with gold and jewelled trappings, a silver stirrup from the Grand Vizir's horse,* quivers mounted with rubies and sapphires, sabres set in gold.

The Turks never returned to Vienna. Jan Sobieski had begun the liquidation of their threat to Europe, the initiation of Fisher's 'long process of Turkish decline which was sealed by the Treaty of Lausanne in 1923'. At the abolition of the Sultanate and Caliphate, Ataturk (Kemal Pasha) spoke in the National Assembly: 'Sovereignty is acquired by force, by power, by violence. It was by violence that the sons of Ottoman acquired the power to rule over the Turkish nation and to maintain their rule for more than six centuries. It is now the nation that revolts against these usurpers, puts them in their right place, and carries on their sovereignty.' Only one voice cried again, 'I am against it.'

---

* According to Loyd Grossman's *Bread of Heaven*, bagels – hard, little, stirrup-shaped loaves – derive from the German word for stirrup (*Steigbugel*), sold in 1683 and afterwards to commemorate the heroism of the Polish cavalry. Some suggest that croissants (crescents) derive similarly from the siege, but it seems possible that their origin was Budapest in 1686, where bakers at night heard the Turks tunnelling and gave the alarm; or so reports Larousse.

SYNOPSIS OF EVENTS BETWEEN
THE SIEGE OF VIENNA AND PLASSEY

In 1685 Louis XIV continued to persecute the Protestants in France but, in England, through the Glorious Revolution, William III took the throne in 1688. The Grand Alliance (under William III) of the Austrian Empire, England and others was mounted against France. On her succession to the throne in 1702 Queen Anne continued the war against the French.

In the War of the Spanish Succession, Marlborough at Blenheim, Ramillies and Oudenaarde defeated the French from 1704 to 1708. At Pultowa in 1709, the Russians against Charles XII destroyed the coherence of the Swedish Empire. The Treaty of Utrecht, with principal advantages to Austria and the Netherlands, was signed in 1713. Queen Anne and King Louis XIV both died in 1714; the Hanoverians succeeded to the English throne.

Frederick of Prussia attacked Austria under Maria Theresa, taking Silesia, conquests reversed at the battle of Dettingen (1743) by French arms over an English army. The war was settled by the Treaty of Aix-la-Chapelle, Silesia, then Austria, awarded to Frederick II.

CHAPTER TWELVE

PLASSEY, 1757, AND QUEBEC, 1759

Plassey arouses the emotions like few other battles. To the British, it was the true beginning of their rule in India and the creation of the British Empire in Asia. For the Indians, it marked the beginning of 200 years of colonial repression. To the British, Plassey was an extraordinary feat of arms, where 3,000 well-disciplined Redcoats took on 50,000 native troops. To the Indians, Plassey was the supreme example of British duplicity and cunning: it was won by a trick. For Robert Clive it marked a high point in a brilliant career that would be tarnished by accusations of corruption and greed, ended by suicide, and commemorated by the statue that stands today between the Foreign Office and the Treasury in London.

Robert Clive, later the first Baron Clive, was born on 25 September 1725 near to Market Drayton in Shropshire, the son of Richard Clive, whose family had held land in the area since the reign of Henry II. He spent much of his childhood away from home and was educated variously, in Market Drayton, the Merchant Taylors' School in London and finally, when he was about thirteen, in Hemel Hempstead with a Mr Sterling. When Clive was seventeen his father managed to secure for him an appointment as a writer with the East India Company and in March 1743 he sailed for India with small regret at leaving England. His childhood had been spent mainly in trouble and it can only be assumed that his choleric father was glad to be rid of his impulsive and wild son. Within only a few years, Robert Clive would repay his father for sending him to India by ensuring that the family name would always be associated with this vast country.

Plassey was a result of the great 'atrocity' of the colonial era. Throughout this time, colonial explorers and their sponsors – usually governments – looked to justify their exploits and conquests. India was no exception. Prior to Plassey, India had proved a difficult place for the British and the East India Company. The Moghul emperor, and the princes below him, did not wish to see British power expand, while the French appeared to be gaining a better grip of India. By the time Clive arrived in 1744, Britain held the main ports of Calcutta, Bombay and Madras, but only tenuously. Over the following decade the French would demonstrate just how precarious was the British hold, making Clive himself a prisoner for two years. By 1756 the situation was slightly healthier for the British: Clive's great stand at Arcot in 1751 had revived British prestige and made him a minor celebrity, while the French were having their own leadership difficulties, unsure of their aims and of whom to put in charge. Moreover, both Great Powers did not always know whether they were at war with each other. Before the telegraph, it was quite possible for nations to be at peace in one part of the world while their armies battled elsewhere. So it was with the French and the British in India: they connived against each other but fell short of continual hostility.

However, the catalyst for Plassey, and for British hegemony in India, was the death of Alivardi Khan, nawab of Bengal, and the appointment of Siraj-ud-Daula as his successor. Siraj was perverted, ill-tempered, avaricious, dissipated, cunning and vicious. He soon attacked Calcutta on the grounds that the British had not greeted his ascension with appropriate fanfare or presents, nor handed over captives whom he wanted to try for treason. After desperate fighting and hopeless tactics by civilian commanders, the fort surrendered to the nawab. The reason for this dismal British performance was that those in charge were not soldiers of any sort. Furthermore, Roger Drake, the acting governor, was desperately unpopular among those he was supposed to govern, and was treated almost with contempt by his officials. Acting governor for four years, he had yet to be confirmed in his post, with neither the wit nor the skill to deal with Siraj-ud-Daula, as he amply demonstrated throughout the battle for Calcutta. Drake could easily have placated Siraj but chose not to do so, a decision that he would not have made had he believed that, if the worst came to the worst, he could rely on his soldiers. To even the most untrained eye, Calcutta was in no state to defend itself. The defences were barely built, there were few stores of ammunition and the soldiers numbered some 165 men, mainly of Portuguese-Indian descent. In the end, Siraj overcame Calcutta with ease. Most of the British garrison were drunk by the end of the battle. Their shambolic defence was easily swept aside. Eventually the council ordered the evacuation of the fort and left the garrison to their fate, Roger Drake among those to escape down the river: it would have been better for Clive if he had stayed where he was.

James Holwell, the British magistrate and de facto commander after the evacuation of the fort, was taken to Siraj, who, in a good mood, promised that the British prisoners would be well treated. The opposite happened. All the prisoners were forced into the fort's legendary Black Hole, measuring 18 feet by 14 feet. There are doubts about how many were placed in the cell, Macaulay's famous account quoting 146, Holwell reducing it to about 70, while Indian sources claim the number was no higher than 39. (It was a barbaric act anyway, which Siraj should have known would arouse the anger of any western power.) By morning, there were twenty-three survivors caked in vomit, excrement and blood, who were then paraded naked through the city while the rest of the garrison and other Europeans were ordered to leave. Siraj had created a massive stick with which the British would beat the Indians for 200 years, the 'Black Hole of Calcutta', that atrocity which could provide the justification for an empire.

At the time of the fall of Calcutta Clive was at Madras, where it seemed likely that hostilities would break out again with the French. The nizam of Hyderabad had asked the British to assist him in overthrowing his French overlords under the marquis de Bussy, an excellent chance for the British to take control of the Deccan and extend their influence inland from Madras. The news from Calcutta soon put paid to any expansion in the south, and the British were faced with an awkward dilemma: to send a force to the north while relations were so tense in the south was risky, but could they risk the opprobrium that would be heaped upon them in Britain by the government, the Company and by public opinion if they failed to respond to this national humiliation? The British were hampered not only by their own indecision about the action to be taken, but also by the identity of their commander, a familiar story of regular military men refusing command by Company soldiers. Eventually, after the monsoon floods abated and a land campaign was deemed possible, a Company expedition under the command of Clive set out for Bengal without regular military assistance. Colonel John Aldercron, the pompous commander of the King's Regiment's several hundred troops in Madras, would have been the obvious choice as commander of the expedition, but had insisted that he control all land troops. He refused to guarantee to share any booty with the Company. When he heard that Clive was to be the expedition leader he ordered his artillery removed from the ships and disembarked all his men. In the end he very reluctantly allowed three companies of his men to go with the expedition, but classed them as marines so that they would be under the command of the admiral, Charles Watson, and not Robert Clive, the Company's man.

Clive was fairly relaxed about what awaited him in Bengal, believing firmly that fate had marked him out, once again, for glory. He wrote to his father, 'This expedition, if attended with any success may enable me to do great things. It is by far the greatest of my undertakings; I go with great forces and great authority.' He might not have been quite so bullish had he realised the extent of the forces being raised by the nawab. He was also ambitious about the potential achievements of his mission. Even before he left Madras, Clive intended not only to retake Calcutta and force a new settlement on more favourable terms, but also to expand Company interests within the entire Bengal district. He realised how much latitude his orders and his situation had given him: in Calcutta, he would be hundreds of miles from Madras and could act as he pleased. There would be no constraints on him. He had been given unprecedented powers and, with no civilian power in Calcutta to deal with, Clive was master of the situation. The force that sailed with him on 16 October 1756 was proof of this, four ships of the line, a destroyer and a fire ship from the Royal Navy, and the Company's three warships. He also had 500 British Company soldiers, 150 marines and nearly 1,000 sepoys; in total over 2,500 men sailed.

The expedition began badly when two of the ships of the line were forced by a typhoon to return to Madras. Clive consequently lost the services of 243 infantry and 430 sepoys. He was still faced with problems, especially concerning his fellow leaders. Admiral Watson thought little of Clive as the latter had behaved poorly during the journey north, and shown dislike at being under Watson's command while aboard the flagship. On arrival at the Hugli, Watson conspired with Richard Drake, the ousted governor of Calcutta, that if Calcutta were retaken, control would pass to Drake and his council, not to Clive who, when he arrived at the Hugli, was thus in command of a fractured, sickly and divided force. Nevertheless, he pursued the task in hand, taking Budge Budge and Fort William.

Clive was also undermined at this stage by Captain Eyre Coote, the commander of Aldercron's 'marines', who thought him a John Company upstart. Coote had his own agenda: the resurrection of a career that had almost been destroyed after court-martial for cowardice at the battle of Falkirk. He had been acquitted, though forced to resign his commission, and had only been pardoned and able to restart his career after an intervention by the duke of

Cumberland. These personality clashes did not make for an auspicious start to the campaign, made worse by news that war had broken out again between France and Britain in Europe. (Would, for example, the French with their 300-strong garrison at Chandernagore assist the nawab?) The nawab began to form a new army north of the Hugli and north of Fort William. At Fort William, Clive set out with a small force to attack the nawab's vast army, in retrospect suicidal folly. But, after a day's fighting, which Clive and his soldiers were extraordinarily fortunate to survive, the nawab took fright and retreated several miles north of Calcutta out of range. The city was suddenly open to Clive and his reputation as 'the man who retook Calcutta' was practically secured.

Clive followed this spectacular and lucky success by neutralising the French force at Chandernagore. Using his ships of the line as huge mobile gun batteries, he pounded the French fort into submission. Beaten by overwhelming advantage in numbers, Renault, the leader of the French force, was in no mood to contemplate fighting hand-to-hand for the fort itself. The French had been crushed decisively in Bengal. The battle for the mastery of the region would now be a straight fight between Clive and Siraj-ud-Daula.

The interlude between Chandernagore and Plassey provided Clive with time to put out feelers to Siraj's court, and discover exactly where loyalty could be bought. In the end, there were two conspiracies against Siraj-ud-Daula: Mir Jaffir and the Muslim aristocracy, and Yar Latuf Khan and the Hindu aristocracy. The betrayal of Siraj-ud-Daula by Mir Jaffir, his commander-in-chief, was the vital blow. The capricious Siraj had only himself to blame for Jaffir's defection by goading the proud Jaffir into showing deference to the new court favourite, Mohan Lal. Furious, Jaffir announced to the British that he would be happy to lead any revolt against the nawab.

The Seths, furthermore, under General Yar Latuf Khan, keen to safeguard their possessions and encouraged by the Hindu merchant Omichand, also pledged their support to the British.

169

Omichand was a rich but murky individual whose support for the British was no more than convenient. When Siraj had taken Calcutta, Omichand had been quick to switch allegiance to the winning side; now it seemed that he was doing the same thing in different circumstances. But as the leading Hindu merchant in Bengal, his influence was vital. The conspiracy ran very deep: turning against the nawab were not only leading generals, but also leading politicians, including the second minister, Rai Durlabh, and businessmen who believed their prosperity would be better served under the British than under the nawab.

Amid all this intrigue a steady flow of correspondence shuttled back and forth between Clive and the nawab. The double-dealing reached its height with the formation of a double treaty signed by the leading conspirators, Mir Jaffir and Omichand. Both believed they were signing the same treaty. In fact, articles in each treaty reflected their personal concerns, the only way for Clive to ensure the loyalty of the two traitors. In later life, the act would haunt him: a House of Commons committee would question his judgement in allowing such an occurrence to happen with his full knowledge. With both treaties signed, however, Clive could afford to advance his campaign: on 10 June 1757, he decided to march south towards the nawab's army and so engage him in battle.

After a march lasting ten days and including a couple of minor skirmishes, Clive and his small force reached Plassey, hoping and believing that Mir Jaffir would remain loyal to his conspiracy. The monsoon had broken. Tempers and health were greatly improved. It was a signal that Clive could not afford to fail: the swollen rivers of Bengal and the deterioration in roads that the monsoon brought made it plain that any retreat to the fort at Chandernagore was out of the question, and he had already surrendered to the fates with his agonised decision to cross the Ganges delta to Plassey. He hoped desperately that Mir Jaffir would keep to the terms of the treaty and supply the cavalry he would so badly need if he were to retreat across the river, hounded by enemy troops.

On 23 June 1757 Clive and his army encamped at Plassey Grove. They occupied a strong defensive position at the nawab's hunting lodge and in a mango grove that adjoined it, their position made stronger by the fact that the grove was bordered by an earth ditch and bank forming an entrenchment some 800 yards long and 300 yards wide. Clive took over the hunting lodge as his headquarters and wrote a last letter to Mir Jaffir, seeking help.

As dawn broke, it seemed that Mir Jaffir had broken his promise to Clive. Lookouts on the roof of the hunting lodge watched in horror as the nawab's army of 50,000 arrived at Plassey. Retreat was impossible. The river crossing could not be attempted till nightfall and, by then, it would almost certainly be too late. Clive acted quickly: he formed his European infantry into four companies of 180 men. On either side he put 1,000 sepoys. Between the various units, Clive placed his guns. He held no reserve. The thin red line spread about 1,000 yards, three men deep. Clive had put a brave face on what seemed a desperate situation. In front, the nawab's army was preparing to begin the battle, artillery at the centre and, behind the guns, vast ranks of infantry and cavalry.

The British were in obvious danger at their front, but also at the open right flank, where horse- and foot-soldiers were beginning to mass: Clive was thus forced to fire half his meagre artillery at the cavalry on his right flank to ensure they came no closer. Only three guns could threaten the main body of the enemy. Soon, the nawab's army began to return fire and with some effect as a small body of French artillery opened up as well, a total of twelve guns pounding the British line. The French battery was beginning to do damage. Clive ordered his men to fall back to the protection of the orchard. They waited, a little protected by the ditch and the orchard. Then came the key moment of the battle: it started to rain, very hard. The nawab's cavalry advanced, seeing the chance to attack while British powder was drenched, but were beaten off: the British gunners had kept their powder dry.

The Bengali and French gunners had less success. Their guns fell almost silent as the rain soaked their powder. Much of the nawab's army began to lose heart after their cavalry attack failed and drifted back towards their entrenched camp. Clive's army began to move forward but Clive, still very nervous about his right flank, did not stray far from the protection of the orchard. Meanwhile, Kilpatrick, one of the company commanders, moved forward to begin an artillery duel with such French guns as functioned under St Frais. When the nawab attacked again, the British beat off his combined artillery and infantry attack, killing several 'generals'. It was now four o'clock in the afternoon. Clive sensed that the nawab's cavalry that had been lurking on his right flank would not now attack, and launched a frontal attack on the visibly wavering enemy.

Clive ordered Eyre Coote and his men to take the French guns, while he, 350 Europeans and two to three companies of sepoys headed straight for the body of the nawab's army. The Bengalis fled and by five o'clock the battle was over. At the entrenched camp there was no sign of the nawab himself: the wretched Siraj-ud-Daula had listened from the comfort of his tent to the defeat of his army and fled to Murshidabad.

Clive had won an extraordinary victory but, given the factors on his side, not an unlikely one. Faced by an army that was divided by a pay dispute and torn asunder by the treachery of its senior commanders, it is unsurprising that Clive's well-disciplined troops were able to overcome a force that probably numbered around 12,000. Clive's artillery was important in the battle, his four guns as effective as the nawab's dozen, which were fired at an almost lackadaisical pace. However, the key to the battle was probably Mir Jaffir's defection on Clive's right flank. As Clive was painfully aware, this area was very vulnerable to cavalry. Had Mir not kept his promise and instead attacked there with a well-disciplined cavalry charge, Clive might not have won.

Mir's help was an obvious advantage, but Clive also made several vital tactical decisions: first, he chose an excellent, though exposed camp, which suited his purpose admirably; second, he kept his guns in exceptional order and concentrated them in the right positions; and, third, he made his final attack at a vital time. Had he waited till nightfall, as he had originally intended, it is possible that the nawab would have had time to regroup. But the most important decision came before the battle. By crossing the river Clive forced a pitched battle from entrenched positions. Unsure about Mir Jaffir's intentions, Clive still crossed over to Plassey and sealed the fate of India for the next 200 years. If Mir Jaffir had attacked Clive's right flank, Clive could have lost at Plassey. If Clive had not crossed the river, there would have been no battle.

Following the battle, Siraj was hunted down and expediently murdered on the initiative of Miran, Mir Jaffir's son, despite the orders of both Jaffir and Clive that Siraj's life should be spared. Mir Jaffir was created nawab. Omichand, the duplicitous merchant, was informed that the treaty he had signed was not genuine. His influence faded away. Clive now emerged as the real power-broker in Bengal. The new nawab signed a treaty with Clive which restored the Calcutta merchants to their original position and compensated them for their losses. Clive and the select committee all received vast sums of money from the treasury of Mir Jaffir. It was this gift that caused Clive his difficulties with the House of Commons in later years. He recalled it being worth about £160,000 and had few scruples about taking the money, which he saw as part of his due salary. The Company paid its employees virtually nothing, and expected them to take advantage of whatever they could make while in India.

The French presented the final problem in Bengal. Once they were dealt with, the British would be masters of a vast region of eastern India. After an epic march involving mutiny, rebellion and liberal use of the cat o' nine tails among his own troops, Eyre Coote chased the French into Oudh, where British troops would be neither welcome nor successful. Clive was now master of Bengal and the surrounding district, in an unassailable position controlling a vast area made up of modern-day Bengal, Orissa and Bihar. Mir Jaffir could do little to reverse this situation, further enhanced by the Moghul emperor's recognition of Clive as an *orma* or imperial councillor. Over the following four years, Clive would continue to rule Bengal as his own fiefdom. He kept Mir Jaffir in power and crushed rebellions against the aged nawab, although Jaffir did forget his place, eventually asking the Dutch to help him expel the British. Clive did not, however, appear to hold any grudge and was furious when, while he was away in London, Jaffir was deposed. Neither did he neglect Madras, sending troops under Colonel Forde to assist the struggle against the French, who were short of money and had severely weakened themselves by recalling to Paris de Bussy, the only Frenchman who understood the Carnatic. They were soon neutralised, and Lally's quest to control south India swiftly fell away.*

Plassey is a decisive battle for several reasons. Clive's campaign neutralised the French in Bengal. It created a legend around Clive

---

* Thomas Arthur, comte de Lally and baron de Tollendal, was a French general, son of Sir Gerald O'Lally, an Irish Jacobite married to a French lady of noble birth. The younger Lally served in the war against Austria, was present at Dettingen, and commanded the famous (French) Irish brigade of Fontenoy. He was also involved in Jacobite plots, accompanying Charles Edward to Scotland. He later fought under Saxe in the Low Countries, and at Maastricht.

At the outbreak of war with England in 1756 he commanded – as lieutenant-general and commandant-general of the Compagnie des Indes – a French expedition to India, unsuccessfully on the whole, losing at Tanjore and Madras, and at Wandiwash to Sir Eyre Coote. He seems to have been a contentious officer, quarrelling with his peers such as Bussy and d'Aché, detested by both native and metropolitan other ranks. After capture at Pondicherry, he became a prisoner of war in England whence, accused of treachery by French enemies, he returned voluntarily to France for trial and sentence of death. His name was later vindicated in a determined campaign mounted by Voltaire.

His son escaped to England during the French Revolution and survived there, thanks to subsidies probably arranged by Burke.

and the British that they could win pitched battles with tiny numbers of troops. They were prepared to fight and expected to win. Victory created a solid base for expansion within India. By controlling Bengal, the British and the East India Company were able to consolidate, and then advance. All provincial leaders owed allegiance to the Moghul emperor but India was a very decentralised and fractured 'country', in certain regions of which the British could make advances, knowing that their actions would be approved by other local leaders. It sapped French morale in the south and freed troops from Bengal for use in the Carnatic.

Plassey marked the start of British control of India, the site of the birth of the British Empire in Asia. But in India, 200 years is not so long a time.

QUEBEC

Maritime war between England and France, like that between England and Spain, did not end with the Armada. Instead, it continued to take place on the oceans, Atlantic, Pacific and Indian, almost unaffected by governments, wherever financial or territorial gain was to be made by sailors and merchants. It ended, nevertheless, with the acquisition in 1763 at the Peace of Paris of vast Anglo-Saxon empires in the Americas and in Asia.

These triumphs were, of course, a direct consequence of France's decision to engage in land hostilities in Europe, initially to damage or destroy her ancient enemy, Austria, in a continental war, the Seven Years War, demanding vast resources of men and matériel. Not only did France fail in that undertaking, but the effort and expense enforced distraction from the real task, the construction of a maritime empire, otherwise within her capacity.

Certainly there was an Anglo-Saxon predominance of numbers in Canada and the English colonies in America, albeit not properly coordinated until William Pitt's arrival as secretary of state in 1757. (Nor was virtual exclusion from emigration to Canada of Huguenots, the most disciplined and hard working of the French, at all helpful to Paris's colonial policy.) But France, more than any other deficiency, most woundingly lacked concentration on the defence of her existing possessions on the Ohio and in the Deccan. She also lacked an adequate navy. When the time came for the Quebec campaign, the French Atlantic and Mediterranean fleets, which would otherwise have constituted at least fleets in being, had already been crippled, if not destroyed, by Hawke and Boscawen at the great naval battles of Quiberon Bay and Lagos.

Apart from British claims around Hudson Bay, the French of 'La Nouvelle France' owned much of America from the North Pole through the Rockies and the Alleghenies, along the Mississippi and Ohio rivers, via Louisiana, to Florida and Mexico. France's claim was her 'right of discovery and occupation'. England's, or Pitt's, was based on future conquest and settlement in farming and fishing communities, starting northward from the Thirteen Colonies, through the forests, over the mountain ranges, and along fast, wide rivers.

In 1755, Lieutenant-Colonel George Washington, then in British service, finding that the French had already built Fort Duquesne, today's Pittsburgh, constructed Fort Necessity at Great Meadows near the present Uniontown in Pennsylvania, before being forced by the French to capitulate. General Braddock, a beefy, red-faced officer, the new English commander-in-chief, with two English regiments, including gaolbirds, was killed in July at Monongahela with half his force of 1,850 men by French and (mainly) Indians.

This frightful action, fought on the English side by blue-coated Virginians and regulars in red coats, encumbered by howitzers, wagons, cannon, pack horses and cattle, was distinguished by the bravery and courage of the officers, in particular George Washington, and by the shameful flight of many of the local colonial soldiery. It was also marked by the tradecraft of the Indians which began – it was a lengthy business – the process of converting English tactics from conventional to guerrilla, resulting eventually in the formation of the Royal American Light Infantry, ancestors of today's Green Jackets. This change was accelerated by fear of the consequences of defeat: running the gauntlet of 'savages daubed in red, blue, black and brown, and armed with clubs'; blacking prisoners' bodies and burning them alive, at stakes, with fire-brands and red-hot irons, to the sound of their applauded screams.

In May 1756 the marquis de Montcalm, the new French commander-in-chief, brought reinforcements to Ticonderoga. In August 1756 he captured Oswego whence, in 1757, he took Fort William Henry. 'His' Indians massacred the garrison as it marched out under safe conduct, disobeying his direct order. In the same year, a British expedition to take Louisbourg on Cape Breton north of Halifax was abandoned, but the port was taken by Lord Amherst and Brigadier James Wolfe in 1758. Later that year a force including the Royal Americans took Fort Duquesne and Fort Frontenac, but the British under Abercrombie failed to seize Ticonderoga. The French remained there until July 1759 when Amherst captured it; Johnson took Fort Niagara for Britain, isolating Detroit and other French posts in the interior.

William Pitt in 1759 had ordered a triple offensive, up the Mohawk river to cut Canada off at Fort Niagara from the St Lawrence, from Ticonderoga under Jeffrey Amherst up the valley of Lake Champlain to Montreal, and an assault upstream from the north on the St Lawrence itself to Quebec. As commander of the third operation, Pitt appointed Wolfe in brevet rank of major-general, pay at £14 a week, under the overall command of Jeffrey Amherst, C-in-C in America. Wolfe selected the Hon. Robert Monckton and James Murray to serve as brigadiers under him and reluctantly accepted from Lord Ligonier, C-in-C of the army, a third, Hon. George Townshend, described by Horace Walpole as 'clever, unlikeable and maliciously witty. So far as wrong-headedness went, he is very proper for a hero.' On one occasion, when a shell took off a German officer's head, spraying the debris on Townshend's coat, the latter remarked – cleaning himself with a handkerchief – 'I never knew that Scheiger had so many brains.'

177

Wolfe had not been satisfied by the extent of the English victory at Louisbourg and had pressed, before returning briefly to England, for further operations in the Gulf of St Lawrence and the Bay of Fundy. (When told by the duke of Newcastle that Wolfe was mad, King George II replied only that 'I hope he will bite some others of my generals.') Wolfe, tall, thin, narrow in the shoulder, with receding chin and forehead, upturned nose, red hair in a queue, always sickly, presented an unusual figure for a military officer, albeit in scarlet frock coat and black tricorne hat. His career, when not in Canada, had been passed in the 'dirty and barbarous town' of Inverness, in Stirling, Flanders, Perth and Glasgow, seeing action at Dettingen, Rochefort, Culloden, earning high opinions of his ability as a fighting soldier and commander of men, 'most complete in his mastery over himself and over others'. He was, none the less, highly strung, fearless, ardent in his duties, impatient and unwilling to decentralise; a solitary.

On 17 February 1758 Wolfe's fleet sailed for Louisbourg, arriving there three months later, months – for the young general – of devastating seasickness. The fleet, led by Admiral Saunders (the naval commander), found Louisbourg harbour blocked by ice and had to sail on to Halifax. Admiral Holmes made for New York to take on board troops for the Quebec expedition, while Admiral Durell's squadron sailed for the mouth of the St Lawrence to intercept French reinforcements. The whole fleet consisted of twenty-two ships of the line, plus frigates, sloops and transports.

Pierre Rigaud, marquis de Vaudreuil, governor general of all French Canada, was facile, corrupt, egotistic, cowardly and indecisive. He shared, with extreme reluctance, military command of French forces in Canada with Louis, marquis de Montcalm, whom he distrusted as representative of that France which was neither colonial nor feudal, nor given to unquestioning acceptance of king and Church. But both Frances excluded Huguenots, as well as the harsh criticism and doctrines of Voltaire, from its Canadian settlements.

In boastful and grandiloquent terms, Rigaud spoke of his intentions: 'the zeal with which I am animated to the service of the King will be ardent and indefatigable . . . I will hold my ground even to annihilation'. His belief, that the main attack on Quebec would come from the south – Ticonderoga, the Ohio and Ontario – was diluted by a warning from Bougainville, Montcalm's ADC, that a great British fleet was on its way to attack Quebec from the north.

In the event, the only vessels immediately to appear were a fleet from France carrying supplies, for sale by the dishonest contractor Cadet at exorbitant prices to the wretched consumers, and at vast profit to Cadet and his masters, including Vaudreuil. The fleet arrived almost intact, Durell having reached Canada too late to catch more than three stragglers. Meanwhile, French and Canadian troops hurried north from Montreal under Montcalm and Vaudreuil, the latter pledging to 'fight the British with ardour and even fury', his council of officers pushing, shoving and elbowing, until Montcalm had to take individuals aside and seek their views in writing.

Five battalions from France, colonial troops and militia from all over Canada, and 1,000 Indians with scalping knives now filled Quebec. Montcalm dispersed his troops below the city of Quebec, his right on the St Charles river and his left on the Montmorency, entrenchments and redoubts extending all along the main river fronting the tents and huts of the white soldiers and the squalid wigwams of the *indigènes*. Vaudreuil's headquarters were sited mid-way between the St Charles and the Beauport stream, to the west of Montcalm's HQ, the latter in a largish stone house. A bridge of boats crossed the St Charles about a mile from the St Lawrence, forming the main link between the city and the army. The river mouth was guarded by a boom and by two hulks armed with cannon.

The gates of the city itself, except the Palace Gate to the bridge, were barricaded, and over 100 guns were mounted on the walls. Gunboats, a floating battery and fire ships constituted the water-borne defences, manned by the crews of 'Cadet's ships' moored downstream. About 14,000 men – not including Indians – were billeted above the shoals of Beauport. With the city's garrison of about 2,000, the total force available to the French was some 16,000 men of all arms, to the eventual 9,000 commanded by Wolfe.

Weeks passed before the main English fleet came up the traverse between Cape Tourmente and the island of Orléans. By the time of their arrival, food ashore had become scarce, meat rationed to two ounces a day, except to Cadet, Vaudreuil and others of the *gratin*. Three captured British midshipmen increased apprehension by 'grossly exaggerating the English force'.

Pilots for this river, parts of which were said to be very dangerous, had been acquired by a British ruse. The French flag had been hoisted in one of Durell's ships, to be lowered – and the red cross flag of St George raised – only when the pilots had been gulled into believing that the vessel towards which they had rowed was French. A priest watching dropped dead from shock. One British captain, an old salt named Killick, who 'despised the entire Gallic race', would not tolerate the pilot allocated to him. Studying the ripple and colour of the water, distinguishing rocks from sand, mud and gravel: 'Damn me if there are not a thousand places in the Thames fifty times more hazardous than this,' grunted the genial Killick.

On 26 June the entire British fleet moored in perfect safety off the island of Orléans, a few miles from Quebec. 'The enemy passed sixty ships of war, where we [the French] hardly dared risk a vessel of a hundred tons,' possibly because Vaudreuil had neglected to site cannon on the mountainside. 'Here we are,' said Captain Knox, 'entertained with a most agreeable prospect . . . windmills, churches, watermills, chapels and compact farm-houses . . . the land well cultivated and sown with flax, wheat, barley and peas.' Above the city rose the palaces, barracks, mansions, hospitals, churches, the cathedral, convents and fortifications of Quebec, an inviting if intimidating goal.

The first British troops, forty New England Rangers, landed on the island of Orléans, followed by Wolfe and the main army. The general could now see the task ahead: Quebec, the natural fortress covered by earthworks 'at the brink of abrupt and lofty heights', the St Lawrence walled in by difficult, if not inaccessible 'steeps' which could each be defended by very small numbers. Bougainville had already claimed that the city could be held by only 3–4,000 men and there were 16,000 actually in place. Against this impregnable bastion, unless Amherst got to Ticonderoga and beyond to take the French from the south, it seemed that Montcalm had only to hold his position until winter came, or supplies for Wolfe ran out.

A brief but violent storm failed to destroy the fleet, and an attack by a squadron of French fire ships failed because the commander set fire to his vessel thirty minutes too soon. The bombs, grenades and fully laden cannon hideously exploded, but without damage to the British, whose intrepid sailors grappled the ships and stranded them, as the Spanish had done with the English fire ships in the Channel nearly 200 years earlier. It was 'the grandest fireworks that can possibly be conceived', but Montcalm had been right in foreseeing earlier that they 'would be good for nothing after all'.

Montcalm continued to avoid battle. Wolfe did not have that option. Instead, he sent Monckton's brigade to the island, taking possession of Point Levi next day, entrenching opposite Beauport. Next he installed batteries of cannon which, although they could not take the city, encouraged the troops by the destruction they wrought. As he could not launch a frontal attack on the French across the Beauport shoals, on 8 July he bombarded Lévis' militia above the Montmorency cataract before landing 3,000 men from Murray's and Townshend's brigades just below the waterfall, scaling the heights in order to take the enemy behind or in the flank, from the forest. If the French under Lévis had attacked them here in strength, the fate of the English would have been in doubt: 'a Canadian in the woods is worth three disciplined soldiers, as a soldier in a plain is worth three Canadians'.

Wolfe thus had time to fortify his position. But he still could not take the offensive. Nor, still, would Montcalm. When urged to do so, he replied: 'Let him amuse himself where he is. If we drive him off, he may go to some place where he can do us harm.' In the meanwhile, the cannon roared out from Montmorency in its forested gorge, across the vast misty waterfall, and from Point Levi across the basin, accompanied by ship-to-shore artillery duels between floating batteries. Ashore, skirmishing took place between Indians – or Canadians painted like Indians – with feathers on their heads and British Rangers as skilled and brutal as their foe. The inhabitants began to desert the wounded city and its pillaged houses, more and faster, as rumours spread of the British advance to Ticonderoga and Niagara. Only fear of Indian reprisal now kept the French Canadian colonists in their homes.

On 18 July, under cover of cannon from Point Levi, the *Sutherland*, a frigate, and some small ships reached the river above Quebec outfacing the town's batteries. News was also received in the city that the British had embarked troops above town in boats which they had dragged from Point Levi, presenting a new threat to the French, who were thus required to weaken existing defences and strengthen their precipices by a further 1,000 men. Two days later, Colonel Carleton with 600 men landed from rowed boats at Pointe-aux-Trembles, eighteen miles upstream on the north shore. On 20 July Vaudreuil mounted another, larger fire-ship attack on the British, similarly repelled by the seamen, who towed the blazing vessels ashore. 'Damme, Jack,' said one sailor to another as the grenades, muskets and swivel guns burst into flame and smoke around them, 'didst thee ever take hell in tow before?' A hellish fleet indeed: seventy rafts, boats and schooners.

Montcalm would not fight on Wolfe's terms. The heights from Cap-Rouge to Beauport were impregnably manned. Wolfe, however, believed in the gallantry of his men, and held nothing but contempt for the French Canadian militia. But to ensure the safety of Montmorency and Point Levi, he could command no more than 5,000 men with whom to take a strand defended by French redoubts with cannon at the foot of the cataract leading to the heights. And he had not seen that these redoubts were commanded by musketry from above.

On 31 July the British bombardment of the redoubts began, from two armed transports of fourteen guns, the sixty-four-gun *Centurion*, batteries across the Montmorency and the cannon of Point Levi toward the high cliffs of the St Lawrence. These salvos were preparatory to a landing at the redoubts which would, Wolfe hoped, force the French to defend them in the open or, at least, enable a British reconnaissance and successful assault.

The craft bearing the landing parties moved to and fro between Beauport and Montmorency in attempts at deception, finally going ashore at low tide, where the river had left the mud bare. The grenadiers and Royal Americans led, drenched in the warm day by a gathering summer storm, Monckton's brigade close behind. At that point, without waiting for Monckton or for further orders, the grenadiers rushed the redoubts at the foot of the cataract. Under terrible crossfire from massed musketry high at the top of the hill, they fell, dead, wounded or unable to master the slippery grass. ('We could not see halfway down the hill,' said Johnstone, a renegade Jacobite Scot who had defected to Montcalm.) Howling and whooping, the Indians hurtled down the greasy slope, tomahawks and scalping knives in hand, to dispose of over 400 dead and dying grenadiers and Royal Americans.

Wolfe was horrified by this disaster. On the following day, he rebuked his grenadiers for their impetuous indiscipline: 'You could not suppose that you could beat the French alone.' A colonel, eight captains, twenty-one lieutenants and three ensigns were lost, some to unspeakable deaths, along with 410 other ranks. The French were delighted. Vaudreuil wrote to Montreal: 'I have no more anxiety about Quebec. M. Wolfe, I can assure you, will make no progress. Deserters say that he will try us again in a few days. Trial is what we want.' He thought, as perhaps did Montcalm, that the English had been mad, and would be mad again. They hoped so; or, perhaps, those did who did not think that the English might just go away.

In August Wolfe spent time sacking and burning Canadian settlements in reprisal for widespread scalping of sentries, his actions aimed at exhausting the colony and causing the militia to desert. Montcalm would not respond. British ships were now sent upstream above the town in increasing numbers, where they formed a squadron under Admiral Holmes, joined by 1,200 troops under Brigadier Murray, who conducted three rather unsuccessful raids at Pointe-aux-Trembles and elsewhere. Dysentery and fever had broken out. Desertion spread in the French camp, where Bougainville monitored the river westward from Beauport, at the rate of 200 Canadians a night. Supplies were running short; the bombardment of Quebec had caused serious damage. Ticonderoga and Niagara had fallen to British arms, although Amherst was not making progress towards Montreal.

Wolfe became very ill with a high fever. After consulting his brigadiers, and somewhat recovering on 31 August, he left his house for the first time since the sickness began. Before doing so, he had written to his mother, whom he loved, and to Pitt. To the latter, he declared his intention of conveying above the town a corps of 4–500 men, 3,600 in ships off Cap Rouge, 'to draw the enemy from their present situation and bring them to an action'. He knew now that there was no longer hope of reinforcement by Amherst. He knew also that his own disease had taken hold irrevocably.

To Admiral Saunders, who was anxious to get his fleet out of the St Lawrence before winter descended, Wolfe was able directly to indicate that a place had been found where the heights could successfully be scaled by 150 men, followed by what remained of his weakened army, now lacking 850 killed, wounded or missing. Saunders agreed 'to await the result; and the force, Monckton and Townshend's battalions after evacuating Montmorency and Point

Levi, was joined in Holmes' vessels upstream by Murray's battalion, having marched up the Etchemin River under fire from Silbery'. Vaudreuil believed that these movements indicated imminent *departure*: 'Everything proves that the grand design of the English has failed.'

Bougainville's force above Quebec was raised to 3,000 men, ordered to follow Holmes's movements on the river. Even Montcalm believed the heights were inaccessible. 'We need not suppose that the enemy has wings,' pointing precisely at the spot where Wolfe was to land. 'I swear to you that a hundred men posted there would stop their whole army.'

Those hundred men, at the Anse du Foulon, a mile and a half from Quebec, and similar detachments with cannon at Sarnes and Sillery, were indeed there. However, a British officer, Stobo, escaped from French custody and, familiar with the landscape, indicated to the general a landing place from which led a path up a forested cliff. At the top were only ten or twelve tents, which Wolfe believed could soon be taken. Their commanding officer, Vergor, had already been court-martialled for misconduct and cowardice. Certainly his subsequent behaviour indicates gross incompetence, an unwilling spirit or even French treachery.

Another day was spent sailing up and down the river to Cap Rouge and back, red coats prominent on deck, in a further deception operation, to which Admiral Saunders added his own in the Basin of Quebec, bombarding Beauport and constantly lowering boats loaded with troops. Montcalm *was* deceived, believing that the main attack would be directed below and not above the city.

At Cap Rouge, in the darkness, 1,700 men boarded the British landing boats which, at the ebb, went downriver under the guise of French provision boats, due to make the routine voyage that night. Challenged twice by sentries, the boats passed safely, without – since the posts thought them French supplies – being asked the night's password. To add to British good fortune, Vergor on the heights had let most of his men go home for the harvest, himself keeping only a careless watch, before going to bed. The Guienne battalion, furthermore, had not left its encampment on the St Charles for its designated post on the Plains of Abraham.

Wolfe in *Sutherland*, accompanied by his old school friend, the great John Jervis, later Earl St Vincent, victor of the eponymous battle in 1797 when Nelson himself boarded two enemy ships, had said that he expected to die fighting next day. He gave Jervis a miniature of Miss Lowther, the woman to whom he had become engaged. In the boats, he recited Gray's *Elegy* to his officers, including the line: 'The paths of glory lead but to the grave,' on which he observed: 'Gentlemen, I would rather have written these lines than take Quebec.' Christopher Hibbert alleged, in *Wolfe at Quebec*, that Wolfe's companions had been embarrassed.

The advance party, twenty-four volunteers, followed by a larger body, reached the top of the path without hindrance, stormed the tents, captured or routed the little garrison and shot Vergor in the heel before taking him prisoner as he jumped out of bed. Wolfe, down below, heard the cheering over the tide, the falling water of a little brook and the heavy footsteps of the climbers. The main body in their scarlet now moved up the track to the plateau, detaching parties en route to silence the guns at Sillery and Samos.

Colonel Burton's 1,200 from Point Levi had joined the assault force, now totalling 4,800, to drag themselves up the heights, muskets slung, hauling themselves on by shrubs and trees. 'You can try it,' said the ailing Wolfe to a nearby officer, 'but I don't think you'll get up.' Both of them did. At the top, his army drew up on the mile-wide Plains of Abraham – named for a pilot of that name who had owned land there – a mile from Quebec. The order of battle consisted of grenadiers and six battalions, three ranks deep, in a front line of 3,500 men, under Wolfe, Monckton and Murray. Colonel Burton, commanding Webb's regiment, took the reserve, the Royal Americans guarding the landing at Anse du Foulon, Howe's light infantry in woods to the rear. To the left, to avoid outflanking, Townshend's two battalions stood at right angles, facing the St Charles.

Quebec was invisible, hidden behind a ridge on which suddenly appeared the Guiennes in their white uniforms with coloured facings. To the rear, two miles away opposite Vaudreuil's HQ, Montcalm riding with his ADC saw red coats. 'This is a serious business,' he said, ordering Johnstone to bring up troops, and rode off without a word, mouth set, towards the confrontation. In front of him rose the long scarlet line of Wolfe's regulars, 'a silent wall of red', then the kilted Highlanders and the wild skirl of the pipes beginning. No troops came to help Montcalm from the left, Vaudreuil preferring to cover the Beauport shoals, where in fact no English ever came. Nor were all twenty-five guns requested sent forward by the garrison, the commander despatching only three. Nor did the general contact Bougainville to the west, with whom a coordinated attack against both the English front and rear could have been mounted if, indeed, battle had to be joined at all.

But because he believed that Wolfe could block all his supplies from Montreal and the south, and perhaps because his men could no longer be easily restrained, Montcalm at last *had* to do battle. 'He rode a black or dark bay horse, brandishing his sword as if to excite us to do our duty. He wore a coat with wide sleeves, which fell back as he raised his arm, and showed the white lines of his wrist band.' Behind him his army had poured through the narrow streets of Quebec, the regulars of France in white and blue, Indians in war paint, the steady, unwarlike Canadians, storming out on to the plain through the city gates.

French snipers fired from the shelter of trees, bushes and houses. The garrison's three guns with canister-shot did damage in the front line of Wolfe's regulars. British light infantry, thrown out before the lines, reduced the sharpshooters' accuracy in violent skirmishes, while the main French body on the ridge, regulars and Canadians, came forward in broken order under fire from British field guns. The infantry held their fire until the French advance was within forty paces, when the first devastating volley sounded to the French like cannon-shot, quickly succeeded by another and then by 'furious clattering fire that lasted but a minute or two'.

British fire was remarkably accurate. 'When the smoke rose, a miserable sight was revealed: the ground cumbered with dead and wounded, the advancing masses stopped short and turned into a frantic mob, shouting, cursing, gesticulating', fleeing for refuge.

Wolfe's troops moved into the charge, either with the bayonet or firing and reloading as they advanced, the Highlanders wielding broadswords, still continually under musket fire from the sharp-shooters concealed in cornfields, behind bushes or on the grassy plain.

During the charge Wolfe was hit three times. At the third shot, he staggered and fell. Four men carried him to the rear in their arms. He ordered them to put him down. They did so. He told them that there was no need for a surgeon: 'It's all over with me.' When he had learned that the enemy were in full retreat, he cried: 'Tell Colonel Burton to cut off their flight at the bridge on the River Charles with Webb's regiment.' Turning on his side, he murmured: 'Now God be praised, I will die in peace,' and so he did, this lonely man.

After the battle, a sergeant of the 58th asked rhetorically: 'How could this [victory] be otherwise, being at the heels of gentlemen whose whole thirst, equal with their General, was for glory? We had seen them tried and always found them sterling. We knew that they would stand by us to the last extremity.'

Montcalm, fleeing towards the sanctuary of Quebec among his beaten troops, was shot through the body, then propped up on his horse and led through the St Louis Gate. A woman seeing him called, 'O mon Dieu! Mon Dieu! Le Marquis est tué.' 'Ce n'est rien, ce n'est rien,' replied this brave officer. 'Ne vous affligez pas pour moi, mes bonnes amies.' He died that night, without seeing again the house and family in France for which he longed continually.

Quebec capitulated in mid-September. The British expedition returned home, leaving only a garrison to survive the long, icy winter of disease and hunger. In April 1760, General Lévis, the best of Montcalm's subordinates, put the city under siege after a fierce and bloody engagement with Brigadier James Murray's troops. The siege was lifted in May by the arrival in the basin of *Lowestoft, Diana* and *Vanguard*. Lévis retreated to Montreal with a force diminished by desertion, pursued by Amherst with 11,000 men, Haviland with 3,000 from the south, and Murray's garrison, reduced from 7,000 to 2,500 through illness and war.

On 8 September Vaudreuil signed the surrender which brought a final end to French dominion in Canada.

Little was left by the nineteenth century to France in America except St Pierre and Miquelon on the Newfoundland coast, 'two rocks . . . for drying her cod fish' contemptuously awarded by the Treaty of Paris. Her navy, creature of the great Colbert, had been reduced to forty ships. In the east, Pondicherry was left as her best settlement in the subcontinent; her imperial dreams, after Plassey, quite dissolved. France's failure in the field even hastened and confirmed the destruction of the French monarchy itself.

'New France' died on the Plains of Abraham and in the steaming heat of the Carnatic. The British Empire of the west and east was born.

'All that France lost, England had won. Almost undisputed on the high seas, ruler of vast Empires in east and west, possessor of a flourishing agriculture and manufacturing base, dominant in commerce and finance, yet soon to be challenged at the height of her power by colonies exploiting in America the very absence of France to bring about England's Nemesis, the United States of America.'

SYNOPSIS OF EVENTS BETWEEN
QUEBEC AND YORKTOWN

Between 1756 and 1763, the Seven Years War set Prussia against Austria, France and Russia. England, under Chatham, opposed France and Spain. At the Treaty of Paris in 1763 cessions and acquisitions by and to France, England, Spain and Portugal were awarded.

In America General Burgoyne's army surrendered at Saratoga, bringing vengeful France into alliance with the colonists, joined by Holland and a league of neutral northern powers, including Russia under Catherine the Great, ready to strike at Britain on the oceans.

CHAPTER THIRTEEN

YORKTOWN, 1781

Skirmishes in 1775 between British troops under General Thomas Gage and local militias – including Minutemen – at Concord and Lexington, led to a massive increase, of 15,000 men, in armed support for revolution. At Lexington, Major John Pitcairn had called, 'Lay down your arms, you damned rebels and disperse': the rebel, Captain John Parker, cried: 'If they mean war, let it begin here.' Then the fatal shot rang out 'heard around the world'. At first, the Americans blockaded the British who had retreated to Boston after Concord. But at the battle of Bunker Hill the rebels lost half of their force. Although they were defeated there, their ammunition exhausted, General Sir William Howe – soon to succeed Gage as C-in-C – commented that the success had been 'too dearly bought'.

More troops were therefore brought from Europe to serve under Howe, 'Handsome Jack' Burgoyne and Henry Clinton. Meanwhile, the remarkable Benedict Arnold, later to defect spectacularly from the revolutionary to the colonial cause, in May seized Ticonderoga for the rebels with Ethan Allen's Green Mountain Boys, then Crown Point, St Johns and Montreal. Betrayed by a captured letter, he was defeated at the approaches to Quebec by General Sir Guy Carleton, the British commander in Canada, once with Wolfe at the taking of that city.

George Washington's arrival south of Boston obliged Howe to move his army of 9,000 men to Halifax, returning to New York in July 1776, defeating the Americans at Long Island in August. The rebel army, pursued by Lord Cornwallis, retreated to the Delaware. At Trenton, on Boxing Day, despite fever and sickness among his soldiers, General Washington captured 900 out of 1,300 Hessian mercenaries at the Old Barracks. On New Year's Day 1777 he secured another victory, at Princeton, both battles fought in snow and ice. Lord Germaine, secretary of state for war in London, generally despised for his incompetent, even pusillanimous behaviour at Minden, observed: 'all our hopes were blasted by the unhappy affair at Trenton', while sedulously not mentioning the improvement in *American* morale.

Jefferson's Declaration of Independence, read in July to the assembled army, made plain to every officer and soldier that 'now the peace and safety of our country depend, under God, solely on the success of our arms'. The rebellion had become a war, which divided colonists into loyalists, known as Tories, and 'patriots' or Whigs, possibly predominant in the country as a whole.

Germaine's incompetence permitted him to forget to sign orders instructing General Howe to march north on Albany. There he was to meet Burgoyne coming down from Canada with a planned 7,700 men, and take him under command. Howe himself, then discovering that he was to receive only 2,900 out of 13,000 reinforcements expected from England, 'relinquished the idea of all the expeditions, except that to the southward and a diversion occasionally up Hudson's River'. Muddle ensued.

British strategy, given these and other lacunae, had been for Burgoyne to invade from Canada to Albany, where he would be joined by Howe, opening the link to New York. Clinton would hold that city, keep Washington's army in check and cover Philadelphia. Lieutenant-Colonel Barry St Leger would move down the Mohawk with a mixed British and Indian force of some 2,000 men to join Burgoyne. But having won a small engagement at Oriskany, St Leger was deceived by Benedict Arnold into thinking that an overwhelming American force was upon him, whereupon his Indians broke and ran.

In September Howe and Cornwallis brought Washington to action at Chadd's Ford on Brandywine Creek among the red leaves of that autumn, turning the American flank as Howe had done at Long Island, 300 Americans killed and 400 taken. The twenty-year-old marquis de Lafayette, just appointed by Washington to a major-general's command, was wounded by a musket ball until 'the blood ran out of the top of his boot', a severe setback at so early a stage of the Frenchman's military career.

After Long Island, a British officer had recorded that 'the Heart of the Rebellion is now nearly broken'. Even Washington thought that, without more men, 'the game will be pretty well up'. Trenton and Princeton had gone some way to dispelling the judgement; but Brandywine and Germantown, which was fought in thick fog, drove the 'whipped Continental army, barefoot and otherwise naked' to Valley Forge. In the vicious cold, a New Englander complained to his diary: 'It snows, I'm sick, eat nothing, no whisky, no forage – Lord – Lord – Lord.' Here, nevertheless, to offset Howe's seizure of Philadelphia by Christmas 1777, a former Prussian general, Baron von Steuben, introduced the raw Americans to drill and discipline over the biting winter, defeating typhus, hunger, smallpox and desertion.

By March 1778, Washington observed that 'our prospects begin to brighten'. In the most hopeful movement of the war, the French government had recognised the independence of the United States, brought about war between Britain and France and also Anglo-Spanish and Anglo-Dutch hostilities. These were the real consequences of the capitulation of Saratoga and Gilbert Lafayette, on hearing of independence, kissed Washington – to his embarrassment – on both cheeks.

In that campaign, Burgoyne's advance from Canada had been plagued by leaks of his plans and intentions, by crippling shortages of transport (carts and horses) and of supply in the primitive country in which – rather than down the lake – he had chosen to move. His opponents, furthermore, were most familiar with the forests, swamps and mountains and were, besides, brilliant marksmen. Since he elected to press straight through 'nearly trackless wilderness' as Fuller described it, in country broken by creek and marsh, these were serious, ultimately fatal difficulties.

His first defeat, at Bennington, was from John Stark, a New Hampshire man, who led the charge against Burgoyne's Colonel Baum and the Brunswickers, shouting: 'We will gain the victory or Molly Stark shall be a widow tonight.' Stark lost only 70 men, Baum 600, the former rewarded by New Hampshire with 'a new suit of cloathes and a piece of linen'.

It was in the same month, August 1777, that Burgoyne first heard from Howe in New York that the general intended to go to Pennsylvania. 'I little foresaw', said Burgoyne, 'that I was to be left to pursue my way through such a tract of country, and hosts of foes, without any cooperation from New York.' (Two days later, the unfortunate Colonel St Leger had had to raise the siege of Fort Stanwix and retreat to Oswego.) But, at that stage, Burgoyne still thought that he would eventually meet Howe, at least at Albany, if not sooner on the Hudson.

Near Saratoga, Burgoyne now sought to break round Bemis Heights at Stillwater which, fortified by a Polish engineer named Kosciusko, was held by Horatio Gates, a costive officer whose army, nevertheless, included Benedict Arnold. General Gates's inaction led Arnold to gallop off, yelling: 'By God, I'll soon put an end to it.' ('Dark skinned, black hair, middling height: no waste of timber in him, he was our fighting general and a bloody fellow he was . . . it was "Come on boys" – it wasn't "go, Boys" – as brave a man as ever lived.') Arnold took the pressure off Brigadier Learned's contingent, and off Colonel Dan Morgan's riflemen. For four hours the battle ebbed and flowed between the Americans (with many sharpshooters in the high timber) and the British infantry and artillery. Gates sent in no reinforcements and, had it not been for Arnold, Burgoyne would have surely one day soon taken Albany.

Gates sacked Arnold notwithstanding. But Arnold, against orders, led Morgan's riflemen against the nearby Freeman's Farm, and stormed the redoubts there of both Colonel Breyman and Lord Balcarres, leading Learned's brigade as well, before being himself wounded. Their own guns had saved the British from total disaster, but it was Arnold who saved Gates and the American defence.

Burgoyne now heard that Sugar Hill near Ticonderoga had been taken by the enemy, and all his supplies on Lake Champlain seized. Clinton could not reach him in time to save his battered men. Howe would not come. Burgoyne's losses were heavy, compared with the Americans', his position overlooked by the enemy. His men were in remarkably good heart but he had no alternative to withdrawal, abandoning all transport and guns that night. It was too late for anything but surrender. Gates granted his army 'a free passage to Great Britain on condition of not serving again in North America during the present contest', a condition which Congress, with Washington's connivance, disgracefully repudiated. Nothing was left to Britain except Philadelphia, a city without outstanding strategic significance. And the surrender led directly to France's entry into the war on America's side; and to Britain's final defeat at Yorktown in October 1781.

In June 1778 Howe was succeeded by Clinton, who evacuated Philadelphia and made for New York, engaging with Washington en route in a long, hot, inconclusive battle at Monmouth Court House. Here, one American corps under Charles Lee bolted. More men died of heatstroke than from their wounds. A water carrier, a 'Molly Pitcher', earned immortality by acting as a loader after her husband had fallen. Washington dispersed his army around New York.

The French admiral, comte d'Estaing, with twelve ships of the line, four frigates and several smaller vessels, confronted a numerically inferior British squadron under Admiral Lord Howe off the Delaware until gales scattered and damaged both fleets, forcing Howe to put into New York for repairs. D'Estaing eventually sailed for Martinique after a short visit to Boston where, incidentally, the first Catholic mass to be held in that city was celebrated.

Lord Germaine now proposed conquest of Florida and Georgia, followed by North and South Carolina, before tackling Virginia and Maryland, in the ultimate expectation of isolating the northern rebel colonies. He anticipated strong initial support from loyalists, and, indeed, Lieutenant-Colonel Archibald Campbell took Savannah on 29 December 1778, a city whose town plan under Colonel Oglethorpe was based on Kubilai Khan's town plan for Beijing. General Lincoln's rebels were beaten by General Benjamin Prevost in March 1779: all Georgia was lost by the end of that month, heat thereafter preventing further operations in South Carolina or Georgia between May and September 1779. In October, 6,000 troops under General Lincoln, Admiral d'Estaing, and in the Polish Legion, were defeated in an attempt to retake Savannah.

On Boxing Day 1779 Clinton and Lord Cornwallis had left for Charleston with 8,500 men escorted by Admiral Arbuthnot's five ships of the line: the weather was so bad that one of the ninety transports ended up on the Cornish coast! On 12 May 1780 after a bombardment lasting forty-five days, Clinton took the city, the commander surrendering in order to 'to spare civilians'. Cornwallis refused to let the garrison march out with colours flying. The Stars and Stripes were cased and the rebels left to 'the Turks' march'. In this, the most severe American defeat of the war, nearly 300 officers and 6,000 men were captured.

In 1780 Clinton returned to New York in force, leaving Cornwallis behind with some 8,000 men. Horatio Gates took over all patriot forces in the south: these troops, meanwhile, had been seriously weakened by the consequences of eating green corn. In a rare show of aggression, he put his incommoded army into action at Camden against Cornwallis's infantry who, although badly affected by the heat, seized Gates's guns and stores and, in repeated bayonet charges, put the rebels to rout. Gates fled to Charlotte, where he was succeeded by General Nathaniel Greene, required to fight a war with only 2,300 men, of whom hardly half were actually present and fewer still properly equipped or physically fit. 'Wretched beyond description', observed Greene.

Cornwallis moved to Charlotte. General Leslie and 3,000 men were despatched by General Clinton to the Chesapeake under his (the C-in-C's) command. In North Carolina, Cornwallis had little difficulty with the militia until Major Patrick Ferguson, commanding 1,000 Tories near the Blue Ridge Mountains, issued a challenge to the 'over mountain men' to disband, or he would 'march his army over the mountains, hang their leaders and lay the country waste with fire and sword'.

That was a mistake. The rebels pursued 'Bulldog' Ferguson up the high peak where he had established his men. From this eminence he mounted both musket volleys and bayonet charges against the guerrillas hidden in the farmland and the forests below. The Americans, however, equipped with superior rifles and precise marksmanship, killed, captured or wounded almost every loyalist, while Ferguson in the saddle was shot seven times. This battle, at King's Mountain, restored American morale, providing the south – since the British went on the defensive – with time to regroup. Cornwallis retired to Winnsborough, where, if need arose, Leslie could join him only by sea.

America in September was shocked by the capture of the British major John André, Clinton's contact with Benedict Arnold, in shabby civilian clothes. Arnold, now commanding at West Point after his demotion by Gates, was secretly working for the British and currently negotiating terms (£6,315) for joining the British army as a brigadier. André, a 'Tory dandy', was found on capture with the plans of West Point, which bastion, under Arnold, controlled the Hudson valley. Arnold escaped on the British sloop *Vulture* for service under the crown and retirement in London, while André was executed as a spy. On the other side, patriots, led by Benjamin Tallmadge, a Yale classmate of Nathan Hale hanged as a spy by the British after Long Island, led a successful sabotage ring against British stores, Elijah Churchill the bizarre name of his sergeant.

Colonel Banastre ('Bloody') Tarleton, a dashing, red-haired cavalryman commanding the British Legion, hated for his supposed brutality, surprised rebels under the great guerrilla fighter Colonel Thomas Sumter at Fishing Creek, inflicting heavy casualties and taking 300 American prisoners. But in January 1781 Cornwallis made the error of dividing his forces, diminishing the effect of that victory by sending Tarleton to confront Colonel Dan Morgan at Cowpens, an American version of Cannae. Tarleton emerged from that defeat as one of its few British survivors, his Highlanders and green-uniformed dragoons almost wiped out by Morgan in a battle of mingled chance, brilliant planning and panic, combining in rebel victory.

In March 1781 Cornwallis and Greene then met at the battle of Guildford Court House on the Haw river. Greene's considerable numerical superiority was negated by the flight of his militiamen, although a giant in his army named Peter Francisco claimed to have killed eleven Redcoats by the sword. (In a painting of a later engagement now in Guildford Court House, he is portrayed as holding off, single-handed, nine dragoons on a field-gun carriage.) Cornwallis, outnumbered, entered the fight himself on a borrowed horse but, in this battle, before using grapeshot on the enemy, the British had suffered over 500 casualties. Greene wisely retired behind the Haw.

Clinton believed that Cornwallis's action had lost a fine army and, ultimately, 'an opulent and important province'. But Cornwallis considered that British control of both Carolinas depended on British dominance over 'the Old Dominion' (Virginia), whither he now moved, leaving Lord Rawdon to defeat Greene, which he did in the second battle of Camden. Greene, lying low after Camden, stubbornly said: 'We fight, get beat, rise and fight again.' Cornwallis at Wilmington in April marched over 200 miles to Petersburg to join Arnold, now in British service, and General Phillips, who died before Cornwallis could reach his destination.

Cornwallis was convinced that Virginia was the key, if not to total victory, at least to control of the Carolinas: Chesapeake, in his view, was the heart of the matter, worth even the abandonment of New York. In South Carolina, in the face of small, local actions, and of one large one, at Eutaw Springs where Greene once again suffered losses as heavy as Cornwallis's, the British took refuge in Charleston. Greene had won the southern war without winning a single battle.

Thanks to the victory at Saratoga, the sea power which eventually brought the triumph envisaged by Washington could now be provided, if only temporarily, by the French. The Americans, through Lafayette, had twice – in 1780 and 1781 – appealed to the comte de Rochambeau, to 'transfer the naval War [from European objectives in the Seven Years War] to America'. These appeals were the more frantic because of grave financial problems – Greene complained that his army was literally naked – and mutinies in Pennsylvania and New Jersey.

The British command, however, was divided in its objectives, Clinton seeking above all to hold New York in order to maintain Canada, and also to ensure that Cornwallis should not, by his advance on Virginia, prejudice the British position in South Carolina and Georgia. The chain of command, furthermore, between Germaine and Clinton in New York, and between Clinton and Cornwallis, was confused. And no one had much confidence in the naval commander, Admiral Arbuthnot, admittedly in a situation where letters took weeks, not days, to arrive.

Both Germaine and Cornwallis were determined on the Virginia policy precisely because success there would guarantee the security of the Carolinas, even if Britain had to yield New York and, by reducing 'the Southern Provinces, give the Death

Wound to the Rebellion', irrespective of French aid to the rebels. Although uninformed about British strategic aims, Washington had already decided in February to send Lafayette to Head of Elk River on Chesapeake Bay, at that time to deal with Arnold whose capture 'would be an event particularly agreeable'. Wayne and Steuben reinforced him there. Lafayette and Cornwallis began to circle one another until the British so badly bruised Lafayette's combined force at Green Springs as to induce Carleton, now in the south, to believe that, with persistence, Cornwallis could have destroyed its entire strength.

When, in mid-campaign, Lafayette returned to Paris after eighteen months in America, he was rapturously received over a seventeen-month period by crown and people alike. His wife gave him a son, he bought the King's Dragoons as 'his' own regiment, and took the most coveted woman at court as his mistress, before returning to his American allies in April 1780. Washington appointed him, since neither de Grasse nor de Rochambeau was Francophone, as his personal representative to those two worthies. Since he was only twenty-two, neither was flattered. But Lafayette pleased his American allies by paying out of his own pocket to dress his indigent Virginian levies. And when all was over, and the peace treaty signed, he exchanged his d'Hunolstein mistress for a new one, Madame de Simiane, the most beautiful woman in France, while naturally continuing to live with his wife, fortunately – since he had spent most of his money – a member of the de Noailles family.

In July Cornwallis decided to fortify two villages, small tobacco ports, on the York river, Yorktown and Gloucester, respectively comprising sixty and twenty houses. Lafayette informed Washington of these landings in a letter which reached the commander-in-chief on 6 August at White Plains, where he stood with four infantry regiments and the duc de Lauzun's legion under de Rochambeau.

In May 1781 Admiral the comte de Barras with a small squadron arrived at Newport, bearing good news – for the rebels

– that a much larger fleet under Admiral the comte de Grasse had left France, although chiefly for predatory action on trade in the Caribbean, rather than on the eastern shore.

For Britain, Admirals Rodney and Hood commanded a fleet of twenty-one ships on the Leeward Islands station, slightly inferior to de Grasse's twenty-eight of the line encountered off Port Royal in Martinique on 29 April and engaged, briefly, at long range. De Grasse avoided further bombardment. Rodney, unwell, sailed for England escorting 150 merchantmen, leaving fourteen of the line with Hood to back Graves's squadron of five off New York, on the completely false assumption that de Grasse himself was also going back to Europe, in convoy with French merchant ships. In fact, by 30 September de Grasse had sailed into Chesapeake Bay 'with all the sea and land forces he could assemble'.

This action had been preceded, indeed brought about, by General Washington's decision, transmitted to de Grasse via Lafayette and de Rochambeau, after failing adequately to raise numbers from the States, to drop his planned attack on Clinton's 16,000 in New York. Instead he prepared an assault on Virginia for which de Grasse's 3,000 troops were an essential addition to the 4,000 French and 2,000 Americans sent from King's Ferry on the Hudson in late August. All or most were to be carried down the bay in de Grasse's transports and landing craft to the Head of Elk. Three thousand Americans remained at West Point to divert Clinton and leave a screen facing him in New York. The main march south of the mixed Franco-American force was designed to persuade the British – at least until the force reached Philadelphia – that the final objective was not Virginia, but New York.

By 18 September all forces under Washington's command had arrived at the nearest landing points to Williamsburg, to join the outnumbered Lafayette.

Hood, after calling in Chesapeake Bay on 27 August, joined Admiral Graves off New York. The combined fleet sailed to intercept de Barras, who had just left Rhode Island and whom they therefore missed. On 5 September they sighted de Grasse's main fleet but, owing to Hood's 'pigheadedness', to both admirals' curious lack of initiative and to a series of signal errors close, major engagement was avoided, although casualties were high. After de Barras then joined de Grasse, the British made for New York. The conclusion is inevitable that had Nelson, St Vincent or any other maritime hero been present, the battle of the Chesapeake would have been a defeat for de Grasse, at least a reprieve for Cornwallis.

When the British learned of the French fleet's arrival ('The Comte de Grasse is within the Capes of Chesapeake'), Clinton sent Arnold to Groton and to New London, the latter which he bloodily and inexcusably ravaged. At the same time, the C-in-C promised Cornwallis a reinforcement of 4,000 men who, in the event, because of 'fleet repairs' did not sail for a further six weeks, when all had been lost. And all the while, Cornwallis, normally professional and energetic, lay inactive on the York river, attempting neither withdrawal to North Carolina nor to destroy Lafayette's vulnerable force from Richmond. Massive American and French superiority over his 7,000 men in Yorktown then supervened. Washington and Rochambeau's force counted, with 16,000 men, approximately the number who formed Clinton's strength far away in New York.

It can only be supposed that Lord Cornwallis was ignorant that sea power had effectively, on the eastern shore, overtaken the land power, on which attribute he seems also grotesquely ill-informed. Certainly Carleton always maintained that, before the arrival of the main force, there were enough boats and other craft available to make evacuation and a night crossing to Gloucester feasible, from which village the British could have cut their way out.

The first American cannonball at Yorktown, allegedly fired by Washington himself on 9 October, is said to have crashed into a house where the officers were sitting down to dinner, 'killing or wounding the one at the head of the table'. Thereafter the French and American artillery bombarded the little garrison incessantly for a full week, broken only by a cavalry engagement between Tarleton's men and the duc de Lauzun, Tarleton himself unhorsed and nearly captured. British casualties mounted to 100 a day.

On 16 October, when Cornwallis finally decided to make for tiny Gloucester across the river, a storm disrupted the boats, causing cancellation of the break-out. It was too late anyway: Redoubts 9 and 10 had yielded and a second siege line at point-blank range was ready next day. Cornwallis ordered a drummer boy in red coat and black tricorne to the parapet, to beat for parley. Three days later, as the British marched out, the band playing 'The World Turned Upside-down'.

Over 8,000 British soldiers surrendered, to end the war, to create the richest and most powerful nation on earth, to start the slow demise of the British Empire and Commonwealth, and to amputate its liveliest limb. The American Revolution sounded the tocsin for absolute monarchy, and pealed the latest bell for individual liberty, equality and democratic choice in government.

SYNOPSIS OF EVENTS BETWEEN
YORKTOWN AND TRAFALGAR

Victory for the colonists in the American War of Independence was followed in 1789 by the beginning of the French Revolution, the death of that monarchy and the defeat at Valmy by French Republican forces of the Prussian army. In 1794 at the battle of 1 June, Admiral Lord Howe defeated the French fleet. Also in 1794, Poland was partitioned, and the Crimea seized by Russia. In the immediately following years, against Napoleon's victories over Austria, English admirals Jervis and Duncan won the battles of Cape St Vincent and Camperdown (1797), and Nelson destroyed Napoleon's fleet at the Battle of the Nile (1798). Napoleon became first consul in 1799 and defeated the Austrians at Marengo in 1800.

The Peace of Amiens was signed in 1802 but, in 1805, Napoleon prepared to invade England. Austria and Russia renewed the war with France. At Austerlitz Napoleon repeated the victory of Marengo and defeated Prussia at Jena and Friedland.

CHAPTER FOURTEEN

TRAFALGAR, 1805

'Men adored him,' an ordinary sailor wrote of Nelson, 'and in fighting under him, every man thought himself sure of success.' Between him and his captains was complete trust which transmitted itself to the men, a combination of authority and love, which resulted in a permanent conviction that, however menacing the circumstances, victory would always lie with the British. 'You are, my Lord,' said one of his captains, 'surrounded by friends whom you inspire with confidence,' a confidence which at least comprehended *l'affaire* Hamilton and the flaw his behaviour to Lady Nelson revealed. A. L. Rowse said of him: 'I can never hear the name of Nelson without tears coming into my eyes – such genius, such courage, so transcendent a fate.'

Villeneuve, his chief opponent, was a sound professional officer. Because he believed in the principles of the French Revolution, he survived it when so many of his colleagues perished under the guillotine or suffered in exile, a few of them aristocrats but, for the most part, 'gentry', as in English wardrooms.

Villeneuve's record in battle, Ireland and the Nile, was uninspiring. There was no counterpart to the 'band of brothers' that surrounded Nelson. Villeneuve knew, and so did his captains, that the French, usually blockaded in their harbours at Brest, Toulon and Rochefort, with their Spanish allies at Cartagena, Ferrol, Vigo and Cadiz, could not match the British. Their own crews, brave enough, but with too high a proportion of landsmen, and delinquent landsmen at that, lacked adequate training as gunners or in seamanship, often prostrated by seasickness in the vital first days of their rare sorties from port. They *expected* defeat or, at least, unlike their enemy, did not assume every encounter would end in victory.

There is a sense, as David Howarth shows in his magnificent *Trafalgar*, that 'Trafalgar had been won before it was fought.' Napoleon Bonaparte had been encamped on the heights of Boulogne since 1797, with the Grande Armée, according to the French press, numbering up to 175,000 men and 2,000 transports large and small, intent upon the invasion of England. But successful seaborne assault obviously depended on protection by the French fleet during the traverse of the Channel, a consideration which the Board of Admiralty also understood: it was indeed the reason why some 50,000 men in the Royal Navy had already spent over two years in blockading the enemy in the Atlantic and the Mediterranean, precisely so that the combined allies should *not* enter the Channel without crippling loss.

For the British, the blockade had been marked by day after endless day of frustrating inaction, filled by the most intensive training, broken only by the rarest of shore visits – to the villages of the Maddalenas in Sardinia for the Mediterranean fleet, and to Plymouth in the vilest of weather – or battling rolling, mountainous seas off Ushant for the Brest squadron. Discomfort, homesickness, monotonous diet varied by judicious purchase through clandestine agents of vegetables and fruit from Sicily and Italy, meat sometimes, from Tangier and Tetuan, onions and fish. 'After twenty months off Toulon, there was only one man sick in *Victory*,' Howarth tells us, but we do not know how many withstood the gales and cold of the Bay of Biscay, or the heat in those wooden walls, damp, noisy, sunless gun decks, of the Mediterranean in mid-summer. 'The smell of tar, bilge water, sodden timber, rum, gun powder and closely packed bodies.'

Bernard Coleridge, eleven years old and besieging Brest, wrote to his father and mother:

The siege of Yorktown, 1781. This painting shows George Washington and the comte de Rochambeau giving orders to attack (*The Art Archive/Musée du Château de Versailles/Dagli Orti*)

The Battle of Trafalgar by Clarkson Stanfield. Nelson's victory led to Napoleon's eventual downfall (*The Art Archive/Institute of Directors/Eileen Tweedy*)

Opposite: 'Men adored him and, in fighting under him, every man thought himself sure of success': an ordinary sailor's view of Lord Nelson. This portrait was painted by F.H. Fuger c.1800 (*The Art Archive/Royal Naval Museum, Portsmouth*)

Ulysses S. Grant, commander-in-chief of Union forces in the American Civil War (*AKG London*)

General Robert E. Lee, commander-in-chief of the Confederate armies (*TRH/US National Archives*)

Below: A scene from the battle of Gettysburg, 1863, the point at which Union victory in the Civil War became assured (*Medford Historical Society Collection/Corbis*)

Columns of Russian prisoners face an uncertain future in the aftermath of the battle of Tannenberg, 1914 (*Robert Hunt Library*)

This photograph was taken in 1939, the year General Zhukov (centre) led the Russians to victory over Japan at Nomonhan (*Robert Hunt Library*)

Spitfires patrolling the south coast of England during the Battle of Britain. As a turning point in the Second World War, the RAF's defeat of the Luftwaffe prevented Nazi Germany's invasion of Britain (*Getty Images/Hulton Archive*)

British forces surrender to the Japanese in Singapore in February 1942, presaging the collapse of western colonialism (*Getty Images/Hulton Archive*)

US shipbuilding went into overdrive during the Second World War, an advantage the Americans were able to press home following the decisive battle of Midway Island in 1942. The photograph shows men in Portland, Oregon, at work on a 10,500-ton freighter, which was constructed in a record time of ten days (*Bettmann/Corbis*)

The Red Army's victory at the battle of Kursk in 1943 turned the tide of war in favour of the Soviet Union and the Allies. With considerable loss of life and matériel, the German defeat signalled the end of Hitler's ambitions in the east (*Novosti, London*)

Indeed we live on beef which has been ten or eleven years in corn and on biscuit which quite makes your throat cold in eating it owing to the maggots which are very cold when you eat them, like calves-foot jelly or blomonge being very fat indeed . . . We drink water the colour of the bark of a pear tree with plenty of little maggots and weevils in it and wine which is exactly like bullock's blood and sawdust mixed together. I hope I shall not learn to swear and by God's assistance I hope I shall not.

Bernard Coleridge was killed aged fourteen, when he fell out of the rigging.

Officers had privacy in their cabins, and could be rowed to dine with friends in sister ships during good weather and calm waters. The sailors were driven in on themselves and, anyway, had little to observe, except the changing contours of the sea. So there were few events to report in letters home, which could themselves take six months to complete the circle of despatch and reply. Few wrote letters anyway, so the ship became their home and their prison. Yet, at least in Nelson's command, although not all were 'happy ships', most were, even when manned by pressed and quota men, uneducated, often criminal, at best 'anti-socials'. Nelson had as much to do with relative content as did reforms following the Nore and Spithead mutinies, those rebellions the consequence not so much of harsh existing law and custom, but of *abuse* of law and custom by bad officers. 'Men felt they had a right to be commanded by gentlemen' who were, in turn, proud of their men.

On his birthday in Boulogne, after coronation in Paris, Bonaparte reviewed his army in the presence on land of the pope, and of a British squadron in the Channel, monitoring events ashore through minatory telescope. (St Vincent's earlier comment: 'I do not say they cannot come, I only say they cannot come by sea,' will be recalled.) His orders to Villeneuve were for the combined French and Spanish fleets to evade the British blockade, make for Martinique in the French West Indies, where up to fifty vessels were to harass British shipping and territory, before proceeding to Ushant, where the fleets would destroy Cornwallis's Brest squadron and cover Bonaparte's invasion fleet, 'avenging six centuries of British shame and insult'.

Although the strategy collapsed after Ganteaume, with twenty-one ships and captains from other ports, had failed to break the British blockades and join Villeneuve at Martinique, Napoleon did not then change his order to Villeneuve to defeat Cornwallis, releasing Ganteaume for the projected action off Boulogne.

Villeneuve, correctly assessing the impossibility of tackling Cornwallis outside Brest without Ganteaume, and after considering potentially lethal fleet action between his own inexperienced ships and Nelson, who had chased him to the Caribbean, decided to make for Europe. In July 1805 he was brought to battle by Sir Robert Calder off Finisterre, and after losing two Spanish men-of-war, made for Ferrol and Vigo. Knowing that the British in superior strength must be awaiting him at the entrance to the Channel, he now decided to accept the earlier dispensation offered by the emperor, in case Ganteaume should not reach Martinique, to make for Cadiz. On 22 August Admiral Cuthbert Collingwood let him in, and closed the gate behind him.

But, on that same day, unknowing, Bonaparte from Brest again ordered Villeneuve up the Channel to Boulogne. (Villeneuve's letter announcing his arrival at Cadiz was not received in Paris until the first week in September. Napoleon did not learn of it until a day or two later.) On 27 August, after the admiral had not appeared in the Channel, the emperor dismantled the great camp at Boulogne and marched his army eastward to the glories of Ulm and Austerlitz. Although his navy was safely in Cadiz, Napoleon did not know that. Through his order of 22 August he was prepared to risk its loss in the Channel, the army's support removed, and against a superior and implacable enemy. 'No more serious decision', said the indulgent historian Desbrière, 'can ever have been taken on less solid grounds.'

On 28 September Villeneuve in Cadiz, among fellow admirals and captains, of whom some were loyal to him and some regarded him as a coward, received a letter which ordered him to take the combined fleet to Naples. There he was to land 4,000 French troops and return to Toulon, capturing any convoys sighted, including Russian and Austrian. The admiral, so far having received no rebuke for his absence from northern waters, regarded the order as a compliment rather than the slap that it represented to the navy in its misuse of naval power for trivial ends. And when Villeneuve's enemy, General Lauriston, an ADC to the emperor, slyly told Bonaparte that the admiral had never intended to go to Brest, but always to Cadiz, Napoleon dismissed Villeneuve with accusations of treason and cowardice.

Villeneuve had sailed before learning of his recall and before his successor, Admiral Rosily, arrived at Cadiz, the latter having been delayed in Madrid by a broken carriage spring. Rosily's orders, had he taken command, *would* have provided time for training, opportunities for which had existed neither in blockaded ports nor – sufficiently – during the West Indies operation. Trafalgar, then, might not have taken place.

By dawn on 20 October, under the close eye of Nelson's frigates, *Euryalus* and others, the combined Franco-Spanish fleet had cleared Cadiz for the open sea in a feeble breeze, all its movements reported to Nelson and the main British fleet by flag signals from Captain Blackwood's frigates. Nelson signalled 'general chase' and steered southeast toward the Straits of Gibraltar.

In June, Nelson, after pursuing Villeneuve across the Atlantic, had missed him, learning too late, because of faulty intelligence, that eighteen French ships of the line had passed Prince Rupert's Head in northbound flight. (The action which followed between Calder's squadron and Villeneuve took place on 22 July.) On his return journey to Europe he went ashore for the first time in two years, at Rosia Bay. Having handed over command to Admiral Collingwood, he then used the permission already received from the Admiralty – 'to repair a very shattered constitution' – to bring *Victory* to a tumultuous reception at Portsmouth on 19 August 1805.

At 6 a.m. on 20 August he reached Merton, his elegant new country house, to find Lady Hamilton, his daughter Horatia, nearly five, their friends and relations hoping without much conviction for a period of undisturbed peace. He was allotted precisely twenty-five days by his beloved country. Fourteen of these, from the date when it was learned that Villeneuve had put to sea on 13 August from Ferrol with nearly thirty of the line, were spent in London with Pitt, other ministers and Lord Barham, first sea lord. He had at least time to explain to one of his captains, Keats, his three-division, three-line plan of attack: 'I think it will surprise and confound the enemy. They won't know what I am about. It will bring forward a pell mell Battle and that is what I want.' While in London, he had his coffin made, out of French timber from the Nile.

After Barham had examined Calder's inconclusive encounter, Pitt told Nelson that only he, not even Collingwood, was fit to command those ships which must confront the combined allied fleet, now prophesied by Nelson to be heading for Cadiz or Toulon, 'sixty or seventy sail-of-the-line'. The next day saw the arrival at Merton of Captain Blackwood from the *Euryalus*, with despatches from Collingwood reporting that that fleet had indeed arrived at Cadiz.

Before taking his last post-chaise to Portsmouth from Merton, Nelson said farewell to the sleeping Horatia, whom he much loved. The admiral entered a prayer in his diary:

Friday night, at half-past ten, drove from dear, dear, Merton, where I left all which I hold dear in this world, to go to serve my King and country. May the great God, whom I adore, enable me to fulfil the expectation of my country: and if it is His good pleasure that I should return, my thanks will never cease . . . If it is His good Providence to cut short my days upon earth, I bow with the greatest submission, relying that He will protect those so dear to me, that I may leave behind. His will be done. Amen, Amen, Amen.

Victory rejoined the fleet outside Cadiz, in silence, Nelson not permitting mention or acknowledgement of his return: 'I would not have you salute even if you are out of sight of land,' a fleet action being imminent.

Collingwood's command in the meanwhile had been dour, little fresh food brought out from Africa, no ship-visiting. 'Send us Lord Nelson, you men of power,' prayed Captain Codrington of *Orion*; 'The pleasantest admiral I ever served under,' said Duff of *Mars*. Nelson accordingly wrote: 'The reception I met with on rejoining the Fleet caused the sweetest sensation of my life. The officers forgot my rank as Commander-in-Chief in the enthusiasm with which they greeted me . . . I laid before them the Plan [the plan of attack, or 'Nelson Touch', as named by Nelson and Lady Hamilton] and it was my pleasure to find it not only generally approved, but clearly perceived and understood.'

On 20 October, the combined Franco-Spanish fleet of thirty-three ships, although expecting defeat, had cleared Cadiz. Daylight found the British fleet of twenty-seven vessels in low visibility and heavy rain, without sight of the enemy. Nelson said that he hoped 'to capture twenty to twenty-two' of the enemy fleet: he told some midshipmen that 'tomorrow will be a fortunate day for you young gentlemen'. At first light next day, Dr Beatty expressed the wish that the C-in-C would cover the four great orders of knighthood on his breast: 'there were sharpshooters in the enemy fighting-tops'. But Nelson told Flag Captain Hardy that 'it was now too late to be shifting a coat'. At the same time, Collingwood to leeward had remarked on 'a crowd of great ships' to his steward: 'In a short time, we shall see a great deal more of them.'

The plan was for the order of battle to be the order of sailing when the enemy was sighted. Because he thought that he might have as many as forty ships, Nelson had wished to attack in three separate divisions, one to windward led by himself, one to leeward commanded by Collingwood, and a fast advance squadron. Collingwood, in *Royal Sovereign*, would cut the enemy's single-line, twelve ships from the rear, while Nelson, in *Victory*, would attack at Villeneuve's position in the centre of the rear, abaft his flagship *Bucentaure*. As he had said to Keats, he wanted a pell mell battle, creating the greatest confusion among the enemy, without having deeply considered the course of events after the two British divisions had broken the Franco-Spanish line at right angles. And as his fleet had been reduced to twenty-seven from the earlier estimate of forty, the advance squadron did not form a part of the plan generally agreed.

The aim thus was to overpower the enemy at right angles to their line from two to three ships ahead of their commander-in-chief, supposed to be in the centre, to his rear. If twenty of the enemy were untouched, it would nevertheless be a long time before they could help their own ships or attack the British. 'Something must be left to chance: nothing is sure in a sea-fight beyond all others, but', said Nelson, 'I look with confidence to a victory before the Van of the Enemy could succour their rear and, then, that the British Fleet would, most of them, be ready to receive their twenty sail of the line, or pursue them, should they endeavour to make off.'

Hardy and Blackwood now witnessed a codicil to Nelson's will, leaving Lady Hamilton and Horatia as legacies 'to his king and country'. 'These are the only favours I ask of [them] at this moment, when I am going to fight their battle.' Blackwood then tried but failed to persuade the C-in-C to transfer his flag, for his own sake and the fleet's, to *Euryalus*. Nelson went to his cabin for the last time, where, the furniture cleared away, on his knees he wrote a prayer: 'May the Great God, whom I worship, grant to my country and for the benefit of Europe in general, a great and glorious victory and may no misconduct in anyone tarnish it; and may humanity after victory be the predominant feature in the British fleet. For myself, I commit my life to him who made me.'

Villeneuve had calculated that the British would not attack him in a single line, firing broadsides from van to rear, but would make for a part or parts of his line. His fleet, scattered, was not in line either, and when he hoisted the signal to 'form a line of battle in normal sequence', the subsequent confusion brought it to a virtual standstill. Untrained crews in a heavy swell and very light winds could not surmount the circumstances. 'They had never sailed together as a fleet and there were simply not enough of them who knew how to do it.'

The Frenchman then, on reaching the high seas, faced with the choice between the straits and Cadiz, chose Cadiz. Nelson, to the west, held his course. At eight o'clock, Villeneuve turned his fleet in reverse order to the north. A Spanish captain said: 'The fleet is doomed. The French admiral does not know his business. He has compromised us all.' He was wrong. Had Villeneuve stood on, his van could have survived. Nelson, in Howarth's version, saw the turn, since the combined fleet might have escaped to the Mediterranean, as 'deliberate acceptance of Nelson's challenge. All [Villeneuve] had left was courage and naval pride, these at least shared with his officers.'

At 11.35, perhaps the most famous signal ever made was hoisted in *Victory*: 'England expects [changed from 'Nelson confides'] that every man will do his duty.' Collingwood said grumpily: 'I wish Nelson would stop signalling. We know well enough what to do.' On the gun decks, where Nelson lived in the hearts of men, and where England was neither close nor the precise epitome of the navy, a sailor queried, 'Do my duty? I've always done my duty, haven't you, Jack?' And then *Victory* hoisted the last signal: 'Engage the enemy more closely.'

With that, he sent the frigate captains to their commands. 'God bless you, Blackwood: I shall not speak to you again.'

Thirty-three enemy ships had been visible, heading, before Villeneuve's signal, for the Straits of Gibraltar, the turn back to Cadiz executed by 10 a.m. Admiral Dumanoir now commanded the van, accused after the battle of sailing away from gunfire, court-martialled, but doubtfully acquitted. Villeneuve followed, in *Bucentaure*, with the Spanish admiral Alava astern of him in

Santa Ana, which he later surrendered to Collingwood. Gravina, in *Príncipe de Asturias*, who died of wounds ('I am going, I hope and trust to join Nelson'), and Admiral Magon, a severe critic of Villeneuve, in *Algéciras*, in which he fought until his own death, joined the line with their squadrons.

But the combined line was shaky and inaccurate, a curve five miles long, itself broken by accidental groups of two or three in line abreast, formed by the slack breeze, the incompetent seamanship of crews devoid of the practice acquired by combined exercises as a fleet, and a general failure to manoeuvre. Villeneuve's captains felt themselves the victims, even playthings, of the sea. Nelson knew he was its master. To conquer this deficiency may have been one motive of those French captains, like the gallant Lucas of *Redoubtable*, who used boarding parties and sharpshooters, not cannon with its prior requirement for precise navigation, as their principal weapons.

The British did not favour these tactics, preferring to smash ships with ball, rather than as individuals in hand-to-hand or marksmen's fighting. But individuals in Nelson's fleet were not devoid of initiative, albeit sometimes rash. An Irish sailor named Fitzgerald from *Tennant* boarded Magon's *Algéciras* alone, shinned up the rigging to the topmast, where he secured the French flag round his waist, and came down again, to be shot before reaching the deck.

Royal Sovereign, leading the leeward line under Admiral Collingwood, was the first British ship to fire her main armament, the first to break the allied line astern of Alava's *Santa Ana*, followed three minutes later by *Belleisle*, *Mars*, *Tennant*, passing under the stern of the Spanish flagship. *Royal Sovereign* fired two double-shotted broadsides at thirty yards' range (the admiral and his captains ordered their crews to lie down as they went into the attack). When an officer asked Harwood, captain of *Belleisle*, whether the vessel should not 'show her broadside and fire', the captain replied, 'No, we are ordered to go through, and go through she shall, by God.'

Nelson, watching, remarked: 'See how that noble fellow Collingwood carries his ship into action,' before *Victory* herself in her division came under fire from *Héros*, *Bucentaure* and *Santissima Trinidad*, all firing high and wildly in the heavy swell. (His officers noted that he was in 'that taut omniscient state common to him on such occasions, in calm but very good spirits'.) But British ships suffered, topmasts and rigging shot away. And a splinter tore off the buckle of Captain Hardy's shoe: 'This is too warm work, Hardy, to last long,' said Nelson, as his own broadside tore point blank into Villeneuve's stern.

In the thick smoke of the cannonades, the fleets – hampered by the weak breeze blowing around Cape Trafalgar – performed an infinitely slow *danse macabre*, while *Royal Sovereign* and *Santa Ana*, fast together, hammered broadsides at two to three yards' range. *Victory* was locked with *Téméraire*, and the French *Fougueux* and *Redoubtable*, the gun decks dark infernos of cries, explosions, the crash of shot through timber, blood, shouted orders, flames and, above all, smoke everywhere, the stench of gunpowder.

Battle became fierce, general and close. French and Spanish ships, holed and dismasted, began to lose ground, their steering gone, unable to hoist sail. A few had struck already when, over an hour into the battle, Nelson – walking as usual with Hardy on the quarterdeck, among round-shot and heavy sniper fire – was hit by a sharpshooter from *Redoubtable*'s mizzen. The exact spot where he fell to the deck was that on which his secretary, Mr Scott, had also just fallen to round-shot. Howarth said that, five minutes after Nelson had been shot, a total of fifty men had already been wounded by Lucas's musketeers. The upper deck was almost empty, those unwounded taking cover.

'Hardy, I believe that they have done for me at last,' whispered Nelson.

'I hope not,' replied the flag captain.

'Yes, my backbone is shot through.' He was carried, the escort stumbling, to the cockpit, below the water-line. This and other parts of British ships had been originally painted red by Admiral

Sir Robert Blake so that the blood would be less obvious. (The chaplain said, 'It was like a butcher's shambles,' and never left him thereafter.) The purser and chaplain encouraged Nelson to believe that he would return alive and triumphant in *Victory* to England. 'It is nonsense, Mr Burke, to suppose I will live: my sufferings are great but they will soon be over.' The doctor, Beatty, could only agree, offering lemonade and a fan. A midshipman reported that Hardy would visit him as soon as the battle made it possible. Nelson could not see the boy but, recalling a visit by an old shipmate: 'It is his voice,' the admiral said. 'Remember me to your father,' words treasured for ever by Dick Bulkeley.

When Captain Hardy at last arrived at the death-bed, he reported that *Redoubtable* and *Fougueux* were in silent ruin. *Victory* had freed herself, and *Téméraire* was attacking the *Santissima Trinidad*. 'We have twelve or fourteen of the enemy's ships in our possession, but five of their van [under Dumanoir] have tacked.' Hardy had called up *Spartiate* and *Minotaur* to deal with them.

'I hope none of our ships have struck, Hardy.'

'No, my Lord, there is no fear of that.'

'I am a dead man, Hardy. I am going fast: it will be all over with me soon. Come nearer to me . . .' Hardy shook hands with him, and left to send a warning signal to Collingwood, Nelson's second-in-command. Later, the admiral told Dr Beatty that his pain 'continued so very severe that he wished he were dead . . . Yet, one would like to live a little longer too.' At the concussion of gunfire in that tiny space: 'Oh *Victory*! *Victory*! How you distract my poor brain!' Then, as if in contemplation: 'How dear is life to all men.'

Hardy returned and stood, large and solid, looking down upon the little group in the cockpit drawn by Devis on the homeward voyage. He reported to Nelson 'a brilliant victory, which is complete', but could not answer for more than fourteen or fifteen enemy vessels taken at that juncture.

'That is well, but I bargained for twenty.' Then, perhaps predicting the gales and tempestuous seas to come, '*Anchor*, Hardy, *anchor*.' Hardy asked if Collingwood should give the order. 'Not while I live, I hope. No, do *you* anchor, Hardy.' Hardy did not, nor Collingwood.

'Don't throw me overboard, Hardy,' the fate of the dead from warships in battle. 'Oh, no, certainly not,' replied the captain miserably. Dr Beatty's record now began again, to read: 'Then you know what to do. And take care of my dear Lady Hamilton, Hardy. Take care of poor Lady Hamilton. Kiss me, Hardy.' The captain now knelt down and kissed his cheek, when His Lordship said: 'Now I am satisfied: thank God I have done my duty.'

Captain Hardy stood for a minute or two in silent contemplation. He knelt down again and kissed His Lordship's forehead.

Nelson said, 'Who is that?'

The captain answered, 'It is Hardy,' to which Nelson replied, 'God bless you, Hardy.' Before dying, he said, 'I wish I had not left the deck,' and, to the chaplain, 'I have not been a great sinner.' Then, 'Remember that I leave Lady Hamilton and my daughter as a legacy to my country. Never forget Horatia.' His last words were, again, 'Thank God I have done my duty.'

The log of *Victory* read, in pencil, 'Partial firing continued until 4.30, when a victory having been reported to the Right Hon. Viscount Nelson KB, and Commander-in-Chief, he died of his wounds.'

Eighteen were, in fact, taken, the four ships of the van which escaped to the west under Dumanoir captured by Sir Richard Strachan's squadron. Only four prizes, however, survived the frightful gale and mountainous seas which followed the battle, to anchor still in British hands at Gibraltar. Only eleven of the original thirty-three enemy vessels ever reached Cadiz harbour in safety.

Nelson's 'King and country' did not, of course, respond to his appeal to 'remember Lady Hamilton and Horatia'. The former, in receipt only of the interest on £500 left to her by Lord Nelson, was, after selling Merton for £13,000 to a Mr Abraham Goldsmid who subsequently took his life in the shrubbery, arrested in 1812 for debt. She had engaged in great extravagance and, in 1814, was rearrested. In July of that year she and Horatia settled in a farmhouse at St Pierre near Calais. Her debts were considerable, her drinking heavy. In January 1815 she died. After her death, Horatia revealed that Lady Hamilton had at least always spent the whole of the interest from Nelson's legacy on his daughter's education.

In February 1822 Horatia married the Reverend Philip Ward MA at Burnham and lived happily ever after. 'The child born on a winter's day in the year of Copenhagen, with whom Nelson had played on the carpet at Sloane Street . . . lived to be eighty-one.'

Trafalgar not only dispelled future dreams of an invasion of England, but seized for Britain overwhelming mastery of the seas. For the world, it achieved the Pax Britannica. Without sea-power, the security of the existing French and Spanish colonies could not be maintained nor, more largely, Bonaparte's gigantic ambitions satisfied. 'People will want to know where we are going,' he said, after Russia's defection from the continental system. 'We are going to make an end of Europe, and then to throw ourselves upon other robbers, more daring than ourselves, and *to become mistress of India.*'

The events of 21 October 1805 put an end to that: sea-power lost that day was mortal to Napoleon.

George Orwell, broadcasting in 1942 after that year's Trafalgar Day, reminded his audience that Trafalgar was to the Napoleonic Wars as the Battle of Britain was to the war then raging. In both instances invasion and defeat would have given over Europe to military dictatorship: 'Britain could not be conquered at one blow.'

SYNOPSIS OF EVENTS BETWEEN
TRAFALGAR AND THE WAR BETWEEN THE STATES

The break-up of the Spanish American Empire proceeded throughout 1806–1830, much aided by the Royal Navy. The Peace of Tilsit in 1807 carried the tsar's recognition of Napoleon's pre-eminence. The latter then attacked Spain, fighting against Britain, under Wellington, the Peninsular War: the battles of Vimiero, Corunna and Talavera. In 1810 France annexed Holland.

In 1812 Napoleon invaded Russia, whence followed Borodino, Moscow, the retreat and destruction of the Grande Armée. While Britain fought a destructive little war against America, burning the White House, Napoleon prepared and fought in Europe the battles of Dresden, Ulm, Leipzig and Vittoria. In 1814 the allies invaded France. Napoleon abdicated and went to Elba: Louis XVIII succeeded to the French throne. Napoleon escaped to France from Elba in 1815 and raised his supporters: Louis XVIII fled; Wellington and Blucher defeated Napoleon at Waterloo and he was exiled to St Helena.

In Britain Canning succeeded Castlereagh in 1822, marking a sea change in British foreign policy. In 1823 the Monroe Doctrine was promulgated as the policy of the United States. The liberation of Greece from Turkey was achieved in 1824, the Egyptian and Turkish fleets destroyed. Revolutions of 1830 and an end to Polish independence were succeeded by the revolutions of 1848. Louis Bonaparte became president and subsequently emperor of France. The Hungarian Kossuth was defeated by Austria. The first Prussian parliament was established, and the unifications of Italy and Germany, through the Risorgimento and by Bismarck, were accomplished.

CHAPTER FIFTEEN

VICKSBURG AND GETTYSBURG, 1863

On 19 November 1863, when dedicating the burial ground for those who fell at the battle of Gettysburg in July, Lincoln's address, with which he was dissatisfied, read:

> Four score and seven years ago, our fathers brought forth upon this continent a new nation: conceived in liberty, and dedicated to the proposition that all men are created equal.
>
> Now we are engaged in a great civil war . . . testing whether that nation, or any nation so conceived and so dedicated . . . can long endure. We are met on a great battlefield of that war.
>
> We have come to dedicate a portion of that field as a final resting place for those who here gave their lives that that nation might live. It is altogether fitting and proper that we should do this.
>
> But, in a larger sense, we cannot dedicate . . . we cannot consecrate . . . we cannot hallow this ground. The brave men, living and dead, who struggled here have consecrated it, far above our poor power to add or detract. The world will little note, nor long remember, what we say here, but it can never forget what they did here.
>
> It is for us the living, rather, to be dedicated here to the unfinished work which they who fought here have thus far so nobly advanced. It is rather for us to be here dedicated to the

great task remaining before us . . . that from these honoured dead we take increased devotion to that cause for which they gave the last full measure of devotion . . . that we here highly resolve that these dead shall not have died in vain . . . that this nation, under God, shall have a new birth of freedom . . . and that government of the people . . . by the people . . . for the people . . . shall not perish from the earth.

When Wolfe's enemies pronounced him mad, King George II had wished that the affliction could be transmitted to some of his less active generals. Similarly, when hostile clergymen complained to Lincoln of Grant's drunkenness, the president had asked where he acquired his supplies, so that he could send some to more passive officers.

Ulysses S. Grant was a professional soldier, rather small, slouching, hard-eyed, tight-lipped, with a thin, handsome, bearded face. He had fought gallantly at Monterrey and Mexico City before resigning in 1854 to become an inept and unhappy farmer and, later, salesman. In 1861, he was reinstated in the US army as a colonel, promoted some months after the outbreak of the Civil War to brigadier. In February 1862 an amphibious operation with 17,000 men under his command, accompanied by river gunboats, took Forts Henry and Donaldson on the Cumberland river. 'No terms except an unconditional and immediate surrender can be accepted' was his ultimatum to the rebel enemy commander, a former colleague from West Point.

In April he defeated the Confederates under Pierre Beauregard at Shiloh with severe casualties on both sides, including the brilliant southerner Albert Sydney Johnston, in a battle somewhat carelessly conducted by Grant. (Beauregard, incidentally, at Fort Sumter had fired the first shot in the Civil War.) In response to northern criticism, however, Lincoln said: 'I can't spare this man. He fights.'

Thereafter, the scholarly General Halleck, then commander of the Missouri, who disliked Grant, could no longer keep him out of the fighting. Indeed, when appointed general of the army in Washington, he returned to him command of the army of the Tennessee, and that of the Ohio army to Don Carlos Buell. (Earlier, only the protest of General William Tecumseh Sherman had prevented Grant's second resignation.) But Halleck continued to distrust him, even sending Charles Dana, journalist and politician by trade, to spy on Grant and on his drinking. This channel was, however, admirably exploited by the general himself to forward to Secretary Stanton and President Lincoln in Washington a true account of his views and intentions. Despite the possibility that Grant really was an alcoholic, his reputation in the nation's capital was thus restored, even enhanced.

After a great deal of unworthy politicking by General McLennan, a politician from Lincoln's own Illinois, who wanted to take Vicksburg himself, Grant and Sherman contrived to remove McLennan's two corps from him and to send them down the Mississippi river toward Vicksburg, an attractive, well-made, luxurious town known to Jefferson Davis, president of the Confederacy, as impregnable, 'the Gibraltar of the East'. (It also had a brothel called Mollie Bunch's, which threw a prostitutes' ball that had to be hosed down.) Meanwhile, rebel command of the western campaign was taken from Beauregard by General Braxton Bragg, characterised by Winston Churchill as 'overbearing and ill served', who fought indecisive battles in Tennessee against Buell and Rosencrans: the Confederate navy had been put temporarily out of action off Memphis by a Captain Davis USN.

Between March and April 1862, Commodore David Farragut took a flotilla of twenty mortar-armed vessels, eight sloops and corvettes and nine gunboats past the forts of the Confederate capital at New Orleans, capturing that city and accepting the surrender of Natchez and Baton Rouge. ('Damn the torpedoes' was Farragut's reply when threatened with the new weapon.) But at Vicksburg itself, extensive shelling produced in May from the defenders only: 'Mississippians don't know, and refuse to learn, how to surrender to an enemy,' particularly one, like Farragut, a defected southerner. The northern navy, after failing to sink a large Confederate 'ram' named *Arkansas* off the port, then returned to blockading the gulf. In the meanwhile, the Vicksburgians had survived naval bombardment, sheltering in the countryside or in hillside caves after Confederate reinforcement.

At the end of the year cavalry under Earl Van Dorn, who had previously served under Robert E. Lee, destroyed Grant's supply base at Holly Springs, delaying Grant's advance on Vicksburg and temporarily reducing his rations by half. Grant had separately despatched Sherman with 40,000 men in an amphibious strike north of the city which the latter had originally opposed. The naval element was commanded by Rear Admiral David Porter, an officer with a black beard like a huge bird's nest, enormous even for that era. (Sherman, incidentally, had also resigned from the peacetime army around the time of Grant's resignation, and was a friend.) In a three-day battle at Chickasaw Bluffs on the Yazoo river, the force was driven off with heavy casualties. The Mississippi remained under Confederate control, at least from Vicksburg to Baton Rouge.

The main body of the army of the Tennessee was at Grand Junction under Grant, trying to drive its way, not down the river against heavy garrison artillery, but through the tangled and disgusting snake-infested swamps and marshes of the Mississippi, trying unsuccessfully to dig canals with spades in the pouring rain. Consequent illness, malaria, typhoid and pneumonia among the troops provoked press attacks on Grant and his habits. 'A poor drunken imbecile . . . a poor stick sober, and most of the time more than half drunk and much of the time idiotically drunk.' Lincoln continued to ignore these accusations and, in January 1863, Grant took personal command at Milliken's Bend in Louisiana.

By this time, Lieutenant-General John Pemberton, commander of the Confederate army of the Mississippi, another gallant and resolute West Pointer, had been instructed by President Jefferson Davis to hold Vicksburg. Grant had served in Mexico with Pemberton, a handsome, cultivated, wealthy northerner, and knew that he would never lightly yield although, like Lee, the basis for his adherence to the south was not pro-slavery, but states' rights. Unfortunately for Pemberton, his superior, General Joseph E. Johnston, wanted him – contrary to the former's instructions – not just to ensure the maintenance of Vicksburg in rebel hands, but to take the war to Grant. And Pemberton, as a northerner, did not even have the confidence of the men and women of Vicksburg, hysterically accused of selling the town to the Union: this rather aloof and domineering Yankee was, wherever he went, believed to be working for the other side, and cowardly with it.

Grant now marched his own army, mustering some 40,000 men down the west bank of the Mississippi in Louisiana, aiming to cross the river south of Vicksburg and take it from the east. (The plan had been opposed, because of Confederate artillery superiority, as too dangerous, a view held even by his friend Sherman, who was now initially north of Vicksburg.) Admiral Porter occupied himself by running troops and supplies to Hard Times, Grant's new base, and in ferrying the army to Bruinsburg below Grand Gulf where, on 1 May, the Confederate garrison was driven off.

On 16 April Grant himself, his wife Julia and young sons Fred and Ulysses were embarked in *Magnolia*, part of a convoy of strange, armoured steam gunboats with tall, slim funnels, coal-barges lashed alongside for defence. The convoy survived massive bombardment from guns on the 200-foot Heights of Vicksburg, passing safely downstream, to ensure Union control of the river. Henceforward, the only supply route for the city would be the railway line eastward to Jackson which Grant now decided, in order to cut off Vicksburg completely, to attack. He had learned that General Joe Johnston, a brave, experienced but sensitive Virginian, was, although unwell, assembling an army in Jackson which, if unopposed, could take his campaign against Vicksburg in the flank.

To confuse General Pemberton, Grant sent 1,700 cavalrymen under Colonel Benjamin Grierson (who, according to Grant, was a music teacher by profession and hated horses since being kicked by one) on a brilliant expedition to terrorise civilians and cause damage to installations and property. Sherman, at the same time, was ordered to carry out, with only one unit, a deception operation at Haines Bluff, north of Vicksburg, which led the Confederates to believe that *ten* Union regiments had come ashore there, instead of a solitary one, ten times rotated.

Grant, again contrary to advice from his staff, now put 40,000 men on a fast march to Jackson, living richly off the country except for ammunition, which he carried in everything from wagons to private carriages. (Before leaving, he was observed to drink three full standard-issue tin cups of whiskey.) The Confederates did not believe that such a march, without a supply base, could be undertaken successfully. Johnston ordered Pemberton to attack Grant. Pemberton, who wanted Johnston's help in defending Vicksburg, compromised by digging in east of the city. But there at Champion Hill, after Grant had burned down Jackson, the rebels were soundly defeated, losing 3,800 to Grant's 2,400 men. Vicksburg seemed open to immediate Union victory.

Miserable, dirty, bloodied, the defeated rebel army slouched into the town, abused by their women, sometimes – in their shameful retreat – even without personal weapons. (At the other side of the continent, Lee had just begun planning for that invasion of the north which led to Gettysburg, rather than for measures to save Vicksburg, now on the point of investment by Grant's army of the Tennessee.) But the Yankees did not immediately break in, reinforcements arrived, pride returned, supplies poured in, some on the hoof.

Pemberton took measures to defend his elegant and civilised little city, since should it be abandoned, total control of the Mississippi would be given up to the Union, and the Confederacy split in two.

Johnston, however, recovering from earlier wounds, never came to Pemberton's aid, instead advocating evacuation which his colleague could not accept. Escape was not feasible without the loss of all supplies, including arms, equipment, food, men and, more damaging, honour and the morale of those still struggling. 'I have', said Pemberton, 'decided to hold Vicksburg as long as is possible, with the firm hope that the Government may yet be able to assist me in keeping this obstruction to the enemy's free navigation of the Mississippi River . . . the most important point in the Confederacy.' But Grant had marched nearly 200 miles in twenty days and won five battles, including Champion Hill and the Big Black river. His forces now had a strength of 76,000 men after a campaign which Sherman told him was 'one of the greatest in history'.

But the terrain and fortification of Vicksburg were not favourable to the attacker, high bluffs filled with veterans, rifle pits, timber entanglements, protruding cannon – admittedly some 'fabricated' – causing the bloody failure uphill of two separate Union assaults against sharpened stakes, up scaling ladders, with 3,000 casualties to the rebels' 500, 'bodies swollen and bursting in the unforgiving Mississippi heat'. Grant, to avoid further losses, had no alternative but protracted siege. He was fortunate that Johnston, although reinforced to 25,000 men, still did not consider that his force was strong enough to relieve Pemberton.

To clear the battlefield of the dead and wounded, a truce was proclaimed for two and a half hours on 25 May, during which Union and Confederate officers and men talked, exchanged drink and other provisions, mutually regretting the circumstances. When it was lifted, Grant – who unfortunately was not accompanied by his military secretary Rawlins or by Julia, his steady and helpful wife – went on a three-day drinking bout conducted from his official river steamer. One of his 'minders', however, reported that at breakfast, the general was 'as fresh as a rose, clean shirt and all, quite himself', possibly because the minder threw most of the remaining bottles of whiskey through the window and into the river. John Rawlins, by threatening to leave the general's staff, ensured that the binge was not repeated, at least during the Vicksburg campaign.

Shelling from Porter's batteries on the river and from Grant's 200 cannon could not be matched by Pemberton's 102 guns, lacking as they did adequate ammunition. Unexploded hand-grenades and naval shells were tossed or rolled back instead on the attackers, and 'thunder barrels' full of powder launched at the besiegers. Sharpshooters were engaged on the rebel side, and musketeers firing inflammable ball, stuffed with cotton soaked in turpentine. The northerners, still in heavy woollen uniforms, suffered the most from heat and from the bugs, but their diet, 'coffee, crackers, boiled beef, fried pork, sometimes even cod and potatoes', was infinitely superior to the exiguous peas, bacon rashers and rice rationed to the rebels, some of whom were reduced to begging in the streets.

'Fire-shells, chain-shot, cannon balls, grape-shot, scrap iron, links of chain and rusty nails swept the streets from wall to curb.' Few houses were undamaged, many burned to the ground or shattered: civilians, men, women and children took increasing refuge in deep caves in the hillsides or in basements. Peter Walker described 'a bombshell in the very centre of a pretty dining-room, blowing out the roof and one side, crushing the well-spread tea-table like an eggshell, and making a great yawning hole in the floor, into which disappeared supper, china, furniture and the safe containing [the family's] entire stock of butter and eggs'. One child, when her mother said that God would protect them, replied that she was afraid that God would be killed too.

Running water and washing facilities barely existed in the humid heat of this collapsing town. Insects proliferated, so did snakes. Malaria, dysentery, malnutrition, even starvation spread. Rats and mules were caught and eaten, 'nicely cooked', according to one source. Clothing began to fall apart. Johnston, possibly deterred by Sherman's position between Jackson and Vicksburg, still did not move.

On 2 July Pemberton learned from his officers that the 37,000 troops in Vicksburg, wounded, half-starved, diseased, were incapable of a breakout. On 4 July, Independence Day, to prevent useless losses, he marched out his ill and broken men in surrender; arms and colour stacked. He met Johnston only once thereafter, saluted him, but did not shake his hand. As for the citizens of Vicksburg, Independence Day was not observed in that city until the end of the Second World War in 1945.

Lincoln, informed of Grant's great victory on the Mississippi, remarked: 'The father of Waters again goes unvexed to the Sea.'

GETTYSBURG

The Confederacy *was* split in two. The eastern half was in no better state, and the Union cause could now be reinforced from the west. If Lee also were to be defeated, it could be the end of the rebellion.

In the east, during the winter of 1863, General Robert E. Lee himself lived and slept, admittedly warmed by a stove, in a simple tent, also occupied by a laying hen. Rations for the rebels were 4oz bacon, 18oz flour and 10lb rice to 100 men every three days, with some peas and a very little dried fruit.

To maintain the initiative, take his troops out of battered Virginia into the relative riches of the north, even perhaps to secure European recognition of the southern cause, Lee, grey-bearded and fatherly, proposed to invade the north. Screened by the cavalry of General J. E. B. (Jeb) Stuart, he and over 70,000 rebels moved into the Shenandoah valley.

Jeb Stuart, flamboyant in his ostrich plumes, crimson and yellow sashes and linings, adored by women, a dashing cavalryman with service at Harper's Ferry, Bull Run, Antietam, Fredericksburg, Chancellorsville and against the army of the Potomac in the Peninsular Campaign, had returned to Richmond a hero, not least among the ladies. But now, sidetracked by the prize of 125 captured Union supply wagons, he could not locate his prey, the Union army under General Hooker, or even his own commander,

Lee, depriving that Confederate general, now west of Hanover, of his 'eyes'. At Brandy Station, furthermore, Stuart was surprised by Major-General Alfred Pleasanton in the largest cavalry action of the Civil War, incurring 500 casualties to Pleasanton's 900 in a battle of sabres and handguns.

Lee's father had been a general in the War of Independence. He himself had married a descendant of George Washington, living at Arlington, the house which Washington's adopted son had built to overlook the capital. He was a kind and gentle man, honourable, deeply religious, and opposed to slavery. However, he resigned from the Union army because, for him, the state of Virginia and the principle of states' rights had priority over other considerations. 'I will follow my native state with my sword and if need be with my life.' Four days after resignation, he was appointed commander of the Confederate army of North Virginia, all the forces of the state.

'Stonewall' Jackson, Lee's closest comrade-in-arms, had been accidentally killed by his own men at Chancellorsville in May. Lee wept, and said that he had lost his own right arm. Of the surviving commanders, James Longstreet, Richard Ewell and Ambrose P. Hill took over Jackson's corps.

James 'Old Pete' Longstreet had commanded infantry near Williamsburg, and had defeated the blowhard John Pope at Second Bull Run in the summer of 1862. As a younger officer, he had been decorated for bravery at Mexico City and promoted in the field. Lee, after Jackson's death, referred to Longstreet as 'the staff in my right hand', and 'my old workhorse'. But 'Old Pete' had wanted to relieve Vicksburg – his best friend, at West Point, incidentally, had been Grant – and was opposed to Lee's march on the north, advocating a defensive strategy under which the Union would break themselves, as at Fredericksburg, on entrenched Confederates. He believed, wrongly, that he had also so convinced Lee.

Ambrose Hill was quarrelsome. He had once challenged Longstreet to a duel, and had exchanged words with Jackson. He was, or had been, a noted Indian fighter, but disliked staff and garrison duties. He was nicknamed 'Old Bald Head', and fought all his battles in a bright red shirt. Ewell looked like a bird: like Hill, he much preferred life in the line to command. He is said to have lisped under stress and was frequently unwell. As a pupil of 'Stonewall' Jackson, he tended not to have ideas of his own, and to follow orders blindly without adapting them to circumstances. He had lost a leg at Second Bull Run.

General Lee had crossed the Potomac in the third week of June, moving into Pennsylvania through Chambersburg, preceded by Ewell's II Corps, the troops ragged, dirty, some shoeless, although perfectly controlled and under military discipline. The town reluctantly tolerated the Confederate occupation, but would not meet the full rebel requisition for clothing or for such basic provisions as coffee, bread, sugar and so forth. But Lee thought that his soldiers' morale was high and, although Stuart had not yet communicated Hooker's location, Lee told a colleague that he intended to bring the enemy to battle at a place called Gettysburg.

The rebels – part of Hill's corps – entered Gettysburg much earlier than Lee had even dreamed, but only in order to purchase boots and shoes, an advertisement for which they had read in a Cashtown newspaper. They left abruptly after sighting what they then took to be only a small militia unit, but returned the next day, 30 June, to pick up bargains for the ill-shod soldiers.

The 'small militia unit' was, in fact, a force under John Bulford, a good-looking martinet and Indian fighter, who died of exhaustion six months later. Bulford's two cavalry brigades fought dismounted as infantry. He believed, correctly, that Ewell's rebel II Corps was also on its way, and so informed General Reynolds, now commanding I Union Corps, vacated by Meade, on appointment as commander of the army of the Potomac, vice Hooker, in late June. He in turn informed Meade just before being killed by a rebel marksman. XI Corps under Oliver Howard now arrived at Gettysburg, bringing the Union total in the area to over 21,000 men. 'Once the fighting started,' wrote the American historian

Richard Moe, 'the town became a great magnet, pulling both sides irresistibly towards it. Thus the largest battle ever fought on the North American continent, and the most important engagement of the Civil War began almost as an accident.' XII Corps under Slocum and III Corps under Sickles were on their way to Gettysburg: more than half of Meade's army was either there or en route. The Union II Corps (Hancock's command) reached Taneytown.

Meade at Taneytown sent 'Hancock the superb . . . the most magnificent looking General in the whole Army', large, well shaped, elegant even when fighting, to take charge at Gettysburg. Hancock's report persuaded Meade to fight the battle on the Cemetery Hill position. Meanwhile, Ambrose Hill's corps was strongly resisted by Bulford, and by I Corps, formerly under Reynolds. The Union still held west Gettysburg when Ewell appeared from the north and, under Jubal Early, drove back Oliver Howard's XI Corps. Longstreet's corps followed Hill, and the retreating I and XI Corps fell back through the city to Cemetery Hill. But Ewell did not aggressively pursue his victorious advance, perhaps because the Confederates had lost heavily in both Hill's and Ewell's corps: certainly, Lee wanted to wait until Longstreet was fully engaged on the left. This omission was a capital error.

On 2 July, the second day, the Federal army held the 'horse-shoe ridge', XII Corps on Culp's Hill on the right of the line, I and XI Corps, or what was left, on Cemetery Hill in the centre of the ridge. III Corps initially, then reinforced by V Corps, was on the left ahead of II Corps, Sickles' III Corps forming – to Meade's disapproval – the vulnerable salient where, in the Devil's Den, 'the peach orchard', 'the wheat field', terrible fighting took place with huge casualties. (General Sickles had earlier been a Tammany Hall politician, a senator, a diplomat, who wished to become president, until he not only murdered his wife's lover, but *forgave* her, earning almost universal derision.) Victory, which could have been Lee's but for the hesitation and recalcitrance of Ewell and Longstreet, was nearly achieved again, this time at Round Top and Little Round Top, on 2 July saved for the Union only by the last-minute occupation by V Corps of these empty positions.

Dan Sickles' III Corps was forced back to the peach orchard by Longstreet and Hill. The rebels, with startling momentum, even broke the main Union line but, short of numbers, only temporarily. Longstreet, still bitterly opposed to his general's entire plan, was late in starting and, although fighting ferociously, consequently delayed Ewell's advance. (Ewell took Culp Hill, nevertheless, with one division, that position having been weakened by the withdrawal of XII Corps to fight elsewhere.) Jubal Early did not take Cemetery Hill, nor did the two Confederate divisions in the centre then make a decisive contribution.

Lee had not yet won the conflict, tolerating the 'virtual' insubordination and disobedience of his commanders, as well as their irritation, or Longstreet's frustration at being asked to fight in a mode which he (Longstreet) positively opposed. The general had behaved oddly all day, giving no orders and staying on Seminary Ridge in his command post. He missed Jackson badly, of course, but, according to Duane Schultz's *The Most Glorious Fourth*, he also suffered crippling diarrhoea that day, sending no despatches, not communicating at all with his men or his generals. 'On one of the most crucial days of the war', when George Meade was active all along the front and with his commanders, 'Lee was strangely silent.'

Whatever the reason, it was Lee's failure early that second morning to attack, or oblige his generals to attack, with all the strength available, that had given General Meade and the army of the Potomac time to form a defensive line. It was the proximate cause even for the launch and defeat of 'Pickett's charge' in Lee's four-division assault on 3 July: over 15,000 men, halted under heavy artillery, thrown back, almost annihilated, 'amongst sounds like tearing paper'. (One regiment lost 90 per cent of its men; Pickett's division took over 75 per cent casualties, 3,500 out of 4,500 men, ten regimental commanders killed and five wounded, two out of three brigadiers killed.) Lee said only: 'This has been my fight and upon my shoulders rests the blame,' but there were those who had harsh words for Pickett's wife's post-bellum panegyrics of her husband.

Lee began to retreat on 4 July, having lost 30,000 men out of 75,000. His army was still so formidable, and Meade's losses at 23,000 out of 85,000 so considerable, that he was not pursued in the wind and the rain across the flooded Potomac. But the rebels had lost the war or, at least, shot their bolt, and if Meade had chased him, which – to Lincoln's disgust – he did not, the war would have ended sooner than it did, in April 1865 at the Appomattox Court House.

It has been authoritatively claimed that Nashville in 1863 was 'the most decisive tactical victory by either side in a major engagement in this way', but in the accomplishment of the ends – 'the new birth of freedom', which the Gettysburg Address celebrated – the victories of Grant and Meade were, *à la longue*, the most truly decisive in a war to determine the structure and ideals of a nation destined to become the most powerful and productive in the world. Destined too at least to *try* to implement the objectives of 'Gettysburg', the tabernacle of this new society.

And had Lee won a decisive victory at Gettysburg, English recognition of the Confederacy might have been inevitable. It had already been advocated, with Prince Albert as 'peacemaker', before Antietam, and at Lee's invasion of Pennsylvania, variously by Gladstone, Lord John Russell and Palmerston. Napoleon III had also indicated approval, although his intermediary, an MP called John Roebuck, gave the game away by public disclosure of the details of their conversations. Lincoln's minister in Paris confirmed during the campaign that all depended on a Union victory, while, in London, Charles Adams's son and secretary, Henry, wrote that recognition was certain if the Union were to lose.

In that event, both south and north would have been weakened: by defections from the Confederacy; Georgia and North Carolina, already hostile to Jefferson Davis; Texas, California and Oregon, restive in the Union; other seceding states, such as Florida and Arkansas, small in population, but components in a general Balkanisation, the consequence of exhaustion by war and of demands by rebel sympathisers for a negotiated peace.

Before dismissing the possibilities, or indulging in irresponsible *schadenfreude*, we must ask ourselves what would have been the response of such a country, thus divided and troubled, to the traumatic circumstances of the anarchic worlds of 1917, 1941, 1990 or, indeed, 2001, dates on which our own destiny was most closely affected by a more rather than less United States of America.

SYNOPSIS OF EVENTS BETWEEN
THE WAR BETWEEN THE STATES AND TANNENBERG

The war of 1866 between Bismarck's Prussia and Austria resulted in an overwhelming Austrian defeat at Sadowa (Königgrätz) and the signature of the Treaty of Prague. This was followed by the Franco-Prussian War which, *à la longue*, caused the major phenomenon of the establishment of German unity and, even more dangerously, the cession by France to Germany of Alsace and Lorraine, including Strasbourg and Metz.

CHAPTER SIXTEEN

TANNENBERG, 1914

A t Tannenberg in 1410, a combined Polish and Lithuanian force under King Wladislaw Jagiello destroyed the army of the Order of Teutonic Knights. Five hundred years later, between 26 and 31 August 1914, another battle, which General Ludendorff of the Imperial German Army chose also to christen 'Tannenberg', took place near that village.

In order to divide the potentially hostile forces of the Triple Alliance – Germany, Italy and the Austro-Hungarian Empire – a Franco-Russian alliance had been created in the nineteenth century, of which the first and principal military objective was the defeat of Germany, linchpin of that Triple Alliance. Operations in time of war would begin in the west with a French assault on Germany, only *followed* by a Russian advance in east Prussia, designed to oblige the Germans to weaken their western front by drawing off as many of their divisions as possible to the east, thus relieving France, the main German target in the west.

On 28 June 1914 a young Bosnian misfit, inspired by the revolutionary Black Hand, and violently opposed to Austrian rule, assassinated on the streets of Sarajevo Archduke Franz Ferdinand, heir to the Habsburg throne. Russia, on behalf of her fellow Slavs in Serbia, mobilised, followed by mobilisations and declarations of war throughout Europe, including Germany, France, Austria and Britain. The First World War began, its initial course described above.

Russian roads were as bad and as infrequent as her railways, which themselves had a low freight capacity. On the roads, according to General Sir Geoffrey Evans in *Tannenberg, 1410 and 1914*, the Russian army commanded only 679 vehicles, of which 259 were passenger carrying, 418 transport, and *two* ambulances. All other transport was horse-drawn. Although, furthermore, 3.5 million men could be mustered on mobilisation, of the 3 million reservists in this total few had received any but the most exiguous training and many no training at all.

Communications, including wireless, were inadequate, and not enough had been done to put right the enormous faults in administration, command and armament discovered, as Evans remarks, during the disastrously unsuccessful war of 1904–05 against Japan. Officers, since promotion tended to be concentrated in non-regimental sectors such as the Guard Corps, were often unprofessional, unconcerned with their men and, as bad, uninterested in military developments. General Sukhomlinov, minister for war, observed in 1908 that he could not hear the words 'modern war' without annoyance. 'As war was, so it has remained; all these things are vicious innovations. Look at me, for instance: for the last 25 years I have not read a single military manual.' As for education, however gallant they were, only 50 per cent of enlisted men in 1914 were estimated to be literate, and there were many who believed that even that statistic was an exaggeration.

Ammunition reserves were dangerously low in a country in which ports from the Primorski Kraj to the Baltic were closed by ice for months at a time, even had the Russian artillery order of battle matched its main enemy's – which it emphatically did not. Russia, without machinery or tools, disposed of one factory to every 150 in the UK. Yet, in German and Austrian eyes, the east was dominated by the nightmarish shape of huge Russian armies poised to strike defenders who, in reality, were inferior only numerically, and superior in most other regards. The Russian staff was so bad and the generals so incompetent that the Second Army under Samsonov, initially at Volkovisk, had 'a compass but no maps': that staff also employed a youth solely to draw caricatures, the son of a Warsaw *chocolatier*.

The German army, in arms and armour, in discipline, in training, in morale and transport, was the antithesis of its Slav opponent and, according to H. A. L. Fisher, 'the most formidable instrument of war which the world had ever seen . . . four million three hundred thousand fully trained and one million partially trained men, with overwhelming artillery' and, through its General Staff, capable of an immaculate administration. Moltke, chief of staff, decided to implement the Schlieffen Plan, under which four-fifths of that army were to be thrown against France and her British ally. After France's elimination, which Schlieffen thought would take six to seven weeks, the strength of the entire German army would be turned against Russia, which, according to the plan, would be in the final stages of deployment.

But before that occurred, Moltke saw the prior need for the presence of a full army, the Eighth, under von Prittwitz at Bartenstein, southeast of Königsberg in east Prussia. Reporting to Prittwitz, who was sixty-six years old, were I Corps commanded by Hermann von François, aged fifty-eight, a former chief of staff to Hindenburg, and a brilliant but wilful subordinate, August von Mackensen, once commander of the Death's Head Hussars, now commanding XVII Corps, XX Corps under von Scholz, 1st Reserve Corps under von Below, von Morgen's 3rd Reserve Division, a cavalry division and three Landwehr brigades, plus garrison troops, 160,000 men in all, a relatively small force. Von Prittwitz was permitted to withdraw it beyond the river Vistula, if faced with greatly superior Russian forces.

On 2 August Grand Duke Nikolai Nikolaevich was appointed supreme commander-in-chief of the Russian army, and General Yanushkevitch as his chief of staff. Evans tells us that the latter had never seen service in the field or commanded any unit larger than a company. 'Our Chief of General Staff is still a child.'

Cavalry General Jilinski, sixty, was C-in-C of the northwest front, comprising First and Second Armies, respectively under Rennenkampf, who had done well against Japan in 1904 but possessed, for whatever reasons, 'a low moral reputation', and Samsonov, a simple, kindly man but, as former governor of Turkestan, out of touch with his own service and unsuitable for this command, besides having been ill when the call came and worrying constantly about his wife's welfare.

Jilinski's instructions to his commanders were that the First Army at Vilna advance north of the Masurian Lakes in order to attract the maximum German response, and to turn the left flank of von François's I Corps. Second Army's task was to advance south of the Masurian Lakes and destroy the Germans positioned between the lakes and, to the west, the Vistula, thus blocking retreat to that river.

Rennenkampf's centre in its premature advance on 17 August, widely dispersed, if not strung out, was initially successful at Stalluponen in the north against German advanced units. His cavalry, under Khan Nahichevanski, were, however, so dilatory that Rennenkampf, on 19 August, ordered him 'to be more energetic and mobile and to remember you have forty-eight guns which, if brought into action in rear of the enemy, would have enormous effect upon him ... Your completely unsatisfactory reports ... I know nothing or at any rate very little about your operation and, about your losses, almost nothing.' At that point, a charge by 1st German Cavalry Division inflicted 3,000 casualties on XX Corps.

Although the Russian northwest front under Jilinski disposed of 208 battalions and 228 squadrons as against 100 German battalions, it was now clear that because of the unpreparedness of the various staff, the chaotic supply and transport systems, the huge number of untrained reservists – 'peasants in disguise' – the army was unable to conduct offensive operations. It was the opinion of General Klyuev, on arriving to command XIII Corps, that before advance was contemplated, more time was essential in order to introduce functioning supply, training and signals organisations. In that context, because of the complete absence of systems, messages had frequently to be sent *en clair*, with all the consequences for security: the Germans could nearly always read Russian traffic, without need for human intelligence agents. On one occasion, furthermore, a Russian signals officer found a great pile of telegrams in the Warsaw telegraph office which, because no arrangements had been made for a telegraphic link with the Second Army, reached their addressees only when the officer carried them himself.

Jilinski – or his superiors – had therefore jumped the gun. His armies lacked supply, transport and training. Put plainly, the men, mostly uneducated and untrained peasants, were required to march in the heat of August, on crumbling, dusty roads, with little or no food for sixteen or seventeen miles a day: not the best method of preparing raw soldiers for battle, all in defence not of Russia, but France. 'Nous sommes heureux de tels sacrifices pour nos alliés,' said Grand Duke Nikolai to the French MA.

On 20 August, nevertheless, after their minor victory at Stalluponen, the Russians continued their advance to Gumbinnen where, under François, the Russians were outflanked on the right and left. They held against a 'mixed-race' unit (XVII Corps) under von Mackensen, who reported to the Eighth Army that he had been defeated and that his position was 'extremely grave'.

It was at this point, when Rennenkampf's whole system of supply – such as it was – had broken down, and he also faced a change of railway gauge, that Samsonov commanding the Second Russian Army also crossed into east Prussia, reaching Willenberg, Ortelsberg and Neidenburg by 23 August. General Alfred Knox's *With the Russian Army* quotes a German description of Samsonov's approach: 'Whole Army Corps advanced from Byelostok without bread or oats . . . march discipline was bad . . . the Russian columns had to wade through sand . . . Nerves were so shaky that the troops fired at every airman, occasionally even at their own automobiles.' There was no communication, let alone cooperation, despite Jilinski's prior and specific instructions, between the First and Second Armies, who had no idea of the other's objectives.

Here Knox, incidentally and as a guide to Russian thinking, quotes an incident from the battle of Gumbinnen. 'B— asked the General if he might go to bed and was told that he might, but that he should not undress. He lay down for an hour and was awakened by Rennenkampf, who stood beside his bed, smiling, and said: "You can take off your clothes now: the Germans are retiring." ' Knox observed that this, in other armies, would have been the moment to pursue the retreating enemy, and not one at which undressing was appropriate counsel.

Samsonov's northward advance from the south, as interpreted by von Prittwitz from aerial observation, led the German C-in-C to believe that the Russians could cut the Eighth Army off from the Vistula. Von Prittwitz accordingly decided, so informing von Moltke, as chief of the General Staff, not only that he intended to retreat to the left bank of the river but that he needed reinforcements to hold even that line. His nerve recovered during the day. Persuaded by his staff, he cancelled the order to withdraw, but not the order breaking off the battle against Rennenkampf in favour of concentration against the Second Army.

Moltke, who had opposed von Prittwitz's appointment in the first place, after consulting the latter's corps commanders, replaced him and his chief of staff, von Waldersee, with the enormous General Hindenburg, sixty-seven, already retired for three years, and the younger Major-General Ludendorff, forty-nine, both Prussians, Ludendorff already famous as chief of staff to von Bülow in August and hero of Liège during the conquest of Belgium. This military partnership on the western front would endure through thick and thin to the very end.

On arrival (23 August) at their east Prussian headquarters, they discovered that their own plans had already been foreseen and duplicated by the staff there, in particular by the brilliant and light-hearted Colonel Max Hoffmann. The decision to switch troops against the Second Army under Samsonov, and to do no more than hold Rennenkampf with a single cavalry division, had not only been confirmed, but the staff work already prepared. As the Dupuys state in the *Encyclopaedia of Military History*, 'the bulk of the German army was shifting south by rail and road against the incompetent Samsonov'.

The Germans, through intercepted signals traffic and some agent intelligence, were continuously aware of Samsonov's locations and intentions during his advance with I, VI, XIII and XXIII Corps, from 23 August. Martos, a bearded general commanding XV Corps, and Gourko, commanding the 1st Cavalry Division, were perhaps the only adequate Russian leaders, Martos – before his capture and aided by XIII Corps under Klyuev – forcing the enemy to withdraw on 24 August, albeit with heavy Russian casualties, at the battle of Orlau-Frankenau. XX German Corps on 25 August made a tactical withdrawal to Tannenberg itself, supported by von Mackensen's XVII Corps, I Reserve Corps under von Below, von Scholz's XX Corps, and von François's I Corps. François's customary mulishness was effectively countered by Ludendorff's immediate instruction that he carry out orders without further argument.

The next and final stage of the battle of Tannenberg, fought in terrible heat between a hungry, collapsing body of brave but ignorant and weakened stragglers, formally lasted from 26 to 31 August. On the later date, the Second Army was surrendered, although only after the temporary Russian recapture of Neidenburg by I Corps under Sirelius, which Blagochevski's VI Corps did little to assist. Martos was captured near Neidenburg, Kondratovic deserted his XXIII Corps, which surrendered, and Klyuev was taken prisoner on 30 August. Martos, just before he was shipped out to captivity, met both Hindenburg, who was polite to him, generous and kind, returning his sword, and Ludendorff, who was none of those things, in a 'dirty little inn' in Osterode. He was then taken in a second-class railway carriage to prison in Germany, eventually to be acquitted of charges for which the penalty was death.

The Russian rear had been taken, in the total encirclement of Samsonov's army, by François's I Corps, which had similarly enveloped the left flank. I Reserve Corps and XVII Corps under von Below and von Mackensen broke Samsonov's right flank. No assistance was received, despite Jilinski's instructions, from Rennenkampf, against whose First Army the Germans (I Corps) then moved in the battle of the Masurian Lakes, immediately after Samsonov's surrender.

On 31 August Hindenburg informed the kaiser that the ring had closed round the greater part of the Russian army, annihilating the XII, XV and XXIII Corps, taking 60,000 prisoners including two corps commanders, Matos and Klyuev. Guns abandoned in the forests were still being collected, as were considerable quantities of matériel; I and VI Corps were in retreat and under pursuit. Including the battle of the Masurian Lakes, Russian casualties, killed, captured and wounded, were estimated at approximately 130,000; between 180 and 500 guns were taken or destroyed.

Rennenkampf, who was not a well-loved officer, deserted his army after the battle of the Masurian Lakes in September, and was cashiered. He was said to have had a running quarrel all his life with Samsonov, allegedly including an exchange of blows on Mukden railway station during the Russo-Japanese War. Trying to escape the pursuing Germans, Samsonov was heard frequently to mutter, 'The tsar trusted me. How can I face him after such disaster?' before shooting himself in thick woods near Pivnitz, his body eventually found by the Germans and recovered after the war by his wife for burial at home in Russia.

In the 'general plan', Moltke had allocated six corps for despatch to the east should the situation require the transfer, reduced to two – the XI and Guard Reserve Corps – on 25 August, entraining on 27 August. Colonel Tappen's explanation for this project was that, 'under the impression that the great strategic battle in the West had already been won [by the Germans]', the chief of the General Staff 'decided to send troops to the East in order to seek a decision there also', when, in fact, the battle had ended before their arrival. In referring to the removal of these units from the western front, in particular from the enveloping German right, rather than the left, a French officer close to Joffre said that 'the measure was perhaps our salvation . . . such a mistake made by the CGS must have made his uncle, the other von Moltke, turn in his grave'.

Both Hindenburg and Ludendorff, in the east, had rejected any requirement for reinforcements, except for smaller units which had no relevance for the western campaign, especially for the battle of the Marne. Moltke had already altered the Schlieffen Plan for the worse and now, by removing these two corps, and reducing his right wing from thirty-four to twenty-five divisions, Germany lost the battle of the Marne and, with it, the mobility needed to win the war, a decisive consequence.*

Moltke, in his memoir of 1915, admitted that as a 'result' of Tannenberg, taking two corps to the east from the German right wing was 'a mistake which had its revenge upon us at the Marne', victory at which would have been almost coterminous with the early triumph of German armies in the war as a whole.

Russian casualties, although General Ironside's *Tannenberg* lists 300,000 men and 650 guns against the figures above of 130,000 men and between 180 and 500 guns, were inflicted with shameful facility on a mainly professional regular army by a much smaller enemy. Many of those killed were NCOs and officers whose loss was never redeemed. The Russian economy started to collapse, and society with it, until, despite Brussilov's victories against the Austro-Hungarian armies, there was by 1917 little left of the old Russian policy.

More even than on the Marne in the west, Tannenberg's most terrible effect was thus in Russia itself and, thereafter, in the

---

* The episode was curiously echoed in 1940 when the Wehrmacht conducted a partial demobilisation before France had been completely defeated: the action shocked Milch and Kesselring, who wanted to use the troops for the invasion of Britain, Operation Sea Lion.

world. Revolution may anyway have been inevitable, but the blow struck by defeat at an establishment, feeble, incompetent, even tottering, led directly under Lenin and Stalin to anarchy, starvation, the massacre of innocent millions, the corruption of entire populations, and to the waste and *longueurs* of the Cold War. These were among the consequences of the decisive battle of Tannenberg.

SYNOPSIS OF EVENTS BETWEEN
TANNENBERG AND NOMONHAN

On 11 November 1918 Germany formally sued for peace, surrendering captured territory as well as most of her own armaments. The former governments of Russia, the Austro-Hungarian Empire and Germany ceased to exist and, by the treaties of Versailles, St Germain and Neuilly, a new Europe was born, which included new governments such as Romania, Poland, Yugoslavia and Czechoslovakia – the 'children' of President Wilson, whose own American electorate then proceeded to reject that League of Nations which he had largely created.

Totalitarian governments, led by dictators, in Germany, Russia and Italy, then imposed themselves on their distressed subjects: communism in Russia, fascism in Italy and Germany, aided by a similar movement in Japan. All were expansionist and aggressive abroad, rigid at home. The world, citing the various needs of its components for resources and territories, moved towards total war.

CHAPTER SEVENTEEN

NOMONHAN, 1939

General Georgii Zhukov, later marshal and victor of Berlin, but then deputy commander of the Belorussian military district, was summoned to Moscow on 2 June 1939 by Marshal Voroshilov who briefed him on the current military situation in central Asia and ordered him to fly to Chita to report and recommend on the future conduct of operations already in progress on the Mongolia–Manchukuo border. ('Zhukov and his wife', according to the biographer William Spahr, 'had thought that he might be on his way to prison or worse.') He arrived by air from Chita in the early morning of 4 June to the dry heat of Tamsag Bulag. Zhukov went straight to the headquarters of the LVII Special Corps, incorporating Soviet and Mongol formations, a large, coarse, abusive soldier with the calm decisive mien of a great captain.

Only a very few Japanese still really believe that their country was created by the gods, specifically the Sun Goddess, ancestress of the first emperor. From the twelfth to the nineteenth century the country was governed by warrior families, the shogunates. In the thirteenth century they defeated Mongol invasions and, in the sixteenth, unified Japan under the Tokugawa shogunate. Tokugawa Ieyasu pursued national isolation, 'the closed country', until two visits by US Commodore Perry's squadron of 'black ships' led to the Open Door and the acceptance of modern technology. In 1868, the Tokugawa were overthrown and nominal powers restored to Emperor Meiji, with an eventual diet (parliament) supervising an industrial society.

However, the dominant force in political life lay with the armed forces, for some of whose number the diet was to become too much. Military victories over Korea, China and, in 1905, tsarist Russia provided legitimacy to the regime, expanded the territories of imperial Japan and restored domestic unity.

The war between Japan and Russia from 1904 to 1905 had been one of horror. The Japanese victory was, however, undoubted. It was a war which caused Asians for the first time to question the omnipotence of European colonists, and even produced the first crack in the self-confidence of Europeans themselves. It also included the destruction of two Russian fleets – the second a triumph as massive as Trafalgar – and led to rioting in Tokyo against what was regarded as inadequate exploitation of victory by a Japanese government which was, in fact, too poor to pursue the war further. The exchequer was almost empty; 90,000 men had died in Manchuria; the country was exhausted.

General Sir Ian Hamilton, who later commanded unsuccessfully at Gallipoli and, therefore, had experience of mass death, had been an observer in 1904–05: 'Here the bodies do not so much appear to be escaping from the ground as to be the ground itself. Everywhere there are bodies or parts of bodies, flattened out and stamped into the surface of the earth as if they formed part of it.' The Japanese commander-in-chief described the land battle as employing 'boiling oil, electrified wire, planks with nails hammered through them to spear the feet in the dark, hot, rainy nights; a war in which the yellow races turned green in death'.

The Russians, under the peace settlement, had to give up the use of Port Arthur, that considerable Manchurian port, to cease military occupation of Manchuria, to return part of Sakhalin and part of the Chinese Eastern Railway, to recognise Japanese primacy in Korea, and to give up Mukden from which, in 1937, Japan's attack on China would proceed. It also led to humiliation among the tsar's subjects, and to the Russian Revolution of 1905, thence a step towards the final explosion in 1917.

In twentieth-century Japan, immense industrial advance based on European and Asian markets was damaged by a severe lack of raw materials, and of territory, for a population which more than doubled between 1890 and 1950. Emigration from the Home Islands to ease this problem was almost entirely prohibited by legislation in most 'receiving' countries, while exports were impeded by western trade barriers and hindered by insecure access to foreign, especially western-controlled, natural resources.

To secure these aims – exports, territory and raw materials – and to create a client state of Russia or, at least, of north Manchuria, and of Siberia between Vladivostock and Lake Baikal, and to integrate the Siberian economy with that of Japan had certainly been the undeclared objective of the 70,000-strong Japanese contingent in the Allied intervention of 1918 against the struggling Bolshevik regime. The force remained in Russia until April 1922. But, even then, there were those to cry, 'in the first war it will be enough to reach Baikal. In the second war we shall plant our flag in the Urals and water our horses in the Volga'. The day would come.

The worldwide depression of the 1920s and 1930s led in Japan to virulent nationalism, riots, attempted armed coups, assassinations of statesmen and political leaders. The army and navy, in collaboration with the *zaibatsu* or major industrialists, took over government in an unbreakable, centralised bureaucracy.

Thus, economically frustrated by a west which would not accept racial equality with Japan and offered only discrimination and aggression, the Japanese Kwantung Army staged the 1931 Mukden incident, an act of provocation which led to the occupation of Manchuria by Japanese forces. Huge Manchuria became Manchukuo, Japan's colony and economic and military base on the mainland of Asia. To acquire yet richer prizes, the temporary disappearance of one Japanese private soldier at the Marco Polo Bridge near Beijing in July 1937 was contrived to lead to the invasion of China and to all-out war against Chiang Kai-shek and, later, Mao. This ran on uselessly until 1945, absorbing imperial Japanese troops who could been have more effectively deployed elsewhere.

In China by 1939, the Japanese had conquered Shanghai, Beijing, Nanking and Canton, but not Chungking. No further advances were made for five years: the Chinese quagmire had begun, Korea and Formosa, of course, already Japanese satraps.

Elsewhere in Asia, Outer Mongolia (as opposed to Inner Mongolia in China) had moved in the turbulent days of 1921 from a flimsy independence under her own god-kings to the status of 'first satellite' of the USSR. In that capacity, her value to the Soviet Union lay chiefly in her production of meat and milk and in her position as a buffer state against the Japanese in Manchuria. Because Japanese Manchukuo was encircled in 1938 by Soviet and Mongol territory containing forces twice as large as her own, Japan had plans for an autonomous Greater Mongolia under her influence. Nothing came of it. Had it done so, the Soviet Far Eastern defences would have been torn open.

So stood Japan in 1939, bloated with conceit and resentment at the west, in particular Britain, for patronising, then abandoning this great nation. Ambitious for glory and riches, but prevented by western racism from acquiring either peacefully, Japan was thus determined on the conquest of despised Russian neighbours whose lands should form her own deserved reward and fortune. Japan was about to strike north.

Khalkin Gol or Halha river, east of which lay Nomonhan, was claimed by the Ching dynasty in the eighteenth century approximately to demarcate the border between Mongolia and Manchuria. In 1932 Japan had accepted the arrangement and created the puppet state of Manchukuo out of the vastness of

Manchuria. The USSR, however, extended the territory of its Mongol ally several miles eastward, while for her part accusing the Japanese of pursuing 'geographical warfare' in a *westerly* direction.

The landscape on either side of the river is low and flat, although usually higher on the west or Mongolian bank. The Halha's waters provide some green pasture, even in winter: snow does not lie heavy there or often. But the region is a freezing barren place from autumn onwards, cold even in summer after the sun has set, while fiercely hot in the unpolluted day, a trackless land ocean, thin grasses, dunes and desert sands, stark, empty wastes.

Spring in these latitudes is a trying season, not the joyous rebirth seen in Europe, but a time of winds and sand driven against the eyes and face and ears. The ice starts to break for a little while on the streams and rivers, light rains fall on the soda grass and camel bushes, and on grey rocks covered with red lichen. Dunes border arid, sandy clay, gritty, compressed, eroded. Duck, chiefly teal, are found near the rare stagnant ponds and shallow, dried-out swamps.

The Japanese claimed that hostilities began when 200 Mongol horsemen and 60 machine-gunners of the 7th Border Guards were driven back by Manchukuo Barguts between 10 and 12 May 1939. The Russians, on the other hand, told Zhukov on his arrival that troops of the Japanese Kwantung Army under the dignified, withdrawn General Komatsubara, tall, dapper, almost dandyish, literate and cultured, had crossed the frontier on 11 May and occupied the Khalkin Gol salient. In response, the Russian and Mongolian troops of the LVII Special Corps from Mongolian bases re-established a bridgehead on the eastern bank of the river.

On 5 June Zhukov sacked N. V. Fedlenko, the corps commander. 'Do you believe it possible to command troops 120 kilometres from the battlefield?' 'We are a bit too far from it,' Fedlenko admitted, 'but we were about to send for timber and start building . . .' Moscow agreed to Zhukov's request for three rifle divisions and tank, artillery and aircraft reinforcements; between 24 June and the beginning of July, aerial dogfights took place between the two air forces, about which the Japanese claims seem more plausible. Ground contact resulted in serious casualties in both the Soviet and the imperial Japanese armies, now renamed the First Army Group and the Sixth Army, respectively.

On 3 July the Japanese of the 23rd Division seized the Bain Tsagaan (Rich White) Heights with 10,000 infantrymen. Zhukov sent up to 150 tanks and 150 other armoured vehicles of the 11th Tank Brigade, 7th Armoured Brigade and 8th Mongolian Armoured Battalion to destroy such Japanese as had crossed the Halha. The diary on a Japanese corpse read: 'chaos among our troops . . . Horses stampeded', for the Sixth Army was dependent more on horses than on the internal combustion engine, 'and dragging gun carriages with them: cars scattered in all directions. Morale fell extremely low.' Japanese soldiers could be heard saying more and more frequently that things were 'terrible', 'sad', 'ghastly'.

On 5 July the Japanese began to retreat, but bridges had been blown up by Japanese sappers alarmed by the breakthrough of Soviet tanks. Japanese officers dived headlong into the water in full uniform. Many drowned.

Very large quantities of fuel, ammunition and food were despatched to the Russians by truck in round trips lasting five days, the journey 650 kilometres to and from the Mongolian supply railhead. Zhukov mounted a comprehensive concealment and misinformation campaign to persuade the Japanese that he was planning a defensive rather than an offensive battle. His instruments were radio, telephone, disguised or artificial noise, even leaflets leaked to the enemy apparently designed to teach Soviet soldiers to fight in defence. The 149th Motorised Rifle Regiment was charged with reconnaissance and intelligence gathering.

By 20 August, when the general offensive was due to begin, two Russian rifle divisions, a tank brigade, two artillery regiments and other formations had moved to reinforce the existing units of Zhukov's First Army Group. Against 35 Soviet battalions, 200 heavy guns, about 800 armoured fighting vehicles (AFVs) and 200 aircraft, the Sixth Army under General Ueda Kenkichi could only offer 25 infantry battalions, 180 inferior 'tankettes' fit mainly for reconnaissance, 180 guns, many built between 1905 and 1908, and 400 aircraft. The standard of mechanisation was low: a favourite weapon was the Molotov cocktail, one-third sand and two-thirds petrol in a soft-drink bottle.

Sunday, 20 August was a fine, warm day. Japanese officers, believing that the Soviets had no intention of attacking on that or adjacent days, had taken short leaves, many to destinations far away from their troops. General Yasuoka's armour, outgunned, slow and restricted in range, had already lost in battle half the strength of Colonels Yoshimaru's and Tamada's 3rd and 4th Tank Regiments. Ueda ordered the armour to retire, a departure viewed with pleasure and relief by the Russians and with regret by a Japanese infantry that had looked up to its armoured brothers.

In general, the Red Army had hitherto disposed of more and better vehicles, including tracked or wheeled armour, always supported by artillery and infantry, whereas the Japanese tanks had made their desperate advance into enveloping Russian coil wire, unsupported by infantry or by anything else except samurai spirit. The Soviets fought skilfully, if with less *bushido* dash, using ambush and deception, exploiting technical and numerical superiority through good organisation, beginning with artillery barrages under which tanks and infantry mounted coordinated assaults, professionally and without bravado. The Russians conquered by speed, long-range firepower, reverse-slope and hull-down fire; and by forethought, training and better equipment.

When the battle began again that August, Zhukov planned to encircle the enemy north and south of the Holsten river within a solid ring and smash them, first with a northern, then with a southern group, covered both in the centre and from outside the ring. Japanese troops, on entering the sand dunes, after severe bombardment from Soviet aircraft and artillery, were then devastated by tanks and guns before the infantry went in. Initially, however, the Soviets fled at the grotesque if gallant sight of 72nd Regiment advancing in open order across the wastes, the battalion commander walking forward, his drawn sabre bound in red. Nishikawa, although soon hit, shifted his sword to the other hand and went on under a ferocious sun, even a glint from his field glasses catching the eyes of Soviet snipers.

The Japanese 'at first heard what sounded like birds in the spring in the grass . . . machine-gun bullets whizzing over-head'. Men fell everywhere in the noise and smoke: losses were grave, only thirty surviving in one company from the bombs and shells. 'Corpses were stacked up like cordwood.' The living shivered in their hopeless lightweight uniforms against Zhukov's final tally of five well-fed, clothed and equipped rifle divisions, six or seven tank brigades and the several artillery regiments. 'Only rifles remained' in defence of Japanese positions. Near Heights 742, a gunner heard Japanese soldiers sing the national anthem, then shout cheers for the emperor, the prelude to mass suicide.

Soviet rings or cordons tightened across the whole battlefield at a time when the Japanese lacked weapons, ammunition and, increasingly, men, these not only dying but sometimes running for their lives. Everywhere men could see the desperate struggle and the heart-rending scene of wounded comrades – prostrate or leaping from blazing tanks – being bayoneted by the Russian infantry.

Japanese forces, never good in defence, now began to panic; in one sector, even officers discussed *sauve qui peut* as the 20 tanks and 800 men closed in. 'The dark green Soviet tanks seemed huge . . . blood dyed the dunes; all we could do was fight with an iron will transcending human strength', in combat which included grenades, bayonets, shovels. 'We hadn't eaten for a week and our faces and bodies were so misshapen that we no longer looked human.' The colours were then burned. Three cheers were given for the emperor. Higashi with drawn sword led a charge. When a Japanese soldier at the peace ceremony asked a Russian sergeant to admit that at least the Japanese had been brave, his interlocutor responded: 'Don't be such a jerk: we won the war.'

Komatsubara left the field. His aide in 23rd Division, tears streaming down his cheeks, said that the general's hair had turned entirely white, his face filled with an indescribable sorrow. Two corporals held his arms to prevent him from shooting himself as he staggered along. The pleading in the moonlight of those wounded and abandoned, 'Are you going to leave us behind? . . . Please take us with you', haunted the memories of the survivors, but these, against tracer, flares and machine-gun fire, 'left their fate to the gods and ran and ran until their units lost all formation'.

The battlefield was extremely quiet and both the ground and sky looked still.

Subsequently, Zhukov commented that Soviet troops who had fought at Khalkin Gol were often detached after the battle to pass on their experience to other units. When moved to the Moscow area in 1941, no praise was too high for their conduct against the Wehrmacht. He told Stalin, at a personal interview in May 1940, that Japanese other ranks and junior officers were brave and well trained, especially at close quarters: he was uncomplimentary about their senior officers ('apt to act according to the rule book'), and about Japanese armour and artillery. He spoke almost as favourably of the Mongolian army as of the Russian, although adding that their cavalry was 'sensitive' to air raids and artillery fire.

The Japanese, he told the dictator, had failed to achieve their aim, to seize Mongolian territory beyond the Khalkin Gol and build a fortified line to defend a second strategic railway track, west of the Chinese Eastern Railway and close to the border of the Soviet Trans-Baikal district. Soviet claims of Japanese killed and wounded at Khalkin Gol rise as high as 65,000, although the Japanese themselves have not formally admitted to more than 18,000. An American diplomat in Mukden, presumably counting hospital trains, reached a figure of 30,000. The Soviets put their own losses at 10,000 men.

This was the first test of war employing combined armour, artillery, infantry and aircraft on a large scale. It ensured, first, the defence of Mongolia and, second, a realisation in Tokyo that Japan could not defeat, still less conquer and occupy, modern Russia. A weaker Japanese force may have taken on four rifle divisions and five mechanised brigades, but Japan had suffered the double shame of defeat by the despised Russians and of 'treason' elsewhere – the almost simultaneous signature on 23 August 1939 of the Nazi–Soviet Pact by her German ally. No amount of hand-to-hand glory could eliminate that.

There were central consequences. Stalin and Zhukov now knew, because they had penetrated the Japanese establishment through the German spy Richard Sorge, that Russian victory at Nomonhan meant that the Japanese had no plans, during the forthcoming Great Patriotic War, to attack Russia. The Soviets could therefore, while maintaining an essential Far Eastern shield, release large Siberian and other formations, otherwise allocated to defence against Japan, to reinforce the western front against the Axis, providing themselves with a decisive freedom of manoeuvre on the main field of battle, that between Russia and Germany.

And that consequence did not even include the even more fateful swing given to history by this terrible encounter. Japan, after the trauma of defeat, still nevertheless needed land and territory. Since Russia was *chasse gardée*, South East Asia and the Pacific became Japan's targets. A battle fought three years before in the wastes of central Asia led thus, after Japanese action at Pearl Harbor, Java, Indo-China, Malaya, Bataan and Rangoon, to the fall in Asia during 1942 of the vast American, British, French and Dutch empires, recovered for a moment in 1945 but lost again, to independence, in the years that followed: the world turned upside down. The western Allies did not foresee this outcome. Nomonhan in 1939 and its consequence did not appear to have been noted in London and Washington. The overriding importance also to Japan of Asian oil and other resources seems to have been discounted in favour of a conviction that Japan could not resist the temptation to strike north. The Allies averted their eyes from the disagreeable likelihood of a Japanese strike south for economic salvation, in fact Japan's only, if ultimately doomed, alternative.

They had, indeed, little choice. While all *that* was going on, the British were mounting operations to drive the Germans and Italians out of Cyrenaica, and denying to the Asian theatre, for the sake of the USSR, the troops and matériel which could have saved the British Empire in the east while concurrently fighting, almost alone, the battles of Greece, North Africa, the Mediterranean and the Atlantic, not to mention the Battle of Britain.

SYNOPSIS OF EVENTS BETWEEN
NOMONHAN AND THE BATTLE OF BRITAIN

The world was shocked in August 1939 by the signature between the world's principal ideological enemies of the Nazi–Soviet Pact. On 1 September 1939 Germany invaded Poland; on 3 September Britain and France declared war on Germany; and in April and May 1940 Germany invaded Denmark, Norway, Holland, Belgium and France. Also in May 1940 Winston Churchill despatched his first message as prime minister to President Roosevelt. On 4 June of the same year, British, French and Belgian troops, defeated by the Germans, were evacuated to the UK from Dunkirk. The Franco-German armistice was signed on 25 June 1940 and in August fifty US destroyers were acquired by Britain in exchange for Caribbean naval and air bases.

CHAPTER EIGHTEEN

THE BATTLE OF BRITAIN, 1940

And what the dead had no speech for, when living,
They can tell you, being dead: the communication
Of the dead is tongued with fire beyond the language of the living.
Here, the intersection of the timeless moment
Is England and nowhere. Never and always.

T. S. Eliot

In 1933 a psychotic bullyboy, aided by a royalist aristocrat, Franz von Papen, and by the aging General von Hindenburg, became chancellor of the German Reich, replacing the former government of the Weimar Republic. That administration had, nevertheless, before its displacement, at least ended foreign (Allied) occupation of Germany, reduced reparations, restored the currency and brought its defeated country into the League of Nations.

Thereafter, uttering anti-Semitic, nationalist and anti-communist tribal cries, Herr Hitler pursued internally a course of dictatorial terrorism, involving creation of a slave state, and externally embarked on armed aggression in defiance of the Versailles Treaty. By June 1940, with a revived Wehrmacht, he had ended the sovereign existence of Austria, Czechoslovakia, Poland, Norway, Belgium, the Netherlands and France. Italy, furthermore, under Mussolini, had volunteered for him and against Britain, just before France, on 17 June 1940, had sought armistice. The United Kingdom and its empire were left as his only active democratic opponents.

Earlier, in August 1939, Hitler had confused and alarmed an already terrified world by signature of a non-aggression treaty between Berlin and Moscow, the Nazi–Soviet Pact. At that stage and throughout the autumn of 1939, he had no plans for an invasion of Great Britain. He anyway probably considered the step otiose in light of the likely defeat of France in the forthcoming war in the west. After his victory in 1940, however, following unsuccessful peace approaches to the UK through Dutch, Turkish, Italian and Swedish intermediaries, Hitler began to understand that, against all reason, Britain would not surrender.

On 18 June 1940, the anniversary of Waterloo, Winston Churchill had addressed the House of Commons:

> The battle of Britain is about to begin . . . Hitler knows that he will have to break us in this island or lose the war. If we can stand up to him, all Europe may be free and the life of the world may move forward into broad, sunlit uplands . . . But if we fail, then the whole world, including the United States, including all that we have known and cared for, will sink into the abyss of a new Dark Age . . . Let us therefore brace ourselves to our duties and so bear ourselves that, if the British Empire and Commonwealth last for a thousand years, men will still say, 'This was their finest hour.'

And those words only served to confirm – despite the surrender of France – his rallying call of 28 May:

> We shall go on to the end . . . we shall fight on the seas and oceans, we shall fight with growing confidence and growing strength in the air, we shall defend our island whatever the cost may be, we shall fight on the landing grounds, we shall fight in the fields and in the streets, we shall fight in the hills; we shall never surrender and even if, which I do not for a moment believe,

this island or a large part of it were subjugated and starving, then our Empire beyond the seas, armed and guarded by the British Fleet, would carry on the struggle until in God's good time, the new world with all its power and might steps forth to the rescue and the liberation of the old.

Some of his listeners knew that Churchill gave this speech when Britain's military might comprised merely thirty under-strength, partly trained infantry divisions, some fresh from humiliating defeat, and Local Defence Volunteers (later Home Guard) often equipped only with shotguns and pikes, in circumstances which sometimes required initial unit training in mock-up tanks made of wood.

Few, nevertheless, as is usual with the British, concluded that defeat was inevitable, because of reliance on the Royal Navy's history, on the Royal Air Force, and on national self-confidence. Hitler, at least temporarily certain that Churchill meant what he so brilliantly declared, issued a directive in mid-July for the invasion of England, 'to eliminate, if necessary through occupation, Great Britain as a base for war against Germany'. The project was to be known as Sea Lion and, with thirty-nine divisions and corresponding shipping, was to be prepared by mid-August, a deadline so ridiculous that it may help to explain the conviction of 'Boney' Fuller that Hitler had been bluffing all the time.

Some, then as now, agreed with Fuller. Some also believed, whether because of Hitler's alleged respect for Britain and her empire, or because of their own conviction that radical enfeeblement of the empire was the sole result possible from continued hostilities with Germany, that Britain's future lay in a compromise peace. (Stafford Cripps told a neutral that an attack on the island would probably succeed.) Churchill believed quite otherwise or, rather, he saw the Nazi challenge as more terrible in its consequences for civilisation than even the loss, through resistance, of that empire which he loved over everything.

Stephen Bungay's magisterial *The Most Dangerous Enemy* plainly states that it was in defence of liberal democracy, a concept shared with the United States, that the British had to fight, '*because they were there*. As long as Nazism flourished, none would be safe.' In other words Churchill's own refutation of the assertion in *Mein Kampf* that 'Britain had no essential conflict with Germany in Europe' because, in fact, their interests were wholly incompatible.

The British were fighting for ideals again. Until they could be stopped, Hitler could not securely acquire the *Lebensraum* in Russia that he needed to accommodate his countrymen. Attempts at settlement with London, such as a halt of German armour before the Channel ports, had failed in the face of British obstinacy. Hitler had to drop negotiations in favour either of siege or of the invasion that General Jodl advocated.

Invasion, however, was possible only if air superiority could be achieved over southeast England; if British security and production were to be so diminished that either option – siege or invasion – would become feasible. The Luftwaffe's role was to defeat the RAF and neutralise the Royal Navy. The task was simplified after the fall and capture of airfields along the coast of occupied Europe, air and sea then both cleared for combat.

General Halder, German chief of army staff, considered that Britain's position was hopeless: 'The war is won by us. A reversal in the prospects of success is impossible.' In the meanwhile, in case Sea Lion did not work, or Britain still refused Germany's terms, Hitler had begun preparations for Barbarossa, the invasion of the Soviet Union which, if successful, should certainly make it impossible for Churchill to continue his war, whether or not the RAF had been by that time destroyed. But the preparations now under way for Sea Lion at least made plain that allegations of 'bluff' about the operation were mistaken. By 17 September 1940 there were 1,700 barges and 200 seagoing ships in continental ports selected as bases for invasion, with a potential load of 500,000 troops. AOC 11 Group, Air Vice-Marshal Keith Park, a brilliant New Zealander, was at one with Downing Street and, indeed, the White House in believing invasion to be then imminent.

Headquarters of Fighter Command, the Luftwaffe's principal target, was at Bentley Priory near Stanmore, in an eighteenth-century mansion, and had been there under 'Stuffy' Dowding, the RAF's oldest commander, since 1936. Although apparently aloof and withdrawn, Dowding 'knew all the issues'; he had been able between the wars to convince Prime Minister Chamberlain of the need for a strong fighter force – as opposed to the Douhet–Trenchard bomber strategy – and for a comprehensive system of fighter control, including input from wireless interception (insecure aircrew conversation), Enigma (signals intelligence) and radar. Thirty-one radar stations were built during the Battle of Britain, supplemented visually by 30,000 men in the Observer Corps. Anti-aircraft and Balloon Commands were also under Dowding's control. No mention is made of radar in the Air Ministry's *Battle of Britain* published in March 1941: a curious obsession with security after the fact.

Information was passed from the Operations Room at Bentley to 10, 11, 12 and 13 Groups (South West, South East, Midlands and the North), thence to sectors known by letters and by the names of their stations, controlling between two and six squadrons each. Fighter Command devolved tactical command to the groups, in the case of the Battle of Britain largely to 11 Group, Keith Park, thence to the sectors and squadrons. The system was simple and robust. Communications were the province of an efficient and experienced General Post Office. Even the radar towers, although several times put out of action, were small and hard to hit. The pilots were well practised. According to Bungay, only ninety seconds were required for the last aircraft of any squadron to reach take-off from scramble. But in air–sea rescue over the Channel, and in cooperation between 11 Group and Trafford Leigh-Malloy's 12 Group, influenced by Douglas Bader's concepts, there were serious lacunae.

'From the first, however,' said the German fighter-ace Adolf Galland, quoted by Bungay, 'the British had an extraordinary advantage, never to be balanced out at any time during the whole war, which was their radar and fighter control network organisation. It was for us a very bitter surprise.' Galland added, 'We could do no other than knock frontally against the outstandingly well-organised and resolute direct defence of the British Isles.'

The squadrons, sectors, groups and Fighter Command itself were all responsible, through the Air Staff in London – led by Air Chief Marshal Sir Cyril Newall and Air Marshal Sholto Douglas, the latter no supporter of Dowding – to the minister for air, Sir Archibald Sinclair, Liberal MP and former soldier in a battalion led by Churchill during the First World War, an intelligent, honest, steady Scot, and a far cry from his German opposite number.

The massive, flamboyant Hermann Goering had been a fighter ace with von Richthofen's squadron in the Great War. Now both air minister and commander-in-chief of the Luftwaffe, although addicted to morphine prescribed after he was shot in the Munich coup, he forcefully expanded the air force over the six years until 1939, and exercised direct authority over the Battle of Britain. On assuming command he had at his disposal 20,000 men and 1,800 aircraft, developed under cover of the German airline, Deutsche Lufthansa, many of the pilots trained clandestinely in the USSR.

By 1939, according to Williamson Murray's *Luftwaffe*, his service had 15,000 officers and 370,000 men in five air fleets, the most important of which, and the closest to the battle area, being Fleets 2 and 3. (German air fleets, unlike British functional commands, were mixed: fighters, bombers, training, coastal, combined.) Fleet 2 was commanded by Albert Kesselring, a veteran of the battle for France and, later, in charge of the great fighting retreat against the Allies in Italy. Fleet 3 was under the fat, relatively genial, Hugo Sperrle, both he and Kesselring professional soldiers, although Sperrle had also commanded the Condor Legion in Spain; because of his alarming appearance, he was, on occasion, also employed by Hitler to intimidate nervous foreign leaders.

Richard Overy's *The Air War 1939–1945* has told us that, at the outbreak of war with Poland, the Luftwaffe had a first-line strength of 3,609 aircraft, of which 2,893 were serviceable, with 900 reserves. Contemporary figures for the RAF were 1,911 first-line, 1,600 serviceable, and 2,200 reserves (all types for both air forces). The total first-line and reserves were therefore, respectively, 4,509 and 4,111.

After the battles for Poland and France, in which the Luftwaffe suffered substantial losses, the Germans mustered 805 operational fighters, reduced during the Battle of Britain to 533 and, briefly, on 1 October to 275. British fighters, at the same time, numbered a total of 1,032, of which 715 were operational in August. Dowding, because of the astonishing efforts of British aircraft factory workers, was able to create a reserve for 11 Group, the sharpest end of Fighter Command's defence campaign, out of this increase in production, redistributing the 'excess' to 12 and 13 Groups to be summoned as required.

In Germany, until Speer took over, industry could not reproduce the production targets earlier set by Marshal Erhard Milch. Goering's short-termism and lack of vision caused similar shortfalls in technology – other than in *Knickebein* navigation – and in training, particularly of bomber pilots.

The Battle of Britain was very 'untidy'. Even the start-date is subject to argument. Regular but relatively low-key attacks from June and July, in the sunlight and blue skies of that extraordinary and heroic summer, were mounted by the Luftwaffe against British shipping, including convoys in the Channel, and against ports, partly in the framework of blockade. It is, however, generally agreed that the first phase in the battle itself was from 5–8 August, following Hitler's directive of 1 August to his airmen 'to overpower the English air force in the shortest possible time'.

The method adopted to eliminate Fighter Command was to bring the RAF to battle by using German bombers as the bait. This meant 'drawing up' the fighters, on the Luftwaffe's terms, for destruction by Me110s, and by Me109s, the fastest and most manoeuvrable fighter extant, while the escorted bombers sailed serenely on to their targets in superior numbers. But those bombers, including the Dornier 17 and Heinkel 111, were inadequately armed, carried small bomb loads inaccurately aimed and, other than the Ju88, were too slow. Even the Ju88 was vulnerable in daylight to the more manoeuvrable, faster Hurricanes and Spitfires, both with eight machine-guns, speeds between 325 and 340 m.p.h. and ceilings of 34–35,000 feet. The deficiencies of both British aircraft lay in armament, in dangerous (non-self-sealing) fuel tanks and, initially, two-pitch propellers. The main German fighter weaknesses were, surprisingly, shortage of aircrew, although not of skilled and experienced pilots, and of range, which severely limited the Me109's combat time.

On 6 August at his lair at Carinhall, resplendent with stolen goods, Goering gave his instructions to Kesselring, Sperrle, and to General Stumpff's Air Fleet 5 in Norway. Their orders were to destroy Fighter Command across the south of England in four days by day and night and then to move the battle to East Anglia, the Midlands, eventually to dominate all the skies of Britain.

In the phase of 8–18 August Dowding's 52 squadrons of 650 operational fighters had faced about 900 German fighters and 1,300 bombers. (The probing phase from June to July when bombing attacks had been carried out all over the country, in particular in the West Country, was over: these, however irritating, had given Fighter Command at least an opportunity to watch Luftwaffe techniques, to drop the 'vic' or 'V' formation in favour of German 'loose pairs', and to improve communications.) Tactics moved to Air Vice-Marshal Park's deployment of fighters in small groups, forcing German fighters to stick to escorting the bombers instead of the preferred pursuit of their British counterparts. At the end of this phase, although the Luftwaffe made over 1,500 sorties a day, Fighter Command still had air superiority over the islands.

Starting on the abortive Day of the Eagles, *Adlertag*, some attacks had been carried out against the main fighter bases: the main *Adlertag*, however, was continually delayed by the weather, too good or too bad. The 'end' of Fighter Command was, nevertheless, planned by Goering to be coincident with the seaborne invasion, now again postponed until 15 September. Fifty-three attacks were mounted against airfields, thirty-two of them fighter bases, all but two in the 11 Group area. Raids were also directed against radar stations, communication and supply routes. Damage – especially at Ventnor, Manston, Biggin Hill and Lympne – was very severe indeed, and not always rapidly repaired. And nearly sixty aircraft were destroyed on the ground in one day.

But Park then deployed his fighters inland, away from the coast, under the protection of 10 and 12 Groups, his 11 Group fighters employed against Me109s and Me110s, strictly avoiding battle over water. Hurricanes concentrated on bombers and Spitfires on fighters. Each side, between early August and early September, lost about 450 fighters. The Luftwaffe, always overestimating their successes, believed that they had reduced Fighter Command to 100 aircraft, instead of the 730 operational and 250 stored aircraft on 6 September.

Still, by that date, in the second phase, 103 pilots from The Few were killed and 128 wounded. (The Germans fared no better.) Exhaustion and strain were intense. Park reported to Dowding that the cumulative impact of the pounding received by airfields had had 'a serious effect on the fighting efficiency of the fighter squadrons'. Richard Overy describes the damage suffered by 'men swept around on a carousel of noise, danger and fear', palliated only by games and PE, by the occasional night of untroubled sleep in distant refuges, and by 'free electric light in airfield squash courts'. The C-in-C, at this critical stage, tried to arrange twenty-four hours off every week for his pilots, described with affection by the American reporter Virginia Cowles as like overgrown children, 'little boys with blond hair and pink cheeks who looked as though they ought to be in school'.

Their stress was the greater because of British intelligence failure which, unlike the German, was consistently to overestimate Luftwaffe numbers of aircraft and – although German pilots were certainly older and, after Spain, Poland and France, more experienced – of men as well, so the task always seemed even more perilously overwhelming than it was.

In early September, round the clock, the Germans switched their daylight attacks away from airfields and control centres to London and to other major urban areas, at the very time when success for the Luftwaffe had begun to seem possible through the earlier strategy. Assuming, wrongly, that Fighter Command was on its last legs, Hitler believed that this new tactic would so reduce Britain's will and capacity that, even if she did not surrender, Sea Lion would become practical. Between 7 and 15 September, however, the Luftwaffe lost nearly 300 aircraft (99 fighters) and, in the first week of the new phase, 199 bombers against 120 RAF fighters.

On 15 September, now known as Battle of Britain Day, 1,000 bombers in three giant waves, escorted by 700 fighters, struck London in the largest, and one of the last, of the major daylight raids, opposed by 300 Hurricanes and Spitfires. The Luftwaffe suffered losses which no air force could sustain for more than a few days. Thereafter, operations moved mostly to the night, ultimately increasing bomber losses further and increasing Fighter Command's successes.

Including the subsequent Blitz on London, Coventry, Southampton and elsewhere, over 40,000 civilians were killed and 50,000 seriously injured, with equally heartbreaking destruction of buildings. But in September, Hitler suspended Sea Lion. On 12 October he cancelled it.

Radar, RAF 'Y' and Ultra signals intelligence, in terms of technology, German error in diverting strength from essential to 'secondary' targets and a tested system of command and force control, brilliantly executed, had been handmaidens to the determination and will of the British and the skilled courage of Britain's pilots. 'Never,' said Churchull, 'in the field of human conflict, was so much owed by so many to so few': 900 British aircraft were shot down, but so were over 1,700 of the Luftwaffe, and they could not be replaced. The German losses were so large that the decisive air victory needed to launch Sea Lion safely could not be achieved.

Britain had, in those days, other fish to fry than the Battle of Britain, including the now forgotten major war against Italy in North Africa and in the Mediterranean, which drew so many ships of the Royal Navy away from the vital Battle of the Atlantic and the protection of Britain's trade and supplies. By January 1941, furthermore, despite the cancellation of Sea Lion, Hitler had still not entirely ruled out the collapse of Britain under aerial and maritime blockade, or, at least, had not discounted a successful invasion, while recognising the disastrous consequences of failure in that regard.

There were, however, glories and bright stars. Fighter Command had certainly not conquered the Luftwaffe (nor vice versa), but had ensured that no invasion could be carried out on the existing schedule. (The watching presence of the Royal Navy and of a rejuvenated army had made their contributions to that argument, as did Hitler's ambivalent attitude to all-out struggle with Britain.) Because of radar, increased aircraft production, Enigma, Ultra, greater losses among trained German pilots and inadequate Luftwaffe intelligence on numerical British air strength, the terrible ordeal of defeat was prevented. As at Trafalgar, the wary gallantry of Britain held the line against a dictatorship imposed on an entire continent.

What we really know about the Battle of Britain is the lesson that Stephen Bungay gave at the end of *The Most Dangerous Enemy*: 'Probably most people fought because Churchill told them they had to, so they just got on with it in an act of sacrifice which saved civilisation . . . Sacrifice it certainly was. The fate of Europe, and not just of Britain, depended upon it. However it was conceived and understood at the time, it was not the meanest of acts among nations.'

SYNOPSIS OF EVENTS BETWEEN THE BATTLE OF BRITAIN AND THE FALL OF SINGAPORE

In July 1940 the Royal Navy, to prevent use by the enemy of the French squadrons at Oran, sank these vessels in that port. 'The Blitz' over Britain followed the Battle of Britain through to November 1940 when simultaneously the British Mediterranean Fleet was reinforced. The Anglo-Free French assault on Dakar failed.

In December 1940 recognition of the U-boat menace was balanced by the better news of the defeat of the Italian armies in North Africa, although by April and May 1941 British troops were being evacuated from Greece in large numbers, with heavy naval and military casualties.

In Operation Barbarossa Hitler invaded the USSR in June 1941. Later that year troops under General Auchinleck relieved the threat to the Suez Canal.

In December 1941 Japanese aircraft from carriers bombed the US fleet at Pearl Harbor, causing Hitler to make the cardinal error of declaring war on the USA. Japanese troops attacked and took the British, French and Dutch colonies of Malaysia, Singapore, Hong Kong, the Netherlands East Indies, Burma, French Indo-China, encroaching into India, Ceylon and US possessions and associates in the Philippines and the Pacific islands.

CHAPTER NINETEEN

SINGAPORE AND MALAYA, 1941–2

In a letter dated 19 July 1886 to the governor of the Straits Settlement, Lord Granville informed His Excellency that Her Majesty's government did not 'intend to create a naval fortress at Singapore, nor to provide a defence which is theoretically perfect, but to establish a means of protection bearing due relation to the geographical position of the Colony'. In 1911, however, the Colonial Defence Committee, opposing Mr Winston Churchill, said that a fortress should protect its *rear* against besieging infantry. 'Fixed defences, however formidable, will not render a fortress secure against attack by an expeditionary force. This form of attack can only be dealt with by mobile troops and guns capable of being moved to any threatened point.'

In 1918 the Royal Navy had nearly as many capital ships – not yet replaced as a measure of strength by submarine and aircraft – as the rest of the world combined. This preponderance, with ports under her sovereignty, guaranteed to Britain the command of the sea necessary for the safety of empire, the protection of trade, the security of raw materials and superiority over the most probable combination of two opponents.

That latter formula, a 'two-power navy', had itself been amended for the Far East, after the defeat in 1905 of the Russian navies by Admiral Togo in the Tsushima straits, to a 'combination' of the British and Japanese fleets in these waters. Since the arrangement included no British capital ships, it had enabled the British to deal on more than equal terms with her principal European enemies, first the Russians and French, then the Imperial German Navy.

In 1921, for political and especially economic reasons, Britain could not return to the two-power standard. But since the possibility of war with Japan, if not with the United States, was 'thinkable', if unlikely, Britain chose no longer to maintain her alliance with Japan, rather to establish a naval base in Asia, avoiding what Lord Beatty described as the 'intolerable sufferance' of another power, Japan. The choice fell on Singapore, purchased in 1819 by Sir Stamford Raffles for the East India Company, now a huge commercial port with adequate anchorage for a great fleet and potential storage of oil fuel, the navy's new motive power.

Lord Neidpath in his dazzling *Singapore Naval Base* showed that a UK pause in shipbuilding had been matched by no such holiday in Japan or the USA. The deficit was estimated to lead, by 1923, to Britain becoming only the second naval power (behind the USA), at least in capital ships. As a foreign policy directed against the USA was not envisaged, an alliance with that country based on equality was preferred to the alternatives of massive construction or a formal Anglo-Japanese alliance. Furthermore, in order to avoid a naval race, capital ship ratios for the USA, UK and Japan were stabilised by the Washington Conference at 5 : 5 : 3. It was understood that, in wartime, the British Main Fleet would be despatched from Europe (Home and Mediterranean) to Asia. Lord Jellicoe's report of 1919, which had referred to Japan as the Germany of the Far East, was alone in contemplating a fleet of eight battleships and eight battle cruisers *on permanent station* in Asia.

Even at this stage, however, other voices had agreed that the speed at which the British position in the Far East could be reinforced depended on the threat to the UK, which would, in turn, also determine the strength of such reinforcements and, indeed, the length of time during which Singapore, Australia and New Zealand would lack adequate naval protection. Three months might pass before relief could arrive, during which there was little or no prospect of defending at least the island colony of Hong Kong from massive successful attack by the Japanese army in China, without even considering other British possessions.

Renewal of the Anglo-Japanese alliance could only have been undertaken if it did not disturb Anglo-American relations. But the Foreign Office had communicated to the Committee of Imperial Defence in 1920 seven substantive areas of disagreement between British and Japanese interests, most of which applied equally to Japan–US relations. Both sets of differences applied to Japanese expansion, commercial rivalry, and to Japanese intentions towards Russia and China unacceptable to Washington. Lloyd George and the first lord of the Admiralty, Lord Lee, were only the foremost in warning against a naval race with America ('up against the greatest resources of the world'; 'political relations of this country and America are of transcendent importance, and outweigh in every way those with other powers or combination of powers'). To save Japanese face, the Anglo-Japanese alliance was supplanted in 1921 by the Four Power alliance of the UK, USA, Japan and France.

Although few thought that Japanese aggression was imminent, or even probable, the British government decided in June 1921 to submit to the Imperial Conference a proposal to build a naval base at Singapore, in order to confirm Britain's traditional capacity to exercise naval power upon those oceans where the interests of empire were predominant. Oil supplies, trade, territory including India, Ceylon, Burma and Hong Kong, could all otherwise be lost, with grave consequence for Oriental markets, imperial security, and for London's undertakings to the loyal dominions that had supported her throughout the Great War. To whom would Australia and New Zealand turn, should the empire appear unwilling or unable to defend her own, other than to the USA?

The base, in the early stages, was not much more than a 'promise' to protect British possessions, including the dominions. It was not yet a barrier or defence against Japanese aggression, which was anyway not yet manifest. And there were serious objections to the project, such as the RAF's advocacy of torpedo bombers for the defence of Singapore rather than the 15-inch guns planned.

Others staked claims for submarines and aircraft carriers as principal weapons of the future, making battleships – and hence the base itself – redundant. Many objected on the grounds of economy, preferring reduction of income tax and of national debt. Others again clamoured for general disarmament. Some believed that the naval base could only provoke and humiliate an ally, Japan, which it certainly and most regrettably did. And, while ministers defending the project claimed that in the last resort the USA would be present in support of Singapore, concessions incorporated under the Washington Treaty meant that the American navy might have no base within range of the China Sea.

In military thinking during the 1920s, the object of any putative Japanese attack was predicted as the capture or destruction of the base, whether the attack were mounted from the north via Johore, or directly against the island. For this purpose, eighteen transports carrying between 60,000 and 100,000 men were presumed. The defences should, in a 1924 war memorandum, include six to eight 15-inch guns against battleships, six 9.2-inch, eighteen 6-inch and a similar number of 4.7-inch guns against vessels ranging from cruisers to transports. Ashore, infantry, field artillery and fixed or mobile defences, wire, mines and so forth, would be required. But the base could not survive without the rapid arrival of the 'Far Eastern War Fleet', planned in 1925 to consist of fourteen capital ships (including four battle cruisers already to be on station), and four aircraft carriers, reaching Singapore 'in 28–42 days'.

These figures, arbitrary as they seem today, were further complicated through continual advocacy by the Royal Air Force under 'Boom' Trenchard, chief of the Air Staff and 'Father of the RAF', of a much greater role for his service in the defence of the eastern empire and, in particular, the substitution of torpedo bombers for 15-inch guns, an obvious argument, incidentally, against the existence itself of the base.

A first stage, 'the Red Scheme', was devised to provide oil storage, docks, wharves and other facilities, which would initially accommodate the four-battle-cruiser force and, eventually, the Far Eastern War Fleet, in collaboration with other British dockyards, at a total cost of £11 million, part of which was to be contributed by the dominions and other components of the empire. In the event, because of continuing technical and political controversy, and because major war still appeared improbable, by the end of 1930 only £4 million had been spent on the scheme, which by then had been further reduced, even though to complete it fully now required a further £15 million. Work on the defences had been stopped, although after the London Naval Conference no increase in capital ships had been authorised and the relative strength of Japan had been increased.

We have seen that the Singapore base was a product of the conviction that imperial defence could no longer be built on dependable Japanese friendship or cooperation with that nation's navy. At the same time, however, the urgency of the project had been lessened by the ten-year rule ('no major war for ten years') and by relative Japanese quiescence in Asia, at least until the Mukden incident of September 1931. But, thereafter, with the repeal in March 1932 of the ten-year rule, 1938 – and then 1936 – were identified as the dates for completion at least of the graving dock. But by that time, not only had Germany already started to rearm, but Japan was demanding a 5 : 5 : 5 ratio. At a time when it seemed plain that Japan respected nothing but force, the power to stop her had been surrendered in the Washington Treaty.

By 1937 the Joint Planning Committee in London was working on the basis of a two-division landing on the west coast of Malaya, escorted by the entire Japanese navy, 9 battleships, 29 cruisers, 5 aircraft carriers, 100 destroyers, 60 submarines and nearly 300 aircraft! The British order of battle comprised only five regular and seven volunteer battalions, thirty-eight aircraft, and a small British fleet, with one aircraft carrier and no battleships. The success or failure of the operation would be entirely dependent on

275

the arrival within sixty days of the British Main Fleet. If Germany had not been defeated by that time, the Main Fleet might not arrive at all, to deter or defeat invasion, and to fulfil its role of severing Japan's trade routes, the first modern war – in Neidpath's words – 'between two insular, as opposed to continental, Great Powers'. Nevertheless, the first lord of the Admiralty, now Sir Samuel Hoare, told the Imperial Conference of 1937 that it would then still be his government's policy to send a fleet to Singapore 'in the event of aggression against British interests in the Far East', adequate, if inferior to Japan's, to contain that navy: 'the very existence of the Commonwealth rested on our ability to do so . . . nothing specific could be relied on from the United States'. In the meanwhile, Britain's capital ship balance, even with France, diminished further in relation to the Axis by 1939–40, although, in 1937, some slight relief was felt on the British side by preliminary Anglo-American naval staff talks.

British hopes really rested, until the USA could or would deploy its strength against Japan, on China's ability to maintain its resistance to Japan, a tacit acceptance therefore of the situation which the base was designed to avoid: a two-hemisphere policy and a one-hemisphere navy. But in 1939 Chamberlain reiterated to the Australian prime minister his intention to despatch a fleet to the east, the size of which would be determined in the event of a war involving the triple enemy combination not envisaged in earlier plans, a skilful formula, if vague promise, which continued until 1941.

Earlier, the US chief of naval operations, Admiral Leahy, later ambassador to Vichy France, caused a delighted Admiralty to be informed that, if the USA should find itself at war with Japan and/or Germany, the Americans would send their Main Fleet to Singapore, provided that the Royal Navy sent 'an adequate token force' there too. Grounds not for assurance, only for hope, lay in this undertaking, which was not a guarantee, nor available to the eyes of dominion governments, nor, in the end, operable.

The Chiefs of Staff had understood by the end of 1938 that

since an immediate sailing of the British Main Fleet to meet a Japanese attack might not be possible, action against Japanese communications must now be more dependent on air activity in the ninety-day relief period. This extended period would greatly improve Japan's chances, despite the completion of fixed defences at the 'fortress' and Kota Tinggi in order to try to hold all Malaya, thought essential in the light of improved, sophisticated Japanese forces, and despite also four new British bomber squadrons and a brigade group. It required a greatly increased RAF role and an infantry establishment of twenty-five battalions – since the provision of thirty-two was judged impractical – three anti-tank batteries and one company of AFVs. The prognosis of attack from the rear predicted in 1937 by Lieutenant-Colonel A. E. Percival, then chief staff officer, later to become GOC and to surrender Singapore, was accepted, in the shape of an assault launched by Japanese landings through Johore and on the south-east coast of Singapore Island. Percival did not anticipate Japanese landings in northern Malaya to promote an advance down the peninsula, thus circumscribing a task which was to appear, in Neidpath's words, 'less easy' than in the Malaya Command of 1940. A subsequent appreciation by General Dobbie, then GOC, referred to landings on both east and west coasts and to the risk to British forces of recently improved facilities available in Thailand to invaders, and of more developed Japanese training, aircraft and landing-craft construction.

Resources for the defence of Singapore by 1941 in the midst of global war were thin. Churchill misunderstood Japan and never believed a major Japanese attack likely, even were the Middle East to be lost to Germany, so long as the Japanese recognised even the possibility of US entry into the war against them. Consequently, he placed the security of Malaya, despite opposition by the Chiefs of Staff, as a requirement below that for the UK, the USSR or the Middle East. In May 1941 the British garrison consisted of 23 battalions and 115 aircraft, including elderly Buffaloes, against the Chiefs' requirement of 336 and the Far

East commander's proposal for 556 modern aircraft. But even as late as November 1941, the prime minister could not agree that further reinforcements of scale should be sent to the Far East.

Churchill feared above all the collapse of Russia under the hammer of Barbarossa and the diversion thence to the Middle East of successful, battle-hardened Wehrmacht troops and Luftwaffe aircraft, which nightmare would have overthrown the already shaky British position in that theatre. Nor was he confident, on the other hand, that his government could withstand the shock to public opinion of diversion to Malaya, even as an emergency measure, of Anglo-American aid to Russia, already 676 aircraft and 446 tanks in the latter part of 1941, in whatever shipping could be found.

When the Japanese struck in Malaya, Britain's forces there had been increased to 31 battalions and 158 combat aircraft, still far below the numbers estimated by the experts as necessary for the defence of the area. Even so, Churchill's personal attention, so long distracted from the tactics and even the strategy of war in South East Asia, could at least have directed or supported efforts on the ground of those officers and men attempting, against lethargy, neglect, bureaucracy and incompetence, to build a coherent defence. At least, as Neidpath remarks, 'Johore, the north shores of Singapore Island and the whole length of the trunk road up Malaya might have bristled with barbed-wire entanglements, anti-tank obstacles, minefields and pillboxes.' And honour would have been spared against a Blitzkrieg, the speed and violence of which might have been measurably reduced by better British training, leadership and equipment.

Malaya, however, was lost primarily because Japan had almost total command of air and sea, a situation – as Neidpath reminds us – previously experienced only by Britain at Yorktown against de Grasse and George Washington. The collapse of France and Italy's defection had made impossible the despatch of any fleet capable of deterring, let alone engaging, Japan's capital ships, at a time when Germany with up to seven capital ships could command, unless correspondingly opposed, the trade and military approaches to the homeland itself. Nor from September 1939 to December 1941 was any US aid, other than the most indirect and exiguous, available. By 1941, even Leahy's imprecise but welcome assurance had been withdrawn. The concept of the Singapore base was not wrong. It could, under the pressure of events, no longer be implemented. No alternative, from a joint Anglo-American fleet to massive intervention by the RAF, was practical.

Little could have changed in the peninsula in 'the days before the barbarians came'. The thick scent of white frangipani, incense, coconut oil and sandalwood filled the hot, drenching night air, against the tonal screech and croak of Cantonese. Unchecked, the green mass of shiny leaf pursued its remorseless upward onslaught. Huge, brown silent rivers flowed down to the sea. The rubber stood in regulated battalions. Great wounds appeared in the jungle, white or orange among the tin tailings. The foul scent of durian . . . Huge, cream, colonial houses with enormous lawns, tok-tok birds in the rain trees, the flashing plumage of the kingfisher, geckoes groaning like 'old man's laughter'. Rattan furniture in the suburbia of Tanglin. Orchids, red and purple hibiscus, cannas yellow and scarlet, rickshaws, bullock carts, fruit bats, the thunderous, sudden rains of evening. The ant-like activity of, it seemed, the entire Chinese race, and the marmoreal dignity of a good Chinese butler. On the stalls suspended, lacquered duck, chickens, frogs' legs, succulent intestines; beside these creatures, mango, papaya, mangosteen, chiku, durian again, all the fruit and vegetables of the Chinese world, prawns large and small, wonton soup, fishes of every shape and size, nasi goreng. Then the strange, clanging extempore Chinese opera and the slow, threatening, silent mystery of the Malay and Javanese wayang. Formal parties, black tie and white dinner jacket, where the drinking went on so long that the food was always ruined.

To this colony after eight months' leave returned Sir Shenton Thomas, governor of the Straits Settlement, whose only other service had been in Africa. Shenton expressed to their face the wish that British soldiers would go away: 'Your presence here will only bring war to this country. We should be much better off without you.' The C-i-C, Far East, Sir Robert Brooke-Popham, for his part, explained Japanese aggression in China by attributing it to excessive consumption of iodine 'in a largely fish diet'.

A prior Japanese estimate from the first landing in northern Malaya to the occupation of Singapore island was a hundred days, an objective they in fact achieved in seventy, with three divisions, on a plan based on intelligence acquired from loyal Japanese residents over twenty years.

The success of any British defence of northern Malaya depended on Operation Matador, designed to cross the Thai border and occupy Singora and Patani, after evidence had made plain that the Japanese intended to invade. (A position known as The Ledge was later substituted for Patani.) Despite the sighting on 6 December 1941 of twenty-three Japanese transports heading for the expected Japanese landing beaches, Brooke-Popham, advised by Percival, failed to order Matador and, at dawn on 8 December, the enemy's 5th and 18th Divisions started to land at Singora and Patani, with another landing at Kota Bahru in Malaya itself. The Japanese air force bombed Singapore for the first time.

Since Matador was not executed, the main Japanese thrust should have been held by 11th Indian Division under Sir Lewis Heath's III Corps with eight battalions in the Jitra area. The subsequent battle, with heavy losses of men and matériel, ended in British withdrawal on 13 December behind the Kedah river. Every mistake within the capacity of British officials to make – although there were plenty to follow as the steamy, tropical weeks drifted on – was made: ignoring professional advice, neglecting training, underrating the opposition, command indecision. General Kirby's incisive *Singapore: The Chain of Disaster* observed that, after Jitra, the Japanese onrush could have been delayed only by 'brilliant generalship and a rapid deployment of troops', neither of which was provided. At all events, the surrender of the Singapore Island naval base was conditioned almost two months before it occurred by this relatively small engagement, won by an advance guard and a handful of armour.

Thereafter, down the roads, railways, jungle tracks, and through the lines of rubber, along which the chief engineer, Brigadier Ivan Simson, had been forbidden by Command – 'for reasons of morale' – to build road-blocks, blow up bridges, construct pillboxes and other fixed defences, which should have been completed years before, marched the adaptable Japanese army, howling theatrically but fighting man-to-man, in the rubber and jungle which British doctrine had designated as impenetrable.

On 10 December, furthermore and without air cover, the battleship *Prince of Wales* and battle cruiser *Repulse* went to the bottom of the South China Sea off Kuantan, sunk by bombers and torpedo bombers operating without opposition from the RAF. Penang, with its small boats sequestered as a useful coastal force by the Japanese, fell on 19 December, and now the Imperial Guards Division came down by rail from Bangkok to drive down the main trunk road towards Johore and Singapore Island. Half the Blenheims from Butterworth were shot down by Zeros on 9 December, and all the Blenheims left there were that evening destroyed on the airfield. Kuantan was taken on 3 January, Muar and Makri between 15 and 20 January. At Muar, Percival said of the lack of training of British troops, specifically the 45th Indian Brigade: 'This Brigade had never been fit for employment in a theatre of war. It was not that there was anything wrong with the raw material, but it was raw.'

Kirby has said that since it was plain that the RAF's strength was inadequate for its task, there had been little point in concentrating on airfield defence. Rather, Percival should have concentrated his forces west of the main mountain range and, above all, held the bottlenecks on 'the north–south communications route, by field and anti-tank defences, and ensure[d] that the three approaches *in Johore* to Johore Bahru and the Island were covered by permanent defences'. None of these measures was taken, nor was anything done anywhere until Slim's Fourteeth

Army campaign in 1943 in Burma, to deal with Japanese tactical assault from the rear. Had they been, the unfortunate 18th British Division, instead of forming up for long years of captivity after its last-minute arrival in reinforcement, might have held the day against a concerned General Yamashita at the end of his lengthy line of communication.

The British and Australians, piped across the causeway by the two remaining pipers of the Argyll and Sutherland Highlanders, entered Singapore on 31 January 1942, surrendering fifteen days later because the water supply had collapsed, as had the defences of the city against an enemy which had managed everywhere to infiltrate them. In the view of Wint and Calvocoressi's *Total War*, however, since Yamashita had outrun his supplies and since 'the Army in Singapore was twice as large as the besieging force, a prolonged resistance would have been possible . . . [the Japanese] must have fallen back if the garrison had made the determined counter-attack of which it was capable'. But Wavell, now supreme commander, believed that the battle was irretrievably lost. It is certainly the case that continued resistance involving Chinese civilians would have led to horrors unimaginable even to those who experienced Japanese outrage of that era and, perhaps, therefore unacceptable to those still just responsible for the welfare of their loyal and gallant Asian subjects.

The edifice of British colonialism had been so large, so grandiose, so apparently unassailable a symbol of foreign power, that its collapse, rapid and inexcusable, had such a finality that the loss of one small island exceeded the symbolic falls of Batavia, Saigon, Manila and Rangoon. There could be no putting together the pieces after this Humpty Dumpty fell off the wall: despite all the flummery of 1945, no one ever really tried.

SYNOPSIS OF EVENTS BETWEEN
SINGAPORE AND MIDWAY

By July 1941 the Japanese had acquired political control of the whole of Indo-China and by December successfully invaded the Philippines and caused Hong Kong to surrender. In March 1942 the Netherlands East Indies surrendered to Japan, which had already invaded Burma and in February 1942 won the battle of the Java Sea.

CHAPTER TWENTY

MIDWAY ISLAND, 1942

On Japanese Navy Day, 27 May 1905, Admiral Togo annihilated the Imperial Russian Navy in the Tsushima Straits. Thirty-seven years later, Admiral Nagumo's Carrier Task Force, *Akagi, Kaga, Soryu* and *Hiryu* with over 200 aircraft, which had destroyed the American Battle Fleet at Pearl Harbor, moved again down the Inland Sea, in sunshine and under blue skies.

In three days, this deadly squadron with its battleship, cruiser and destroyer escorts was joined or followed by other task groups; invasion troops for the US Aleutians in the Bering Sea, and for Midway (from Saipan); Kurita's heavy cruisers out of Guam; Kondo's two battleships with cruisers and destroyers; finally, the main force under the great Admiral Isoruko Yamamoto, commander-in-chief, with seven battleships, cruisers, destroyers and a carrier. The total force, including also land-based aircraft, comprised 11 battleships, 5 carriers, 23 cruisers, 65 destroyers and 700 aircraft. One of the battleships was the monster *Yamato* with a displacement of 64,000 tons, then much the largest ever built.

Against them was the faint possibility of two or three US carriers, a battleship, some cruisers and rather more destroyers, all – it was supposed – ignorant of Japanese plans.

Yamamoto had studied at Harvard and, as a naval attaché, travelled in the United States and understood its enormous industrial capacity. It would emerge that between 1942 and 1945 the American economy had built 300,000 aircraft and new surface fleets every six months, and a new heavy bomber every sixty-three minutes. In 1941 Yamamoto had told Prime Minister Konoye that, if he had to fight, he would run wild for six months, but had 'utterly no confidence' for the second and third year. He also knew that the American character and view of warfare would permit nothing except the complete surrender or complete devastation of Japan.

His strategy, therefore, however contradictory, was rapidly to destroy the United States fleet and thus control an enormous zone, the Southern Resources Area of the Pacific, so deep and so large that the Americans and their allies would have no option but to sue for peace before their superior industrial resources became effective. This strategy prescribed defensive lines from the Kuriles and Aleutians southward to the Gilbert and Ellice islands, westward enclosing the Solomons and New Guinea, then Java, Sumatra, Malaya and Burma, incorporating Borneo, the Philippines, the Carolines, Marshalls, Wake, Saipan and other island chains within interior lines or segments. Outside this zone, as it were, but accessible from its many new Japanese air bases, lay Fiji, Samoa, New Hebrides and New Caledonia, seizure of which from British, French and American administrations would facilitate the isolation and eventual assault on Australia, already housing General MacArthur's headquarters.

The initial stage of any operation on this objective was planned as invasion from Rabaul in New Britain against Port Moresby in New Guinea on the Coral Sea. This move had been sensed, if not quite predicted, by a brilliantly casual and eccentric intelligence unit, accountable to the C-in-C, Admiral Chester Nimitz in Hawaii, greatly empowered after Pearl Harbor. Subsequent naval intervention from a task force under Rear-Admiral Frank Fletcher, later to command at the Midway battle, caused the Japanese to break off the action. One Japanese carrier was sunk and another hit; *Lexington* in the US squadron went down after an explosion, and *Yorktown* was damaged.

The battle of the Coral Sea was Japan's first defeat in 350 years and, according to Frank King, C-in-C US fleet and chief of naval operations, also the first maritime engagement in which surface ships did not exchange a single shot. The phenomenon was thus another reflection of Admiral Yamamoto's conviction that, since aircraft outranged guns, naval warfare lay henceforward not with battleships, but with aircraft carriers. His earlier hesitation about challenging America might have been terminal, however, had he then known that, only a few months after Midway, not only would the United States have made up all losses from that battle, but that Japanese factory production was already shrinking.

The Aleutians were seen, incorrectly, by the Japanese as dominating the northern Pacific. Port Moresby was selected as a target for the reasons given earlier, but seizure was postponed after the battle of the Coral Sea. Midway Island in the central Pacific was chosen as a potential air and naval base, the 'guardian' of Hawaii. Successful assault would be followed by air strikes and the invasion of Fiji and Samoa, finally by a massive combined action to take and hold Hawaii, too distant yet for a direct strike from Tokyo.

So the key was Midway, remote, only three square miles, a flat atoll in a blue lagoon. Yamamoto wanted it chiefly because he believed that the depleted American fleet would have to try to defend it. When they did, with their pathetic residue after the decimation at Pearl Harbor, his vastly superior ships would be there to exterminate them, finishing the business started on 7 December 1941. Opposition in the capital to this proposal sharply diminished after Doolittle's carrier-borne B25 raid on Tokyo of 18 April, which actually flashed by the Japanese plane carrying the recently installed Prime Minister Tojo, bound for an inspection.

Scholars, whether Fuller or others, have described Yamamoto's plan as 'radically unsound, and the distribution of forces as deplorable'. The admiral should have entrusted the bombardment of Midway to surface ships, not aircraft carriers, reserving his own experienced carriers to deal with the US carriers when or if they appeared: *their* destruction was, or should have been, his principal aim. The Japanese fleet was, furthermore, too variously diffused, against too many different targets: the Aleutians, Port Moresby, as well as Midway; and the unprofessional involvement of Nagumo's carriers against the island was a task rather for battle-ships and cruisers, traditionally suitable bombardiers. Kurita's cruisers and Kondo's battleships could provide additional fire-power needed against Midway to reduce it before Tanaka's twelve transports arrived. Meanwhile, the battleships and carriers of the main force under Takasu and Yamamoto still loomed menacingly to the north of Midway to threaten and destroy any unexpected counter-attack against the largest fleet since the Venetians destroyed the Turkish navy in 1571 at Lepanto, perhaps the largest in naval history.

What the Japanese did not know was that the Combat Intelligence Unit ('Hypo') at Pearl Harbor had been reading the Japanese naval codes – including JN75, the 'highest' – since 1940. By May 1942 at least 15 per cent of most intercepts were legible to Hypo, sometimes more, but when the code changed, rather less. The leading decrypter, the informal Commander Joe Rochefort Jr, had succeeded in convincing Nimitz, commander of the US Pacific Fleet, that a major Japanese offensive was imminent against Midway Island in the central Pacific, employing four carriers each with thirty-six fighters and twenty-seven scout bombers. The approximate date of 28 May was extracted before the coding system suddenly changed.

Nimitz immediately recalled Admiral Halsey's twenty-one-vessel Task Force 16 from the Solomons, with its two large carriers *Hornet* and *Enterprise*. Halsey was ill and, in his place, Nimitz appointed Rear-Admiral Raymond Spruance, then commanding what was left of the Pacific Fleet's carriers and destroyers. Rear-Admiral Frank Fletcher's Task Force 17, with the battered *Yorktown* from the Coral Sea, was at Tongatabu and came in on 27 May, the crews hoping for leave while the flagship recovered in dry dock. But Nimitz gave that badly damaged vessel exactly two days to make herself seaworthy after a direct hit which had buckled, even torn off, whole plates and bulkheads, normally deserving a refit lasting weeks, even months. By working day and night in endless heat, fumes and smoke, in semi-darkness, with only sporadic electricity while, simultaneously, fresh ammunition and stores were being taken on, *Yorktown* was made ready for sea and under main engines by 30 May. Nimitz came on board that day to say 'God speed', and to acknowledge to the crew and dockyard workers their miracle of stamina, energy and devotion.

At Midway, after a visit by Nimitz, barbed wire and other necessities for a siege were delivered, bunkers and slit trenches built. Equipment poured in by air: mortars, bombs, mines, AA guns, even tanks, B17s, B26s, fighters and dive-bombers to replace the ancient Buffaloes and Vindicator dive-bombers from which wing fabric peeled off in the dive. (Buffaloes had been almost the only aircraft available to the RAF to defend the British fleet in Malaya. Two years later, the Fleet Air Arm had to make do with Barracudas, whose wings *fell off* in the dive, or so the pilots coarsely sang.) But the SIGINT detail from Rochefort's desk for indoctrinated readers of CINCPAC Op. Plan 29–42 was such that one officer observed: 'That man of ours in Tokyo is worth every cent we pay him.'

One American destroyer officer in those tense days wrote in his diary:

> we have history in the palm of our hands. If we are able to keep our presence unknown to the enemy and surprise them with a vicious attack on their carriers, the US Navy should once more be supreme in the Pacific . . . But if the Japanese see us first and attack us with their overwhelming number of planes, knock us out of the picture and then take Midway, Pearl Harbor will be almost neutralized and in danger . . . The fate of the nation is in our hands.

His opposite numbers in the Japanese fleet for the most part thought similarly. The more intelligent were concerned about past and future errors, particularly the lack of follow-up by Nagumo after the Pearl Harbor raid. Why had no successful attempt been made to search for the 'missing' US carriers? Was the size of the US fleet underestimated? Why did Yamamoto's advocacy of airpower still allow predominance of the battleship over the carrier? Was Midway really the right point for an advanced air base? Above all, was it really the correct place to which to draw out and destroy the US Pacific Fleet? Was radio communication, with Admiral Yamamoto sea miles back in *Yamato* under W/T silence, really adequate? Had Nagumo lost his fighting spirit? Why, except as a diversion (which the Americans identified as such) did the Japanese occupy useless Alaskan islands? Was concentration not impaired?

In fog, rain and deteriorating weather in the central Pacific, Japanese submarines and flying-boat reconnaissance were unable to identify any US forces at all between 24 and 31 May. And although the volume of signal traffic from Honolulu may have indicated to Yamamoto that the Americans were aware of enemy naval activity in the area, this provided no data which his fleet could exploit. Nagumo therefore assumed that, if he had not sighted their force, neither had the US fleet sighted his. It was, he thought, safe to attack Midway with up to a hundred aircraft in support of the landings, and then to destroy any approaching foe.

Nagumo was wrong. Although very heavy damage was suffered on Midway during the wave of bombing, the defences were forewarned and were at action stations. Shore-based aircraft, B26s, Avengers and Marauders, attacked the task force at low level, losing seven aircraft, but – very slowly – exhausting the enemy which, combined with hubris acquired from earlier victory, caused Japanese crews to take unnecessary risks, to become casual, to neglect preordained procedures.

Suddenly, with the aerial sighting of an American naval formation 200 miles away, the entire position changed. Before, the enemy had neither been seen nor even suspected. In order to deal with this new threat, Nagumo's aircraft in his four carriers, whether on board in reserve or returning from the Midway strike, had all to be sent down below for rearming, not with the armour-piercing bombs with which each had been, or was to be, armed for the second strike against Midway, but with torpedoes against their amended targets, Spruance's and Fletcher's carriers, *Enterprise*, *Hornet* and *Yorktown*. Obviously, not all could be lowered at the same time. Many remained, full of fuel, on the inflammable flight deck while, on the hangar deck, bombs and torpedoes were piled hugger-mugger. The entire rearming operation occupied an hour or more, fighters themselves, as well as bombers, coming in to refuel as cover for the Midway or anti-torpedo-bomber operations.

Nagumo's carriers in box formation, escorted by battleships, cruisers, destroyers and now with only twelve Zeros to protect thirty-four dive-bombers and fifty-four torpedo-bombers, altered course ninety degrees to the east.

The initial American attack was mounted entirely by a class of torpedo-bombers called, unjustifiably, 'Devastator'. Like the British equivalent, the Swordfish, a biplane which sank the Italian fleet at anchor or alongside at Taranto, at a maximum speed of 90 knots *in the dive*, the Devastator and its precious 1,000lb torpedo could just manage 100 knots (but not if the wind were against it). If the target, dead ahead, were moving at 30 knots, the Devastator's relative speed was no more than, at best, 70 knots.

On 4 June 1942, *Hornet*'s attack with fifteen Devastators in 'Torpedo 8' under Lieutenant-Commander Jack Waldron ('Just follow me; I'll take you to them') was covered by thirty-five dive-bombers and ten Wildcats which almost at once overshot their 'charges', losing them in the overcast, missing their targets as well. Waldron, thus in an almost suicidal attack, spotted the carriers himself, not easy in the boundless blue and grey Pacific Ocean. Unprotected by an overhead screen, and knowing that none of his men had the fuel to return to *Hornet*, he and his pilots flew at wave-top height straight into the advancing Japanese fleet with its omnipresent Zeros. Not one American aircraft, and only one crewman, Ensign George Gay, survived: no hits at all were secured by this courageous but almost completely inexperienced band.

Devastators were not supposed to fight in this way, rather to slip in through the gaps in the battle, between Zeros, on the one hand, Dauntless and Wildcats on the other. Victor Davis Hanson described the predicament in *Why the West Has Won* as 'driving a Ford Pinto in the slow lane, loaded with dynamite, while far faster drivers shot at it with machine guns as they passed'. The American pilots that day, sitting on top of explosives and large quantities of gas, died just as they drove.

Enterprise's Torpedo 6, fourteen Devastators under Lieutenant-Commander Eugene Lindsey, headed for the *Kaga*, again without a fighter escort, to be savaged by twenty-five Zeros. No hits were scored on the Japanese. Only four of these aircraft reached a sensible point even to launch their 'fish', the only four also to return to the mother ship.

Twelve Devastators from *Yorktown* in Torpedo 3 under Lem Massey, last seen standing on the wing while the cockpit blazed, attacked *Hiryu*. No torpedoes hit their target, and only two aircraft returned to *Yorktown*.

Of the eighty-two men in ancient two-man monoplanes who had set out that morning into battle, only thirteen lived: thirty-five of forty-one American machines had been shot down. But, however unavailing the practical efforts had been of those brave, innocent and extraordinary young men, in a sacrifice unimaginable today, their continual nagging assaults, with those from the Midway garrison, had unsettled their triumphant opponents for the first time.

The first indicator was the unaccustomed slackness in loading and unloading to which reference has been made. In *Akagi, Kaga, Soryu* and *Hiryu*, torpedoes and bombs cluttered the flight and hangar decks, piled and jumbled in every corner, while the flight decks held aircraft refuelling or just refuelled, forty in *Akagi*, Admiral Nagumo's flagship.

Immediately, however, the Japanese carriers upon which Admiral Yamamoto's master plan depended were in the ascendant. The destruction of the US fleet after the annihilation of its torpedo-bomber strength, and the pulverising attack on the island, seemed inevitable. It was true that the Japanese had no radar, that their decks were wooden, that communications were poor. But so much had already been achieved on the road to final victory that, surely, nothing would go wrong.

However, at 10.05 that day, the morning of 4 June, Lieutenant-Commander Wade McClusky, leading the *Enterprise* Air Group with two squadrons of dive-bombers, sighted four carriers, apparently turning to avoid torpedo attack. It saw no anti-aircraft fire, nor any sign of Zeros, now known to have been pursuing the last Devastators.

Below him in *Akagi*, an invalid Japanese pilot heard a lookout scream: 'Helldivers!', as McClusky's twenty-five Dauntless dive-bombers, plunging at over 250 knots from 20,000 feet, pulled their releases, climbing away from the intolerable blinding flash and explosion of their own bombs. Parked aircraft, already laden with fuel and torpedoes, began to immolate one after another in a series of deafening explosions that ignited fuel, bombs and more aircraft in turn, including the forty on *Akagi*'s flight deck, bursting through the wooden decking until they caught the ammunition magazines and fuel storage below. In *Akagi*, Rear-Admiral Kusaka reported that 'the deck itself was on fire: anti-aircraft and machine-guns were firing automatically, set off by the fires around them. Bodies were all over the place ... Stored torpedoes literally ripped the ship open from within.'

The story aboard *Kaga* was the same. The ship lost all power, stopped dead, and began to explode along her length. The elevator was torn apart, setting fire to all the machines, seventy-two parked in the open and in the hangar. Anything metal was first twisted and then converted into flying 'shrapnel', wounding or killing everything in its path. One bomb destroyed the entire 'island' or control tower. The captain and all officers on the bridge were killed. The ships were filled with dead and dying men, hideously burned, the best pilots and the best technicians of the imperial navy.

Within those terrible six minutes, Lieutenant-Commander Max Leslie then led Bombing Squadron 3 from *Yorktown* in an attack on *Soryu*, slightly northeast in Nagumo's box, catching her with three 1,000lb bombs from a height of no more than 1,500 feet. The whole vessel blossomed into flames; bulkheads collapsed under heat, shock and fire; 'everything was blowing up, planes, bombs, gas tanks'. A little later, her fate similar to her sisters, *Hiryu*, a more modern vessel of 20,000 tons, saw the fire and three columns of smoke from 100 miles away, then to be hit by three or four bombs released by aircraft from *Enterprise* and the others. Admiral Yamaguchi tied himself to the bridge and went down with the ship after she was scuttled by torpedoes fired from Japanese vessels. *Hiryu*'s captain accompanied him. *Akagi* was scuttled in the same way; *Soryu* blew up and sank with 700 men; *Kaga* exploded for the last time and sank, with the loss of 800 lives.

When reminded that there was still money in the ship's safe that might be saved, Yamaguchi said, 'We'll need money for a square meal in hell: leave it alone.'

Yorktown had been struck earlier that afternoon by three bombs and two torpedoes from *Hiryu*'s aircraft. As she listed heavily, 'abandon ship' was ordered by Admiral Fletcher, although an attempt was later made to salvage her by a volunteer party. Two seamen were found wounded on board, but still alive. One of these men recalled an earlier voice saying: 'Leave him and let's go – he's done for anyway.' On 7 June the unfortunate and much loved 'Old Lady' was sunk by two torpedoes from a Japanese submarine, and disappeared for ever.

When Yamamoto heard that all four Japanese carriers had gone, and that two of the Americans' survived, he ordered a general withdrawal. Spruance withdrew *Enterprise* and *Hornet* a little to the eastward, not seeking a direct engagement with the Japanese main force. Aircraft from the US carriers, however, sank one cruiser, *Mikuma*, and badly damaged another. The Japanese mourned 3,500 men against an American death toll of 300 officers and men, the carrier *Yorktown* and a destroyer.

Although Japan was left with other carriers, including two under repair in Japan, this was not enough against US production by 1943 of sixteen Essex-class carriers each carrying Helldivers, Avengers, Corsairs and Hellcats, plus giant battleships of the Iowa class. As Lloyd George said in the 1920s, to confront the USA meant to be 'up against the greatest resources in the world'.

The pendulum had swung to America. Japan had lost her chance, through her aircraft carriers, to destroy the Pacific Fleet, thus to take US and Allied bases before American industrial production made such ambitions unthinkable. From 1941 to 1945, *one hundred* newly built US carriers, against *seven* Japanese, went down the slipways, another statistic to add to the overwhelming figures of this summary.

Yamamoto was unwise in dispersal, not concentration over 1,000 miles of ocean, of his enormous fleet. Unwise also in tying the carriers to the invasion of the island, in neglect of the primary aim of drawing out the enemy for a decisive encounter. Unwise, therefore, in not insisting that the main force, with its battleships, and Nagumo's First Carrier Task Force should act together. Nagumo was unwise, if understandably, in failing to attack the US carriers on sight, instead rearming: technically correct but, in the prison of time, exposing his ships to dive-bombers, the crucial error.

American adaptability, courage and endurance were exemplary. Even more was owed to US technological, predictive intelligence. Without those attributes, the destruction of the US fleet was certain. The balance of power would have then shifted, at least for an extended if not 'permanent' period, to an association of Japanese and European totalitarian powers, damaging, even fatal, not only to the potential democracies of Asia, but to the security of the western seaboard of the United States and to the outcome of the war itself.

SYNOPSIS OF EVENTS BETWEEN
MIDWAY AND KURSK

In 1942 the tide of war began to turn: in North Africa for the Allies at Alam Halfa, El Alamein, Kasserrine Pass and the invasion of Tunisia; in South East Asia and the Pacific with the extraordinary bravery of US infantry at Guadalcanal, General Slim's reconquest of Burma, and the more or less speedy penetration of the Japanese occupied territories.

In April 1943 Admiral Yamamoto was killed; in July the Italian leader Mussolini was overthrown, by which time Malta, by its own endurance and that of British arms, had long been lost to the Axis. Ultra, and the devotion of individual convoy escort and attack groups, had turned in Allied favour the Battle of the Atlantic. Germany was in continual devastation by the RAF and USAAF.

The massive Soviet winter offensive had brought about von Paulus's surrender at Stalingrad. The Russians were moving westwards to join with their western allies in the final defeat of the Third Reich, the end of Hitler and of the Nazi regime.

CHAPTER TWENTY-ONE

KURSK, 1943

The battle of Stalingrad, although certainly a victory, was not decisive. It had been won, after all, against troops including weaker men, 185,000 Italians, 140,000 Hungarians, 250,000 Romanians killed, wounded and captured. The Russians, however, believed there to be only 470,000 Germans on the eastern front in March 1943 when the Soviet winter offensive ended in mud and slush. Sixty-eight Wehrmacht divisions, apart from their allies, had been wrecked.

Leningrad was no longer isolated; both Army Groups A and B had been severely shaken, the latter almost to pieces. Soviet methods of command, from Stalin down, had much improved under Georgii Zhukov, the likeable and brilliant Vasilevski, and Aleksei Antonov, chief of operations, described by Zhukov, of all people, as 'charming and cultured'. The right and power of political commissars to meddle in military operations had been diminished; and officers' uniforms had regained an almost tsarist glitter.

Lend–lease supplies, although only 4 per cent of total munitions, were essential to the Soviet war effort, especially in transport, food and petroleum products, if not matching the contribution made by the amazing mass production of artillery, armour and aircraft provided by the Soviet economy. And, by this time, imported American rails, locomotives and other railway-associated goods had begun to ensure that the astonishing increase in native military industrial products could reach the areas of conflict.

The most immediate such area was the vast Soviet salient facing westward and centred on Kursk, flanked by Orel and Kharkov. In February 1943 Hitler visited the headquarters of Field Marshal Erich von Manstein during the struggle for the south, where Manstein, victor of Sebastopol, former commander of the Eleventh Army and Army Group A, now of Army Group South, eventually to face charges at Nuremberg, persuaded the Führer of the next step for his forces.

His first suggestion, emphatically rejected because of its resemblance to 'withdrawal', was to pull back to the Dnieper, while German armour west of Kharkov was to destroy the Russians there, and eventually to eliminate the enemy at the Sea of Azov. Instead, Hitler agreed to a major attack on the Kursk salient, about the size of England, with – it was thought at that time – a regrouped 1 million men embodying one motorised, one cavalry, forty infantry, twenty panzer, four SS (Adolf Hitler, Das Reich, Death's Head and Gross Deutschland) divisions, a considerable renaissance since Stalingrad, facing Soviet Central (Rokossovski), Voronezh (Vatutin) and South Western (Malinovski) fronts. In addition to Konev's Steppe Front, Generals Popov and Sokolovski commanded the Briansk and Western fronts in the Orel Sector, later attacking von Kluge's army.

The Soviets, reading those dispositions, and with excellent human intelligence from 'Lucy' (Rudolph Rossler) in the main German OKW headquarters, from officers under cover behind the lines, and from Die Rote Kappelle in Switzerland, decided that they would not pre-empt the evidently forthcoming German offensive. They would, rather, mount a strategic defensive, letting the Ostheer initially wear itself down in offence. The Soviets then would crush the Eastern Wall, liberate the eastern Ukraine, eastern Belorussia and the Donbas, smashing Army Group Centre in the process. The German aim in this operation, codenamed *Citadelle*, or Citadel, was the destruction of the Red Army within the salient by von Kluge's Army Group Centre from Orel and von Manstein's Army Group South from Kharkov, coming together at Kursk.

Hitler's delay in authorising the start of Citadel until July meant that, because of Soviet production of AFVs and aircraft, respectively at 2,000 and 2,500 a month, sixty new Russian armoured brigades had by that date arrived behind defensive systems up to fifty miles deep on the Moscow axis, with a large reserve east of Kursk under Konev's Steppe Front. Twenty thousand guns and mortars, 6,000 anti-tank guns, 920 Katyushas, 9 anti-aircraft divisions, 40,000 mines and 3,000 aircraft were deployed. Whereas German divisions mostly numbered around 15,000 men each, Rokossovski's contained only 5,000 to 6,000; each side mustered about 3,000 tanks. It is worth mentioning also that dilution of the commissar system did not much reduce the presence and authority of the secret police, the NKVD, spying and goading in the rear echelons.

Outside the Russian world, the Anglo-American invasion of the continent had been postponed until 1944, to Stalin's chagrin, on the grounds maintained by Churchill that a 'useless massacre would help no one', adding that the 'Mediterranean strategy' had already shown its value by defeating the Germans in Africa, and by bringing southern Europe into imminent danger. War with Japan had, nevertheless, obviously slowed matters, and there was still only one US division in the UK: landing craft and other essentials for seaborne landing were short.

Within the USSR, the Free German Movement was established, with Ulbricht on the board, while a rival grouping to the London Poles had also been founded. The Russian Liberation Army – raised by the Soviet general Vlasov to fight *against* the USSR under German supreme command – was seen by Stalin as 'a serious obstacle on the road to victory', but not one that could not be overturned by a significant victory of Soviet armed forces in the field and by continued, stupid German brutality in the occupied territories.

On 1 July 1943 Hitler told his most senior officers that Citadel would begin in four days' time. He concurrently informed Guderian, commander of 2nd Panzer Group in Army Group Centre, while asserting that 'victory would bring a beacon that would shine around the world', that the concept 'made his stomach turn over'. The operation would be mounted by Model's Ninth Army of fifteen divisions in the north and, in the south, by Kempf's Operational Group with nine divisions and Hoth's Fourth Panzer Army (14–18 divisions), 2,700 tanks and 1,800 aircraft. Hitler's decisions, thanks to 'Lucy', were in Stalin's hands the following day.

At four in the morning of 5 July the Russians captured a German sapper in their minefields, who told them that the Germans would attack at two the next morning, confirming a similar report from a Yugoslav deserter from the German army. At 4.30 a.m., in fact, German guns opened up, followed by tank and infantry assaults in great strength by Model's divisions against the Thirteenth Army. Rokossovski began to give way and by that evening the Germans had achieved a four-mile penetration. Stalin promised reinforcements, an undertaking he had to withdraw because of pressure on Vatutin at Oboyan further south.

Armadas of German tanks in yellow and green camouflage, sometimes 200 at a time, roared clanking forward, Tigers, medium tanks, Ferdinand SP (self-propelled) guns, Panthers, followed by infantry driving for triumph, death, or buckled, burning devastation, all through the smoke-filled day. Between them and the T34s, T70s, heavy KV1s, and Joseph Stalin 1s weighing nearly fifty tons, the battle surged forward and back, the Thirteenth Army rolling back Rokossovski, his Central Front locked hand to hand with ten of Model's infantry divisions and four panzers with massed tanks, past the corpses, wrecked armour and the bloodied wounded, Russian tanks sometimes dug in so deep that only their turrets were visible. The Thirteenth Army drew back to the second defence line in the south, and General Galanin's Seventieth Army to the west was also driven back. Rokossovski counter-attacked but, in the short summer night, General Rodin was slow in launching the Second Tank Army in support: Stalin replaced him at once with General Bogdanov.

Continual air strikes, particularly employing air-to-ground rockets, vast minefields, artillery including anti-tank guns, tanks, SP guns and dive-bombers caused terrible casualties to the Wehrmacht in a series of mass attacks by infantry and armour. On 8 July German armour accompanied by infantry attempted a breakthrough where anti-tank guns were thickest; in one sector, until relieved, three Red Army artillery regiments beat 300 German tanks and their accompanying infantry to a twisted standstill.

The Wehrmacht's attack slackened on the following day. Model's army on this benighted battlefield with its shattered AFVs, burned-out aircraft, dead and wounded soldiers, moved over to the defensive, having reported 50,000 men killed, 400 armoured fighting vehicles destroyed and 500 Luftwaffe machines lost. Only ten miles had been gained on a twenty-five-mile front. Zhukov told Stalin that the Germans were no longer strong enough to break the Red Army's defences in the Kursk salient.

On his advice, the Briansk and Western fronts now began the great Russian counter-offensive, followed by the Central Front, in an attack against von Kluge's defences north and northeast of Orel. In the south, Vasilevski 'supervised' Vatutin's Voronezh Front as it took on Hoth's Fourth Panzer Army and the Kempf Group supported by the four SS divisions, in an enormous battle with Soviet tanks dug in as static firing points. The Germans continued to advance in swarms of between 100 and 400 tanks, the Soviet line holding at the village of Prokhorovka on 16 July.

On 11 July Rotmistrov's Fifth Guards Tank Army, three armoured corps of 1,000 tanks, had joined the Voronezh Front against Manstein and Kempf. Overy, in *Russia's War*, said, 'the Guards, in a phalanx twenty miles wide, in unbearable heat, threw up thick grey dust that covered men, vehicles and horses with a grimy film . . . the soldiers soon soaked with sweat in the Russian summer, oppressed by choking thirst'. The battle, still supervised by the chief of the General Staff, Vasilevski, from his command post at Briansk was, oddly, also coordinated at Stalin's express command by Zhukov himself, who had already sent another ten regiments of artillery into position round Prokhorovka before arriving personally on the field.

Rotmistrov and his men had had to undertake a forced march to the battlefield in this great heat. On arrival, he found that Vatutin's Sixth and Seventh Guards and the Sixty-ninth Armies were fully engaged by Hoth and Manstein with 1,000 tanks and SP guns, so that Rotmistrov had to mount his counter-attack almost single-handed. Richard Overy's beautiful, almost hypnotic account of the greatest tank battle in the history of the world describes the dark forests at dawn where the Germans had slept before the assault, the fields of golden grain. At 8.30 a.m. Rotmistrov ordered the attack in alternate sunlight and torrential rain, when 'fifteen hundred lethal clanking armoured vehicles supported by specialist infantry with automatic weapons, and covered by dug-in tanks of Katukov's First Tank Army under their guns, moved forward to the attack'.

Overhead, hundreds of aircraft from the Soviet air army and the Luftwaffe closed on their Prokhorovka targets, whether Katukov, Manstein or Rotmistrov, 'fighting at point-blank range among the impenetrable clouds', as Malcolm Mackintosh's *Juggernaut* describes, or dive-bombed and machine-gunned their respective infantry enemy.

The Fourth Panzer Army withdrew. On 12 July 300 tanks and 10,000 men were left broken on the Prokhorovka battlefield, followed by their compatriots under Hoth and Kempf, defeated by the Soviet Sixty-seventh, Sixty-ninth and Seventh Guard Armies, the Germans retreating southwards to Belgorod. Konev's Steppe Front, refreshed – as the Germans could not be at that distance – by well-trained reservists, had inserted itself between Vatutin's Voronezh Front and Malinovski's South Western Front, taking Belgorod on 5 August and the ruins of Kharkov itself on 24 August.

Popov and Sokolovski, commanding the Briansk and Western Fronts with the Third, Sixty-first, Sixty-third, Eleventh Guards and Fourth Tank Armies, broke the Germans around Orel by the first week in August.

Zhukov had told Stalin that to retake Kharkov would require, before completion, 20,000 men to reinforce the Sixty-ninth Army, 15,000 for the Fifty-third and Seventh Guards Armies, 100 T70, 35 KV and 200 T34 tanks, 90 fighters, 40 light bombers and 60 IL2 ground-attack aircraft. Stalin had granted the request. Zhukov claimed that German losses from seventy divisions at the whole battle of Kursk had numbered 2,000 tanks and SP guns, 3,000 guns, some 4,000 aircraft and half a million men over fifty days, the duration of the whole battle from start to finish. Even the inclusion of thousands of destroyed motor vehicles does not seem to exaggerate these figures.

The era of victory salutes began:

> Tonight, at twenty-four o'clock, on August 5th, the capital of our country, Moscow, will salute the valiant troops that liberated Orel and Belgorod, with twelve artillery salvos from 120 guns. I express my thanks to all the troops who took part in the offensive ... Eternal glory to the heroes who fell in the struggle for the freedom of our country. Death to the German invaders. The Supreme Commander in Chief, Marshal of the Soviet Union. STALIN

This proclamation was repeated 'more than three hundred times' before VE and VJ Days, to celebrate the victories that now fell like rain on parched earth.

The Germans, having lost the strategic initiative for good, were reduced to the defensive henceforward. At Kursk, twenty-two field-strength armies, five tank and six air armies plus long-range bombers had been deployed, compared to seventeen weakened field armies at Moscow, at Stalingrad fourteen field armies, one tank army and some mechanised corps. At Kursk much wider and deeper use was also made of mechanised and tank units, penetrating the enemy in depth. Mobility had been greatly increased: densities of 250–300 guns and 25–30 tanks were achieved for each mile of the front.

But by 13 July Hitler had called off Operation Citadel, a decision hastened by Allied successes in the Mediterranean against both Italians and Germans. The Russian claims of Germans killed and matériel lost were still enormous, but not implausible.

Victory at Kursk demonstrated that Russia had won the war. Walter Goerlitz said in *Paulus and Stalingrad*: 'Stalingrad was the psychological turning-point of the whole war in the east, but the German defeat at Kursk and Belgorod was the military turning-point.'

Thereafter in 1943, Malinovski's South Western Front and Tolbukhin's Fourth Ukrainian Front captured Mariupol on the Sea of Azov on 10 September, Tolbukhin having taken Taganrog in August. By 8 September, after six days of operations, the whole of the Donbas had been cleared of the enemy who had, however, destroyed factories and mines in 'scorched earth' retribution as they fled. Novorossisk fell to the Soviet navy on 16 September; the Taman peninsula was seized by Petrov's North Caucasian Front, the Wehrmacht fleeing to the Crimea via Kerch.

Zaporozhe and Melitopel were occupied by Malinovski and Tolbukhin in October, but the Soviet army was unable to capture the Crimea in 1943. Malinovski took Dniepropetrovsk on the Dnieper river in October, Rokossovski's Central Front, Konev's Steppe Front and Sokolovski's Western Front captured Chernigov, Poltava and even Smolensk in that same month. Ukraine and Belorussia waited, but not for long.

In *The Road to Berlin*, John Erickson said that after Kursk, the Ostheer, fearful, mangled at the hands of the Red Army, began to wither. The last offensive and the last victories of the German army in Russia had come and gone. Malcolm Mackintosh in *Juggernaut* concurred: 'The Red Army, after the battle of the Kursk salient held the strategic initiative until the end of the war . . . in 1944, it was the Russians who launched the summer campaign.

By this token alone, the Battle deserves to go down in history as the real turning point of the war on the Eastern Front', taking its place with Nomonhan, Midway and Kohima as one of the decisive battles of the Second World War. Or, as Overy's *Russia's War* concluded, 'The Battle of Kursk ended any realistic prospect of German victory in the east.'

SELECT BIBLIOGRAPHY AND SOURCES

GENERAL

COWLEY, Robert (ed.), *What if?*, Macmillan 1999

CREASY, E.S., *Fifteen Decisive Battles of the World*, Bentley 1858

DUPUY, R.E. and DUPUY T.N., *Encyclopaedia of Military History*, Jane's 1986

DURSCHMIED, Erik, *The Hinge Factor*, Hodder & Stoughton General 1999

FISHER, H.A.L., *A History of Europe*, Eyre and Spottiswoode 1935

FULLER, Major-General J.F.C., *Decisive Battles of the Western World*, Eyre and Spottiswoode 1956

GIBBON, Edward, *The Decline and Fall of the Roman Empire*, Penguin Classics 2000

HANSON, Victor D., *Why the West Has Won*, Faber and Faber 2001

KEEGAN, Sir John, *The Face of Battle*, Cape 1979

OVERY, Richard, *The Air War 1939–1945*, Papermac 1987

WINT, Guy and CALVOCORESSI, Peter, *Total War*, Penguin 1977

CHAPTERS 1–4

AESCHYLUS, *Prometheus Bound; The Suppliants; Seven Against Thebes; The Persians*, Penguin Classics 1961

ARRIAN, *Campaigns of Alexander: Life of Alexander the Great*, Book III, Penguin Classics 1971

BEER, Sir Gavin de, *Hannibal: The Struggle for Power in the Mediterranean*, Thames and Hudson 1969

BENGSTON, Herman, *The Greeks and the Persians*, Delacourt Press 1968

BUCHAN, John, *John Buchan: The Complete Short Stories*, Thistle Publishing 1997

BURY, J.B. and MEIGGS, R., *A History of Greece* (chapter 7), Macmillan 1960

BURY, J.D. *et al.* (eds.), *The Cambridge Ancient History*, Cambridge University Press 1927

CARY, Max, *A History of Rome*, Macmillan 1954

CONNOLLY, Peter, *Roman Army* (1975), *Greek Armies* (1977), *Hannibal and the Enemies of Rome* (1978), Macdonald Educational

COTTRELL, Leonard, *Enemy of Rome*, Evans Bros. 1960

CURTIUS RUFUS, Quintus, *History of Alexander* (trans. Rolfe), Book V, Loeb 1946

DIO CASSIUS, *Roman History* (trans. Cary), Book V, William Heinemann 1914

—*Life of Themistocles*, William Heinemann 1935

GOLDSWORTHY, Adrian, *The Punic Wars*, Cassell Military 2000

GRAVES, Robert, *I Claudius*, Arthur Barker 1934

GRUNDY, George B., *Great Persian War and Its Preliminaries*, Ams Press 1901

HAMMOND, Nicholas, *The Genius of Alexander the Great*, Gerald Duckworth and Co. 1997

HERODOTUS, *The Histories*, Book VIII, Penguin Classics 1996

HORACE, *The Odes*, Book I, xxxvii, Penguin Classics 1983

LANE-FOX, Robin, *Alexander the Great*, Allen Lane 1973

LECKIE, Ross, *Hannibal*, Abacus 1996

LIVY, *The War with Hannibal*, Book XXX, Penguin Classics 1964

MORRISON, COATES and RENKOFF, *The Athenian Trireme*, Cambridge University Press 2000

PLUTARCH, *Plutarch's Lives of Themistocles, Pericles, Aristides, Alcibiades and Coriolanus, Demosthenes and Cicero, Caesar and Antony*, Collier & Sons 1969

— *The Rise and Fall of Athens* (1960), *Makers of Rome* (1965), Penguin Classics

RIOTTA, Gianni, *Prince of the Clouds*, Flamingo 2002

SCULLARD, H.H., *Scipio Africanus in the 2nd Punic War*, Cambridge University Press 1930

SUETONIUS, *The Twelve Caesars* (trans. Graves), Penguin Books 2000

TACITUS, *The Annals of Imperial Rome*, Penguin Classics 1956

— *Germania*, Loeb 1969

TARN, W.W., *Alexander the Great*, Ares Publishers 1992

THUCYDIDES, *History of the Peloponnesian War*, Penguin Classics 1954

VANSITTART, Peter, *Paths from a White Horse: A Writer's Memoir*, Quartet Books 1990

— *A Choice of Murder*, Peter Owen 1992

VELLEIUS PATERCULUS, Marcus, *Historiae Romanae*, Book II, Loeb

VIRGIL, *Aeneid VIII*, Penguin Classics 1991

WILCKEN, Ulrich, *Alexander the Great* (trans. Richards), Chatto and Windus 1932

CHAPTER 5

FERRILL, Arthur, *The Fall of the Roman Empire*, Thames and Hudson 1986

GUIZOT, François, *History of Civilisation*, Vol. 2, Penguin Classics 1997

HODGKIN, T., *Italy and Her Invaders*, Oxford Clarenden 1880

JONES, A.H.M., *The Later Roman Empire* (4 vols.), Oxford University Press 1964

MASSIE, Allan, *The Evening of the World*, Phoenix 2002

MIEROW, C.C., *Gothic History of Jordanes*, Princeton 1915

THOMPSON, E.A., *A History of Attila and the Huns*, Oxford University Press 1945

CHAPTER 6

CHANDLER, David, *Battlefields of Europe*, Hugh Evelyn Ltd 1965

EGGLEBERGER, David Y., *Cambridge Mediaeval History*, Vol. 4, Macmillan 1925

— *A Dictionary of Battles*, Thomas Y. Cromwell Co. 1967

HINES, Lieutenant-Colonel, *Gunpowder and Ammunition*, 1904

LAVISSE, Ernest, *Histoire de France*, D.C. Heath & Co. 1923

Readings in Ancient History: Extracts from the Sources (2 vols.), Allyn & Bacon 1913

REINAUD, Joseph Toussaint, *Invasions des Sarrazins en France*, La Librairie Orientale du Vᵉ Dondey-Dupré 1836

CHAPTER 7

The Anglo-Saxon Chronicle (trans. Garmonsway), 1953

ANON, *Vita Aedwardi Regis*, Nelson 1962

BROWN, R. Allen, *The Battle of Hastings (Treasures of Britain)*, Pitkin 1982

— *The Norman Conquest of England*, Boydell Press 1995

CLARKE, Amanda, *The Battle of Hastings*, Dryad Publishers 1988

COAD, J.G., *The Battle of Hastings and the Story of Battle Abbey*, English Heritage 1999

GUY, Bishop of Amiens, *The Carmen de Hastingae Proelis of Guy, Bishop of Amiens* (eds. Morton and Muntz), Oxford University Press 1972

HOWARTH, David, *1066, Year of the Conquest*, Collins 1977

MALMESBURY, William of, *Vita Wulfstani*, Royal Historical Society 1981

— *Gesta Regum Anglorum*, Oxford Medieval Texts 1998

MORILLO, Stephen, *Battle of Hastings: Sources and Interpretations*, Boydell Press 1996

ORDERICUS VITALIS, *Historia Ecclesiastica*

POITIERS, William of, *Gesta Guillelmi*, Oxford Medieval Texts 1998

WACE, *Roman de Rou: A History of the British* (trans. Weiss), University of Exeter Press 1999

CHAPTER 8

BUSSELL, F.W., *The Roman Empire from AD 81 to 1081*, Lawbrook Exchange 2000

GIBBON, Edward, *The Decline and Fall of the Roman Empire*, Vol. 6, Penguin Classics 2000

KUGLER, Bernhard, *Studien zur Geschichte des Zweiten Kreuzzuges*, 1866

LANE-POOLE, Stanley, *Saladin and the Fall of the Kingdom of Jerusalem*, G.P. Putnam & Sons 1898

LAURENT, Joseph, *Byzance et les Turcs seldjoucides dans l'Asie Occidentale jusqu'en 1081*, Berger-Levrault 1913

OMAN, Sir Charles, *The History of the Art of War in the Middle Ages: 1278–1485 AD*, Greenhill Books 1999

OSMANA ibn MOUNKIDH, *Un Amir Syrien au premier siècle des Croisades*, School of Oriental Language 1889

RUNCIMAN, Steven, *A History of the Crusades*, Vol. 1, Penguin Books 1991

CHAPTER 9

BRENT, Peter, *The Mongol Empire: Genghis Khan: His Triumph and His Legacy*, Weidenfeld & Nicolson 1976

LIDDELL HART, B.H., *Great Captains Unveiled*, Da Capo Press 1996

MARSHALL, Robert, *Storm from the East*, BBC Books 1993

MORGAN, David, *The Mongols*, Basil Blackwell 1986

ONON, Urgunge, *History and Life of Genghis Khan*, Bliss 1990

RATCHNEVSKY, Paul, *Genghis Khan: His Life and Legacy* (trans. Nivison Haining), Blackwell 1993

SAUNDERS, J.J., *The History of the Mongol Conquests*, Routledge & Kegan Paul 1971

STEWART, Stanley, *In the Empire of Genghis Khan: A Journey Among Nomads*, HarperCollins 2000

WHALEY, Arthur, *Secret History of the Mongols*, Allen & Unwin 1963

CHAPTER 10

FROUDE, James A., *Spanish Story of the Armada and Other Essays*, AMS Press 1971

LAUGHTON, Sir J.K., *State Papers relating to the defeat of the Spanish Armada anno 1588*, Navy Records Society 1894

LEWIS, Michael, *Armada Guns*, Allen & Unwin 1961

MATTINGLEY, Garrett, *The Defeat of the Spanish Armada*, Jonathan Cape 1959

PARKER, Geoffrey and MARTIN, Colin, *The Spanish Armada*, Manchester University Press 1999

PARKER, Graham, *The Grand Strategy of Philip II*, Yale University Press 2000

ROGERS, Nicholas A.M., *The Safeguard of the Sea: A Naval History of Britain: 660–1649*, HarperCollins 1998

CHAPTER 11

COYER, G.F., *Histoire de Jean Sobieski, Roi de Pologne*, Duchesne 1761

HENRI, duc d'Aumale, *Histoire des Princes de Condé*, 1896

MORFILL, William Richard, *Poland: The Story of the Nations*, T. Fisher Unwin 1893

SALVANDY, Narcisse-Achille de, *Histoire de Pologne avant et sous le Roi Jean Sobieski*, Sautelet 1829

WALISZEWSKI, K., *Marysienka, Queen of Poland and Wife of Sobieski, 1641–1716*, Heinemann 1898

ZAMOYSKI, Adam, *The Polish Way: A Thousand-year History of the Poles and Their Culture*, John Murray 1989

CHAPTER 12

BRADLEY, A.G., *The Fight with France for North America*, Constable 1908

CASGRAIN, H.R., *French War Papers of the Maréchal de Lévis*, Cambridge University Press 1888

— *Guerre du Canada 1756–1760: Montcalm et Lévis*, L.J. Demers & Frère 1891

CAUVAIN, Henri, *Le Grand Vaincu: Dernière Campagne du Marquis de Montcalm au Canada*, Hetzel 1885

CHATTERJI, Tapanmohan, *The Road to Plassey*, Orient Longmans 1960

CHAUDHURY, Sushil, *The Prelude to Empire: Plassey Revolution of 1757*, Manohar Publishers 2000

Collection des Manuscrits contenant Lettres, Mémoires, et autres Documents Historiques relatifs à la Nouvelle France, 1492–1789, 1883–1885

Collection des Manuscrits du Maréchal de Lévis, 1889–1895

Dialogue betwixt General Wolfe and the Marquis Montcalm in the Elysian Fields, 1759

EDWARDES, Michael, *Plassey: The Founding of an Empire*, Hamish Hamilton 1969

ENTICK, John, *The General History of the Late War, containing its Rise, Progress and Event in Europe, Asia, Africa and America 1763–64*, printed for Dilly and Millan 1764

HARRINGTON, Peter, *Plassey 1757: Clive of India's Finest Hour*, Osprey 1994

Extraits des Archives des Ministères de la Marine et de la Guerre à Paris, L.J. Demers & Frère 1890

HIBBERT, Christopher, *Wolfe at Quebec: The Man Who Won the French and Indian War*, Cooper Square Press 1999

JOHNSTONE, James, *A Parallel of Military Errors, of which the French and English Armies were Guilty, during the Campaign of 1759 in Canada*, T.J. Moore & Co. 1927

'Journal of the Expedition up the River St Lawrence', *New York Mercury* 1886

Jugement Impartial sur les Opérations Militaires de la Campagne en Canada en 1759, Memoirs of the History of Canada 1840

KNOX, John, *An Historical Journal of the Campaigns in North America* (ed. Doughty), Champlain Society 1914–16

LYDEKKER, J.W., *The Faithful Mohawks*, Cambridge University Press 1938

MURRAY, J., *Journal of the Siege of Quebec*, Middleton and Dawson 1871

PARKMAN, Francis, *Montcalm and Wolfe*, Macmillan & Co. 1884

SAMUEL, Sigmund, *The Seven Years War in Canada 1756–1763*, Lovat Dickson & Thompson Ltd 1934

'The Siege of Quebec and Conquest of Canada in 1759', by a nun of the General Hospital of Quebec, *Quebec Mercury* 1855

THOMPSON, *Journal of the Quebec Expedition, 1759*, Middleton and Dawson 1872

TOWNSHEND, C.V.F., *The Military Life of Field Marshal George 1st Marquess Townshend 1724–1807*, John Murray 1901

TOWNSHEND, George, *Journal of the Expedition to Quebec*, *University of Toronto Quarterly*, University of Toronto Press

WADDINGTON, R., *La Guerre de Sept Ans*, Firmin-Didot 1899–1914

WALPOLE, Horace, *Memoirs of the Reign of George II*, Colburn 1847

WARBURTON, G.D., *The Conquest of Canada*, Richard Bentley 1849

WAUGH, W.T., *James Wolfe Man and Soldier*, L. Carrier & Co. 1928

WHITTON, Frederick E., *Wolfe and North America*, Ernest Benn 1929

WILLSON, Beckles, *The Life and Letters of James Wolfe*, Heinemann 1909

WINSOR, John, *The Mississippi Basin: The Struggle in America between England and France*, Houghton, Mifflin & Co. 1895

WOLFE, James, *General Orders in Wolfe's Army during the Expedition up the River St Lawrence in 1759*, Dawson and Co. 1875

CHAPTER 13

1862 Peninsula Campaign (Civil War in Tidewater), Virginia Civil War Traits, Williamsburg 2002

BONSAR, Stephen, *When the French Were Here*, Doubleday 1945

BURNHAM, Major John, *Personal Recollections of the Revolutionary War*, Tarrytown 1917

BUTLER, Matthew Calbraith, *General Butler's Narrative*, Confederate Survivors Association 1895

CARTER, William Harding, *From Yorktown to Santiago with the Sixth U.S. Cavalry*, Baltimore Press 1900

CHIDSEY, Donald Barr, *Victory at Yorktown*, Crown Press 1962

DAVIS, Burke, *The Campaign that Won America*, Dial Press 1970

EVANS, Emory G., *Thomas Nelson of Yorktown: Revolutionary Virginian*, Colonial Williamsburg Foundation 1975

FLEMING, Thomas J., *Beat the Last Drum: The Siege of Yorktown*, St Martin's Press 1966

GADRASKOVICH, Karl, *The American Revolution*

JOHNSTON, Henry P., *The Yorktown Campaign*, Harper & Bros. 1881

LUMPKIN, Henry, *From Savannah to Yorktown: The American Revolution in the South*, iUniverse.com 2000

McDONNELL, Bart, *Revolutionary War*, National Geographic 1967

THAYER, Theodore, *Yorktown: Campaign of Strategic Options*, Lippincott 1976

CHAPTER 14

CALLENDER, Sir Geoffrey, *Sea Kings of Britain*, Longman 1916

COLEMAN, Terry, *Nelson: The Man and the Legend*, Bloomsbury 2001

CORBETT, Sir Julian S., *Campaign of Trafalgar*, AMS Press 1970

HOWARTH, David, *Trafalgar: The Nelson Touch*, Collins 1969

MAHAN, A., *The Life of Nelson* (2 vols.), Little, Brown 1892

OMAN, Carola, *Lord Nelson*, Collins 1954

SOUTHEY, Robert, *The Life of Nelson*, Constable Robinson 1999

CHAPTER 15

ALBRIGHT, Harry, *Gettysburg: Crisis of Command*, Hippocrene Books 1989

Battles and Leaders of the Civil War, Vols. 1–4, Century & Co. 1888

BLAKE, Robert, *Disraeli*, Carroll and Graf 1987

CARTER, Samuel, *Final Fortress: Campaign for Vicksburg, 1862–63*, St Martin's Press 1981

CATTON, Bruce, *Gettysburg: The Final Fury*, Gollancz 1975

A Cycle of Adams Letters, 1861–1865 (2 vols.), Boston 1920

DOWDEY, Clifford (ed.), *Wartime Papers of R.E. Lee*, Little, Brown 1961

FOX, Charles K., *Gettysburg*, Yoseloff 1969

GRABAU, Warren E., *98 Days*, University of Tennessee 2000

GRAMM, Kent, *Gettysburg: A Meditation on War and Values*, 1994

JORDAN, Robert Paul, *Civil War*, National Geographic Society 1982

McGILL, *Britain and the War for the Union* (2 vols.), Queen's University Press 1974

McPHERSON, James M., *Battle Cry of Freedom*, Oxford University Press 1988

MIERS, Earl Schenk, *The Web of Victory*, Knopf 1955

OWSLEY, Frank Lawrence, *King Cotton Diplomacy*, Chicago 1931

SCHULTZ, Duane, *The Most Glorious Fourth*, W.W. Norton 2002

WALKER, Peter F., *Vicksburg: A People at War, 1860–65*, University of North Carolina Press 1960

The War of the Rebellion: A Compilation of the Official Records of the Union and Confederate Armies (1880–1901), Government Printing Office

CHAPTER 16

BERLIN, Heinrich Ekkehard, *Von Berlin bis Tannenberg*, Hugo Bermühler Verlag 1915

EVANS, Sir Geoffrey, *Tannenberg, 1410 and 1914*, Hamish Hamilton 1970

FRANÇOIS, Hermann von, *Tannenberg, das Cannae des Weltkrieges*, Verlag Deutsche Jägerbund 1926

GIEHRL, Hermann von, *Tannenberg*, E.S. Mittler & Sohn 1923

HOFFMANN, Carl Adolf Maximilian, *Tannenberg, wie es wirklich war*, 1926

IRONSIDE, William E., *Tannenberg: The First 30 Days in East Prussia*, W. Blackwood & Sons 1925

KNOX, Major-General Alfred, *With the Russian Army 1914–1917*, Hutchinson 1921

SCHAFER, T. von, *Tannenberg 1914*, Gerhard Stalling 1927

SHOWALTER, Dennis E., *Tannenberg: Clash of Empires*, The Shoe String Press 1991

STEFANI, W. von, *Mit Hindenburg bei Tannenberg*, 1919

CHAPTER 17

COLVIN, John, *Nomonhan*, Quartet 1999
COOX, Alvin, *Nomonhan*, Stanford University Press 1985
SPAHR, William J., *Zhukov: The Rise and Fall of a Great Captain*, Presidio Press 1995

CHAPTER 18

ADDISON, P. and CRANG, Jeremy (eds.), *The Burning Blue: A New History of the Battle of Britain*, Pimlico 2000
BUNGAY, Stephen, *The Most Dangerous Enemy: A History of the Battle of Britain*, Aurum Press 2000
CHURCHILL, Winston S., *Their Finest Hour*, Bantam Books 1949
CLAUSEWITZ, Carl von, *On War* (trans. Graham), Vol. 3, Kegan Paul, Trench, Trübner & Co. 1908
COLLIER, R., *Eagle Day*, Hodder & Stoughton 1966
COOKSLEY, Peter G., *1940 Story of 11 Group*, R. Hale 1983
DEIGHTON, Len, *Fighter: The True Story of the Battle of Britain*, Jonathan Cape 1977
GELB, Norman, *Scramble*, Harcourt Inc 1985
GIBSON, Hugh *et al.*, *Ciano's Diary 1939–43*, Simon Publications 1945
HINSLEY, F.H., *Hitler's Strategy*, Cambridge University Press 1951
MARCEL, Julian, *Battle of Britain* (trans. Yvelte and Steward), Cape 1967
MASON, F.K., *Battle over Britain*, McWhirter Twins 1969
The Memoirs of Field Marshal Kesselring, 1953
MURRAY, Williamson, *Luftwaffe*, Brassey's UK 1996
OVERY, Richard, *The Air War 1939–1945*, Papermac 1987
— *The Battle*, Penguin Books 2001
RAYMOND, H.R., *Who Won the Battle of Britain?*, Barker 1974

STAHL, Peter, *Kampfflieger zwischen Eismeer and Sahara*, Motorboch Verlag 1975

CHAPTER 19

ATTIWILL, K., *The Singapore Story*, Muller 1959

BENNETT, H. Gordon, *Why Singapore Fell*, Angus & Robertson 1944

BROOKE-POPHAM, Sir Robert, *Despatch 38183 of 20 January 1945*

BYWATER, Hector, *Sea Power in the Pacific*, Constable 1921

CHURCHILL, Winston S., *The Second World War*, Vols. 2, 3 and 4, Cassell 1949, 1950, 1951

COOPER, Duff, *Old Men Forget*, Pimlico 1986

FEIS, Herbert, *The Road to Pearl Harbor*, Princeton University Press 1950

GRENFELL, Russell, *Main Fleet to Singapore*, Oxford University Press 1987

HASLUCK, Sir Paul, *The Government and the People*, Angus & Robertson 1952

KIRBY, S. *et al.*, *War Against Japan*, Vol. 1, HMSO 1957
— *Singapore: The Chain of Disaster*, Cassell 1971

LAYTON, Vice Admiral Sir Geoffrey, *Despatch 38214 of 26 February 1945*

NEIDPATH, Lord James, *The Singapore Naval Base and the Defence of Britain's Eastern Empire 1019–1941*, Oxford University Press 1981

NISH, Ian S., *Anglo-Japanese Alliance*, Greenwood Press 1977

OWEN, Frank, *The Fall of Singapore*, Penguin Books 2002

PERCIVAL, Lt-Gen. A.E., *Despatch 38215 of 20 February 1945*

WAVELL, Field Marshal Earl, *Despatch*, HMSO 1945

CHAPTER 20

HANSON, Victor D., *Why the West Has Won*, Faber and Faber 2001

LORD, Walter, *Incredible Victory: Battle of Midway*, Hamish Hamilton 1968

Midway: Fuchida and Okumija, US Naval Institute 1955

CHAPTER 21

BEEVOR, Antony, *Stalingrad*, Viking 1998

ERICKSON, John, *The Road to Stalingrad*, Weidenfeld & Nicolson 1975

— *The Road to Berlin*, Weidenfeld & Nicolson 1983

GOERLITZ, Walter, *Paulus and Stalingrad*, Methuen 1963

MACKINTOSH, Malcolm, *Juggernaut*, Secker & Warburg 1967

OVERY, Richard, *Russia's War*, Allen Lane 1998

WERTH, Alexander, *Russia at War*, Barrie and Jenkins 1964

INDEX

Abdur Rahman 89, 90, 91, 92, 113

Actium (battle, 31 BC) 59

Aeschylus 2, 5, 15

Aetius 'the Patrician' 77–8, 80, 81

Ain Jalut (battle, 1260) 136

Akagi (Japanese aircraft carrier) 291, 292, 293

Alcibiades (Greek general) 19

Aldercron, Colonel John 167

Alexander the Great 18, 20, 21–5, 38, 40
  conquest of Greece 26
  at Gaugamela 32–5
  invasion of Asia 26–36 *passim*

Alexander II (king of Macedonia) 6

Alexius I Comnenus (Byzantine emperor) 112, 116

America/Americans
  alliance with France 199

British colonies in 175
  capture of André 197–8
  at Long Island 192
  at Yorktown 202–3
  see also United States

American Civil War 221
  see also Confederacy; Union forces

Amiens, Peace of 204

Ammianus Marcellinus 72, 74

André, Major John 197–8

Antipater (Macedonian general) 26, 36, 38

Antonov, General Aleksei 296

Antony, Mark 59, 60

Arabs 84
  see also Muslim forces

Arbela 32
  see also Gaugamela (battle, 331 BC)

Arcot (siege, 1751) 165

Aristides 2, 10, 14